Pornification

Pornification
Sex and Sexuality in Media Culture

Susanna Paasonen, Kaarina Nikunen
and Laura Saarenmaa

Oxford • New York

First published in 2007 by
Berg
Editorial offices:
1st Floor, Angel Court, 81 St Clements Street, Oxford, OX4 1AW, UK
175 Fifth Avenue, New York, NY 10010, USA

© Susanna Paasonen, Kaarina Nikunen and Laura Saarenmaa 2007

Berg is the imprint of Oxford International Publishers Ltd.

Library of Congress Cataloguing-in-Publication Data
Pornification : sex and sexuality in media culture / [edited by]
Susanna Paasonen, Kaarina Nikunen, and Laura Saarenmaa.
    p. cm.
Includes bibliographical references and index.
ISBN-13: 978-1-84520-703-8 (cloth)
ISBN-10: 1-84520-703-3 (cloth)
ISBN-13: 978-1-84520-704-5 (pbk.)
ISBN-10: 1-84520-704-1 (pbk.)
    1. Pornography. 2. Sex in mass media. 3. Sex in popular
culture. I. Paasonen, Susanna, 1975- II. Nikunen, Kaarina. III.
Saarenmaa, Laura.

HQ471.P595 2007
306.77—dc22   2007030716

British Library Cataloguing-in-Publication Data
A catalogue record for this book is available from the British Library.

ISBN 978 1 84520 703 8 (Cloth)
ISBN 978 1 84520 704 5 (Paper)

Typeset by Avocet Typeset, Chilton, Aylesbury, Bucks
Printed in the United Kingdom by Biddles Ltd, King's Lynn

www.bergpublishers.com

Contents

Part III Porn Media

Illustrations

Notes on Contributors

Michelle Carnes is a doctoral student at American University in Washington DC, completing her PhD in Anthropology. From a working-class family in Indianapolis, Indiana, she is a former stripper, currently a strip club ethnographer and adjunct professor at American University. Her degree is generously funded by The Point Foundation, which provides support to LGBT students who have been marginalized due to their gender and sexualities.

Nathan Scott Epley is a doctoral candidate in media and cultural studies at the University of North Carolina. His research on digital cultures explores the cultural, political and labour practices of 'no collar' professionals and the mobilization of everyday life under contemporary capitalism. He co-edited *Everyday eBay: Culture, Collecting, and Desire.* Currently, he teaches media production and criticism at the University of Northern Iowa.

Kevin Esch is a visiting assistant professor of communication at Tulane University. He teaches film history and genre theory and is writing a book on contemporary Hollywood film performance. His article '"I Don't See Any Method At All": The Problem of Actorly Transformation' appears in the Spring/Summer 2006 issue of *Journal of Film and Video.*

Jenny Kangasvuo is a post-graduate student in the Department of Cultural Anthropology and Art Studies at the University of Oulu. She is co-editor of *Gendered and Sexualised Violence in Educational Environments*, as well as a co-editor of *The Journal of Queer Studies* in Finland. She has published several articles and essays.

Vicki Mayer is Associate Professor of Communication at Tulane University. Author of *Producing Dreams, Consuming Youth* (2003), her most recent book project is entitled *Below the Line: Television Producers and Production Studies in the New Economy.*

Kerstin Mey is Professor in Fine Art at the University of Ulster. She is the author of *Art and Obscenity* (2006), editor of *Art in the Making. Aesthetics, Historicity and Practice* (2004), *Sculpsit: Artist on Contemporary Sculpture and Beyond* (2001); and co-editor of *Communication, Interface, Locality* (2004) and *Kultureller Umbau: Räume, Identitäten, Re/Präsentationen* (2007).

Mireille Miller-Young, PhD is Assistant Professor of Women's Studies at University of California at Santa Barbara. Her research explores racial politics, sexual labour and hardcore porn media. She has written for the Forum of European Contributions to African American Studies (FORECAAST), *$pread, Colorlines Magazine*, Cut-up.com, and has an essay forthcoming in *C'Lick Me: A Netporn Studies Reader* (Amsterdam: The Netherlands: Institute of Network Cultures, 2007).

Sharif Mowlabocus is a lecturer in media and digital media at the University of Sussex, where he also teaches. He has contributed chapters to *Queer Online* (2007) and *Queer Popular Culture* (2007) and his research explores themes of digital immersion, pornography and identity within Western gay male subcultures.

Kaarina Nikunen is postdoctoral researcher for the Academy of Finland at the Department of Journalism and Mass Communication, University of Tampere. Her research interests include feminist media studies, popular culture and audiences. She has written on television fan cultures and popular publicity (*Faniuden aika TUP* 2005; *Nordicom Review* 2007) and Finnish porn stardom (*Velvet Light Trap* issue 59, 2007, together with Susanna Paasonen). Her current research project examines popular media use by teenage immigrants.

Susanna Paasonen is research fellow at the Helsinki Collegium for Advanced Studies, University of Helsinki. She is the author of *Figures of Fantasy* (2005) and co-editor of *Women and Everyday Uses of the Internet* (2002). Her recent research on pornography has appeared in *Feminist Theory, European Journal of Cultural Studies* and the *Velvet Light Trap*.

Diane Railton is the co-author of *Music Video and the Politics of Representation* and has written extensively about gender, popular music and music video. She teaches in the School of Arts and Media at the University of Teesside, UK.

Leena-Maija Rossi is University Lecturer at the Christina Institute for Women's Studies, University of Helsinki. She has written extensively on gender, sexuality and visual culture. She is the author of *Heterotehdas* (Hetero Factory, 2003), and has edited and co-edited several other books. She has also translated the work of several American feminist theorists into Finnish.

Laura Saarenmaa is researcher at the Department of Journalism and Mass Communication, University of Tampere. Her teaching and research interests include historiography of popular culture, celebrity culture and popular film. Her ongoing PhD study addresses gender and sexuality in Finnish celebrity culture in the late 1960s and early 1970s.

Paul Watson is the co-author of *Music Video and the Politics of Representation* and has written extensively on issues of representation in film and music video. He teaches in the School of Arts and Media at the University of Teesside, UK.

Pornification and the Education of Desire

Susanna Paasonen, Kaarina Nikunen and Laura Saarenmaa

From the hypersexualized star image of Paris Hilton to Madame Tussaud's wax modelling of porn star Jenna Jameson, texts citing pornographic styles, gestures and aesthetics – and to a degree pornography itself – have become staple features of popular media culture in Western societies as commodities purchased and consumed, as individual self-representations and independent porn productions. This phenomenon has been discussed and diagnosed as the mainstreaming of pornography, pornographication (McNair 1996; Driver 2004), pornification (Paul 2005; Aucoin 2006), normalization of porn (Poynor 2006), porno chic (McNair 2002; Duits and van Zoonen 2006) and the rise of raunch culture (Levy 2005) by scholars, journalists and representatives of the porn industry.

Pornography is an issue of genre, industry and regulation. The category of pornography has been defined in terms of content (sexually explicit depictions of genitalia and sexual acts), lack thereof (materials without any redeeming artistic, cultural or social value), intention (texts intended to arouse their consumers) and effect (texts arousing their consumers). Definitions of pornography are notoriously ephemeral and purposely used when marking the boundaries of high and low culture, acceptable and obscene, 'normal' and commercial sex. Porn is a dirty word, which is often replaced with the terms adult entertainment or erotica: the former is a concept preferred by the porn industry and journalism whereas erotica is used in separating the artful from the artless, the beautiful from the ugly. The category of pornography is equally divided into hardcore and soft-core, in addition to endless sub-genres and fringes. Soft-core texts lacking in explicitness and featuring simulated sex have probed the limits of the acceptable at least since the 1950s. While such probing is not a novel issue, the boundaries separating the pornographic from the non-pornographic have become increasingly porous and difficult to map. Women's open, moist and lipstick-red lips, half-closed eyelids or hands suggestively placed on a bare bosom or stomach are staple elements in pornography, but also in music videos, cosmetics ads and fashion photography (Juvonen, Kalha, Sorainen and Vänskä 2004; Railton and Watson, Rossi in this volume). As a set of styles, scenarios and conventions, the pornographic cuts across media culture.

Analyses of pornification risk being associated with diagnoses of contemporary culture as one of 'pornication' (in the sense of fornication). Discarding references to degeneracy, this book makes use of the concept of pornification in investigating the intertwining processes of technological development, shifts in modes of representation and the cultural visibility of cultures of sexuality. *Pornification* figures transformations in the cultural position and status of both soft-core and hardcore pornographies, which require a rethinking of the very notion of the pornographic. For the sake of conceptual clarity, pornification can be roughly divided into three levels.

Three Levels of Pornification

Media Technology and the Porn Industry

Firstly, pornification concerns developments in media technology and the expansion of the porn industry. By the 1990s at the latest, porn business became a global industry while the World Wide Web facilitated unprecedented visibility and accessibility of pornography – including various amateur, alternative, independent and niche pornographies that challenge not only the aesthetics of commercial pornography but also its ideologies of capitalist accumulation and centralization (Jacobs 2004a; Paasonen in this volume). The Internet has brought forth considerable transformations in the production, distribution and consumption of pornography: it enables anonymous access to porn without the need of visiting a newspaper stand or a sex shop. Live performances, pornographic images and narratives once available in print or on VHS are now online alongside imageries and practices more specific to the Internet.

Pornography, as understood in this volume, is a phenomenon of media culture and a question of mass production. The 'birth' of pornography can be traced back to the development of print technology: relatively inexpensive print technologies of the eighteenth century made pornographic texts and images available to a wider public beyond the elite, although questions of affordability, availability and literacy continued to limit the consumption of porn (Hunt 1993). It was photography in the nineteenth century – and more specifically, inexpensive and mass-produced postcards in the 1880s and 1890s – that made pornography available to the members of the working classes who had already been established as familiar objects of pornographic representation (Sigel 2000). 'Artistic' nudes were distributed as postcards, stereoscope images and transparencies. Building on already established representational conventions, they also worked to institutionalize colonialist imagery of sexualized and exoticized 'natives', and women in particular (Yee 2004; Sigel 2000: 861–4). Techniques of othering have since been employed in a wide range of pornographies, especially in terms of class, gender and 'race' (see Miller-Young in this volume).

In the context of cinema, films such as the French *Le bain* (1896), featuring a nude woman entering a bath, were produced already in the nineteenth century (Hoffman 1965). Underground 'stag movies' and 'loops' formed the market of hardcore porn from 1908 to 1967, including variations such as the 'nudie cuties' of the 1950s, various educational materials and 'beaver films' of the late 1960s (Schaefer 2004: 371; Williams 1989: 96–8; Johnson 1999; Wyatt 1999). These developments were tied to transformations in film technology. The 1920s saw the standardization of 16 mm film as a medium for the amateur market, in contrast to the professional format of 35 mm. As 8 mm film was introduced in the 1950s (Fig. 1.1), 16 mm became the 'semi-professional' format widely used in the making of sexploitation films (Schaefer 2004: 375–6; Zimmermann 1995: 29, 117). The 1970s saw pornographic feature films shot on 35 mm film whereas the introduction of home video later in the decade marked the beginning of porn productions shot and distributed on video (Paasonen and Saarenmaa; Miller-Young in this volume).

Figure 1.1 Porn loops were also viewed privately in homes. Super 8 mm film projector and reels of German films from the 1970s. Photograph by Susanna Paasonen.

Pornography has been identified as an engine driving the development of media technology, soon adapted to novel platforms and generating fast profits (see O'Toole 1998; Lane 2001; Perdue 2002). The case of VHS and Betamax is often referenced in this respect: Sony introduced Betamax VCRs in 1975 and while they were better in terms of image an sound quality than their competitor, VHS, it was the latter that became the industry standard in the late 1970s. The victory of VHS has been attributed to Betamax not licensing pornography due to which – following the principle 'sex sells' – VHS reigned victorious. While pornography may have played its part in this battle of formats, it certainly was not the only factor contributing to it. The Betamax system was more expensive and its tapes were only one-hour long (as opposed to the longer play time of VHS); Betamax was intended for recording TV programmes for later viewing, while VHS was also oriented toward pre-recorded tapes (Wasko 1994: 40–1; Winston 1998: 128–9). The example of VCR suggests that porn is a factor in the history of media technology (especially so since the early twentieth century), but also that considering the history of technological transformation through the lens of porn is likely to lead to twists in perspective.

More or less affordable tools for the making of amateur porn have been available since the marketing of still and 16 mm film cameras to private households in the late nineteenth century (Slater 1991; Zimmermann 1995). These media, however, involved potential embarrassment since film required developing and exposing the shots to the gaze of others. The introduction of portable video cameras (first in the late 1960s, more affordable amateur models in the 1980s) made it possible to view one's films directly, to efface and redo shots. Similarly, the relatively expensive Polaroid cameras became a medium for amateur porn in the 1960s precisely due to the absence of necessary outside involvement in the imaging process. In the 1990s, digital cameras (both still and video) further effaced third parties from the process. Amateur porn is certainly not a new phenomenon, but the distribution, participation and interaction possibilities of the Internet have given it unprecedented visibility since the 1990s.

The story of porn is often narrated as one from print to film, video, DVD and the Web, and with primary focus on the visual. The development has not, however, been this definite. Print pornographies remain popular and they were the primary format of pornographic consumption in the 1970s and 1980s due to their accessibility and the possibility of private use (in contrast to cinemas screening porn films or peepshow parlours presenting 8 mm loops). In countries such as the Soviet Union where pornography was heavily censored and distribution forms therefore limited, imported pornographic images were distributed in imaginative ways – for example, by photographing them and then distributing playing cards made of the black and white prints (Fig. 1.2).

Technical innovations have been crucial to the growth of the porn industry, which has branched out into new platforms from print media and film to video,

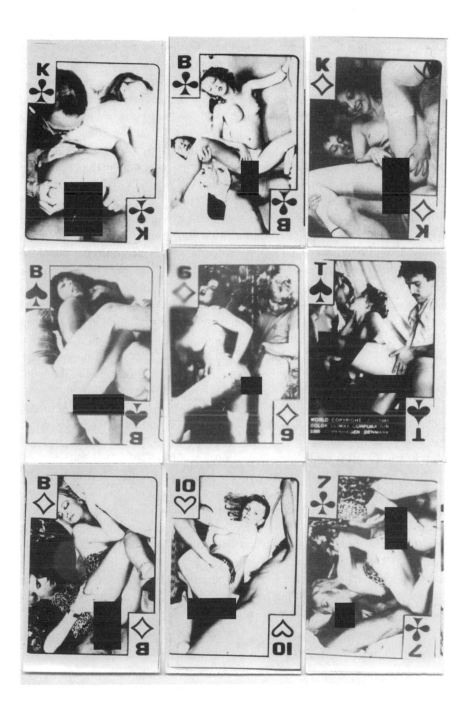

Figure 1.2 Playing cards made with collage-style photographic prints (and with liberal copyright practice) in the last years of the Soviet Union. Image by Susanna Paasonen.

cable television and online distribution. The industry makes use of corporate strategies based on convergence. Content and distribution are developed in order to market the same product in different formats (DVD, Web, print media, pay-per-view TV, mobile media applications, podcasts). Furthermore, companies aim to control both production and distribution. Companies that first made their profits in porn magazines (Larry Flynt Publishing, Playboy) have branched out into DVD and Web production and distribution, pay-per-view TV and retailing. Company strategies also include fusions, as demonstrated in Playboy's move to buy its competitor Spice Entertainment in 1998. On the Internet, pornography has been one of the most successful forms of content production that suffered little from the dot.com collapse of 2000 (Lane 2001).

Social and political transformations such as the deregulation of pornography in Western societies since the late 1960s and the shift to post-socialism in Eastern Europe in the 1990s have – in obviously different ways – facilitated the rise of the porn industry. In addition to France, Germany and Italy, European productions are centred in countries such as Hungary and the Czech Republic, attracting business partners across national boundaries (Milter and Slade 2005). While technological development has facilitated the operation of small companies, the trade seems to glide more and more to the hands of large multinationals such as the Private Media Group in Europe, or the US-based Vivid and VCA. San Fernando Valley – as featured in the semi-reality TV series *Porno Valley* depicting lives around the Vivid studio – is the hub of American porn production. If Hollywood releases approximately 400 films annually, the valley produces over 10,000 DVD titles for the global market. The US porn industry is estimated to be a three to ten billion dollar business annually whereas the estimates of the size of the global industry vary from fifty to sixty billion dollars (Rosen 2006; Ackman 2001; BBC 2005).

The actual profits of the industry remain somewhat unclear since 'legitimate' corporations are unwilling to disclose their involvement in porn distribution. X-rated films are part of the diet of pay-per-view television in hotel chains around the world while major media, software and telecommunication companies provide bandwidth, infrastructure, software and distribution systems for adult companies (Lane 2000: 34; Perdue 2002: 28–59). Porn is an integral part of the media economy, which makes the revenues of the porn industry difficult to isolate. Major corporations generating high profits with porn are likely to downplay its significance in terms of their overall turnover.

Regulation and Media Policy

Technology is by no means the only factor enabling the growth of the porn industry. As suggested above, technological developments have gone in tandem with changes in regulation and media policy. These can be seen as forming the second layer of pornification. Porn is no longer something situated at the boundaries of the public: on the contrary, it is manifest in mainstream publicity, media and (semi)public spaces of various kinds – from wax museums to convention centres, newspapers, magazines, television and department stores. This development is linked to gradual transformations in media regulation and legislation since the 1960s. Denmark was the first European country to legalize pornography in 1969, followed by West Germany in 1970 and Sweden in 1971. This enabled the rise of 'Scandinavian porn', as encapsulated in the productions of Lasse Braun. In the United States, the markets were first opened to pornographic material in 1957 but legislation limited (and banned) the production of pornography well into the 1980s (Williams 1989: 88). The US law on obscenity was written mainly in 1973 and has been constantly challenged since then: *Hustler* producer Larry Flynt waged war against censorship from the 1970s to the late 1980s, while the antipornography movement fought for censoring pornographic materials (Kipnis 1996: 124; Dworkin 1989). Governmental regulation diminished in the late 1980s and new technical solutions resulted in the passing of a series of laws regulating online materials in the mid-1990s (Kleinhans 2004; see O'Toole 1998 for an overview of developments in the UK).

One of the substantial changes in terms of media industry concerns television regulation – television being perhaps the most domestic of media, embedded in the rhythms of everyday life. European television regulation has been transforming in the course of harmonizing the regulatory structures of the EU, following the more global trend of relative decline in the regulatory power of nation states over media content. At the same time, technological convergence is making it more difficult to set regulation on a media-specific basis (Arthurs 2004: 30). Moreover, the emergence of digital TV channels has multiplied the supply of pornographic content – even more so than satellite and cable channels since the 1980s. This has mainly meant the incorporation of porn films into the night-time programming of pay-per-view television. In television, the boundaries of the respectably mainstream and the (soft-core) pornographic can be blurred in quality drama and lifestyle series (legitimized through their educational or aesthetic value) while the more avant-garde or hardcore pornographies remain excluded and pushed to the margins (Arthurs 2004: 24).

In addition to media deregulation, the shifting boundaries of the pornographic and the mainstream can be associated with other diagnoses of contemporary media culture, such as tabloidization and intimization, namely the prioritization of the personal, the emotional and the sexual over information and education – examples of this including reality TV, confessional tabloid stories and celebrity sex scandals (Glynn 2000; Calvert 2000; Attwood 2006). This development has often been lamented as the victory of bad taste over quality media. Brian McNair (2002), however, considers deregulation as a path to pluralization and eventual democratization of desire: increasing accessibility of sexual representations and self-expressions alike. The last decade has witnessed a pluralization of hardcore pornographies and their sexual imagery, yet soft-core porn and its mainstream variants have tended to reproduce rather predictable depictions of gender, desire and sexuality. As Jane Arthurs (2004: 12–13; 41–2) argues, pluralism does not guarantee democracy. The increased visibility of sexual representations previously unaccepted in the national media is not merely a question of democratization through the workings of capitalist market economy. Mainstream applications of porn aesthetics are also efficient in establishing new kinds of norms and regulatory effects. In this sense, deregulation can also be seen as giving rise to new regulatory systems, such as ones based on privatization (Lehtonen 2001: 81).

Porno chic

The third layer of pornification – in practice inseparable from the two addressed above – connects to the general sexualization of culture, or the mainstreaming of sexuality: 'contemporary preoccupation with sexual values, practices and identities; the public shift to more permissive sexual attitudes; the proliferation of sexual texts; the emergence of new forms of sexual experience; the apparent breakdown of rules, categories and regulations designed to keep the obscene at bay; our fondness for scandals controversies and panics around sex' (Attwood 2006: 78–9; also Attwood, Brunt and Cere, forthcoming).

The sexualization of culture refers to a fairly wide range of cultural phenomena while pornification is a more specific term pointing to the increased visibility of hardcore and soft-core pornographies, and the blurring of boundaries between the pornographic and the mainstream. McNair (2002: 61) identifies such increase in sexually explicit representations as porno chic: involving depictions of pornography in non-pornographic contexts in art and culture; pastiche or parody of porn; homage to porn or explorations into it and the incorporation of porn in mainstream cultural products (Fig. 1.3). Examples of porno chic are not difficult to come by: the individual chapters in this volume address the ways of remembering and referencing 1940s' and 1950s' pin-up culture (Epley) and the 1970s' 'golden age of porn' (Paasonen and Saarenmaa), the uses of pornographic elements in online self-representations (Mowlabocus; Nikunen), music videos (Railton and Watson), visual arts (Mey) and street advertising (Rossi). As Kevin Esch and Vicki Mayer, writing on the blurred boundaries of porn and celebrity culture in this volume note, pornography is being defined by its constant reappraisal, both from within (amateur vs. corporate porn; alternative vs. generic) and without (porn vs. 'mainstream' media). The relationship between porn and mainstream media can be seen as symbiotic: 'by covering porn, the media borrows some of its dirty glamour and sense of danger, while in turn it confers legitimacy, making porn a topic of interest and discussion like any other' (Poynor 2006: 132).

Figure 1.3 Porn Star designs – an example of porno chic. Photograph by Susanna Paasonen.

One indication of such symbiosis is the entrance of some porn stars – perhaps most famously Jenna Jameson – into mainstream celebrity status. The first successful example of such crossover was Ron Jeremy, the overweight and middle-aged veteran hero of the American adult business. Emily Shelton describes Jeremy as a figure with 'liminal positioning between the mainstream and its seamy celluloid underbelly' (2002: 177). According to Shelton, Jeremy's secret lies in his repulsiveness: unlike the average fit, groomed and tanned porn star, Jeremy exceeds the bodily requirements and points to pornography's tendency to celebrate the low, the disgusting and the obscene. Moreover, Jeremy's star image indicates a shift in porn's cultural position – not as harmful or repressive but as fun, hilarious and camp. As an old-time porn proletarian, Jeremy's unruly body speaks of camp sensibility (Sontag 1964a: 278) that deliberately re-values the low and the outmoded. Jeremy enjoys a motile form of celebrity that allows him to traverse a range of popular media from *Beavis and Butthead* to Conan O'Brien's sofa. However, as male, American and heterosexual, Ron Jeremy represents the very centre of mainstream pornography, just as his films represent the mainstream of adult film-making.

The question is both similar and different with the young and female Finnish porn star Rakel Liekki who holds an exceptionally flexible, yet far more local intermedia career spanning from hardcore films to television talk shows and art museum performances (Fig. 1.4). Compared to Jeremy, Liekki's performances flirt with the aesthetics of alternative porn and are representative of the more experimental forms of heterosexual hardcore. Liekki's fame owes to the late night cable TV show *Shag School* (2002), which mixed hardcore porn with educational discourse, resulting in a playful mixture of cultural hierarchies. Her other productions have equally contributed to a renegotiation and redefinition of pornography in terms of recreational fun and artistic experimentation while detaching it from notions of shame (Nikunen and Paasonen 2007). Being in charge of her own productions and collaborating with other female porn stars, Liekki represents the 'fair trade' of porn business. Porn made by women for women has, for the past two decades, been seen as possibly offering alternative spaces of agency for both female performers and consumers. The amount of female producers has increased and there are markets for women straight and queer (Juffer 1998; Carnes in this volume), even if women remain a marginal target group in terms of the porn industry as a whole (cf. Attwood 2005) (Fig. 1.5).

The examples of Jeremy and Liekki point to a flux between porn stardom and mainstream celebrity status while also pointing to crucial differences shaped by genre, gender, markets and geography. The move from hardcore porn to prime time lends performers certain legitimacy. The other direction of the flux, namely porno chic in mainstream media or the shifting of mainstream celebrity towards porn stardom, has somewhat different effects. This kind of flirting with porn can be illustrated through the changing star image of Britney Spears. As the former

Figure 1.4 Finnish porn star Rakel Liekki on television interview discussing her show 'Shag School'. Copyright YLE/TV2/ Kaarina Nikunen.

Mickey Mouse Club performer made her breakthrough with the hit song *Baby, One More Time* (1998), her star image was a mixture of a sexy cheerleader, girl next door and abstinence from premarital sex. In Joel Lockard's (2001) view, Spears's hymen was established as a central element of her brand-name chastity,

Figure 1.5 Merchandise for women. Photograph by Laura Saarenmaa.

yet her virginity did not simply signify innocence. On the contrary, low-riding pants, generous cleavages and a perpetually uncovered navel – in Lockard's terms, her 'open-air substitute vulva' – marked her body as firmly and actively heterosexual. Spears eventually gave up her vows of chastity, kissed Madonna in an MTV gala, gained inspiration for her choreographies from strip clubs, married drunk in Las Vegas, divorced quickly and remarried briefly. Gossips of lesbian desires abound, Spears – now mother of two – has since flashed her waxed vulva to the paparazzi and performed an impromptu solo dance on the stage of a topless club.

The development of Spears's star image seems a textbook example of pornification as a media cultural trend. This trajectory is by no means exceptional in the sense that oiled bodies and rhythmic pelvic thrusts have very much become 'the air that we breathe'. In other words, the imageries of commercial sex leak into other realms of media culture without being actual porn (McNair 2002). As several chapters in this volume point out, not all porn acquires similar visibility but pornification largely revolves around predictable gendered poses and scenarios: the soft-core influenced repertoires of music videos and advertising tend to centre on heterosex and largely standard bodily forms (cf. Reichert and Lambiase 2006; Juvonen et al. 2004: 72–3; Rossi in this volume). As the example of Britney Spears illustrates, mainstreamed porno chic draws on conventionally heteronormative imageries. There is indeed little to be considered transgressive in the public/pubic acts of Spears or Paris Hilton (Esch and Mayer in this volume). Contrary to such soft-core references, hardcore pornography has, in its directness and extensiveness, been recognized as the site of the radical potential of porn (Arthurs 2004: 47). The proliferation of hardcore pornographies – queer and straight, kink and vanilla – provides spaces for various tastes, desires and modes of production. Explicit sexual representation escapes the confines of 'good taste' in its focus on bodily orifices, liquids and discharges. Defining hardcore categorically as radical or transgressive is nevertheless simplifying, given that the area of porn culturally most visible and financially profitable, namely commercial heteroporn, relies on highly generic body shapes, styles, acts and scenarios (Paasonen 2006).

Pornification involves a commodification of sexuality: sex is used in selling a variety of products both material and immaterial; the markets of pornography seem to be in continuous increase while porno chic has become part and parcel of youth cultures and the stylization of the self (also Duits and van Zoonen 2005). Framing the question as one of increased sexual self-expression and democratization of desire erases from view the codes and norms that such expressions tend to confine to. In amateur pin-up galleries and music videos alike, bodies repeat sexualized, standard poses and positions. Self-representations straight and queer borrow from the imageries of hardcore and soft-core porn, implying involvement of commercial sex in the processes of self-commodification (see Mowlabocus in this volume). Writing on gay video porn, Richard Fung notes that 'there is such a limited vision of what constitutes the erotic' (1991: 160). The same goes for the proliferating sexual imageries of popular media culture, as well as a large part of hardcore choreographies. Such proliferation should not, however, lead to analytical blindness towards the shifts and transformations simultaneously taking place in their aesthetics and circulation. In other words, while commodification connotes standardization, it cannot be reduced to it. On the one hand, pornification implies reiteration and recycling of representation conventions that are telling of the generic rigidity of porn. On the other hand, and perhaps paradoxically, it also gives rise to media performances subverting the generic conventions and boundaries of porn, facilitates novel representational spaces, ideas and agencies.

Pornography and 'Good Sex'

Porn is a question of genre and embodied practice, not simply sex or sexual expression – although it is often naturalized as such. Generic porn scenarios, stylized displays and iterative conventions teach us moments and movements of pleasure. As Richard Dyer (1992) argues, porn educates desire in highly corporeal ways. The convention of the cum shot (a.k.a. money shot, male ejaculation on a partner's face or body) is a highly literal example of such education. Established by 1977 as a necessary element in porn films gay and straight, the cum shot is a visible verification of sexual gratification: semen functions as indexical evidence of climax while providing closure, a sense of ending, to the act (Williams 1989: 93). Through perpetual repetition, the cum shot – largely a technical convention related to the possibilities of conveying the 'realness' of the acts filmed and the pleasures derived from them – has become a staple feature also in porn stories and amateur erotica. On the Internet, endless image galleries are dedicated to cum shots. In such instances, the sign of male climax becomes *the* focus point of sexual acts, a fantasy figure in itself. If amateur stories and online discussion forums are anything to go by, cum shots have become part of private fantasies and desires – and hence part of everyday sexual practices. This kind of iterative imagery suggests, defines and shapes understandings of sexual acts: what they are and how they can be done (Nikunen in this volume). This implies a certain schooling of desire, as well as the inseparability of public and social fantasies.[1]

As argued by Michael Warner (2000: 177), pornography, with its growing visibility, offers knowledge on the practices, styles and typologies of various sexual cultures. In this sense, porn can be seen as offering means to resist the notion of 'good sex' as monogamous heterosexual and private, produced through regulation and sexual stigmas (Warner 2000; Berlant and Warner 2000). Inherent in the construction of 'good sex' – namely socially acceptable and normative forms of sexuality – is the shame of sex, which is organized in various sets of hierarchies segregating the good from the bad, straight from gay, marital from promiscuous, private from public and non-pornographic from pornographic (Warner 2000: 24–5; also Kulick 2005). The word public (from the Latin *publicus*) refers to that which is considered as the common good, what can be seen, what is on view. Hence it also refers to the cultural understanding of what *should* be seen. Public displays of sexuality, including non-normative intimacies, entail the possibility of reorganizing the boundaries of respectability and normalcy. Making sex public, pornography confronts tendencies to silence or demonize sexualities – and queer sexualities in particular. Seyla Benhabib (1998: 86) argues that morality and religion, commerce and intimacy have traditionally shaped the realm of the private: hence the various modes of pornification stir the lines of the public and the private. As the traditionally intimate has become more visible and public both indoors and outdoors (through confessional media discourses; celebrities flashing their nipples; private people disclosing their lives and bodies in online journals and on Web cams), the meanings of intimacy are obviously under redefinition.

Due to the growing visibility and indeed the 'presentability' of commercial heteroporn, the lines of good sex may have become redrawn. Porn is catered to couples as a means to spice up their sex life, used as reference for various heterosex techniques as well as source material in sex ed programming (Arthurs 2004: 45–6; Nikunen in this volume). In these instances, porn becomes incorporated in the realm of good sex. All this leads to the necessity of defining the pornography discussed – whether this be straight, gay, bi or trans, locally produced or imported, soft-core, educational or one involving variations of gender-fuck. As a general point of reference, 'pornography' tends to suffer from the assumption of homogeneity and it is the mainstream, the heterosexist and largely the American that become its defining factors. Different pornographies, however, contest each other's aesthetics and understandings of things sexual. Commitment to figuring the inner diversity of pornography means that critiques of porn can be specific rather than categorical.

Diagnoses of Pornification

The ubiquity of the pornographic has inspired polemical diagnoses of contemporary North American culture. In her *Female Chauvinist Pigs* (2005), Ariel Levy analyses the spread and implications of porno chic and 'raunch culture' in the lives of women. From *Girls Gone Wild* videos to pole-dancing as a recreational hobby, Levy argues that commercial sex has gained such a normative status that women no longer distance themselves from it but rather apply its aesthetics in their everyday lives in order to present themselves as strong, sexual and independent. The rise of raunch culture, as recounted by Levy, is one with new kinds of disciplinary effects that may in fact make it more difficult for women to define their views on the sexual. In another widely read non-fiction title, Pamela Paul (2005) identifies contemporary American culture as pornified. Focusing on the impact – in her terms, the damage – caused by the increased accessibility and acceptability of pornography on American men, women, children and families, Paul maps pornification in terms of compulsion and alienation while ultimately failing to account for the diverse aesthetics and practices involved (see also Paasonen in this volume).

The last few years have seen the publication of two books with titles similar to this one, namely Paul's *Pornified* and *Pornification* (2006) by Andrew Benjamin. Both books are targeted at a wide audience, the first one in the category of social sciences/relationships and the second in that of humour. Considered together, they make evident some dominant traits in public debates on pornography: while some discuss pornography as a social problem, others de-politicize it as hip and fun. There is little in terms of middle ground.

Benjamin's *Pornification* is a pocket-sized book including listings of 'pornified' film and TV series titles – *The Great Dictator* is transformed into *The Great Dick Taster* and *Freddy Vs. Jason* into *Freddy Does Jason*. In this context, pornification signifies a verbal skill and practice already well established in the porn industry. It is also a social skill, and the book proposes different kinds of games to play with the pornification of familiar film titles. In obvious opposition to Paul's book, pornification is defined as fun and camp and this feel is complemented by the extensive use of pin-up cut-outs, breasts and buttocks in the book layout. According to Rick Poynor (2006: 133–4), visual references to porn on the level of design tend to be explained through the notion of satire or irony. However, if the object of irony remains obscure, satire amounts to little else than a means of framing pin-up imageries as fun and cool. The framework of irony, camp and cult works to mark porn as a question of taste, style and sensibility: as suggested above in a discussion on Ron Jeremy's star image, porn becomes something to be watched and discussed with an attitude. Porn is seen as auto-deconstructive, always reflecting its own artificiality and excess. Those taking porn seriously, then, are the ones who 'don't get it' and fail to understand its carnivalesque dimensions. Camp sensibility seems to go well with pornography since camp serves to create distinctions and celebrate the inappropriate and the low while being aware of the cultural hierarchies at play. The loving and conscious laughter of camp also functions as a means of dismantling possible critique (see Epley; Railton and Watson in this volume).

This volume neither celebrates nor laments the changing status of pornography. In contrast to the publications of a similar title, *Pornification* argues against any simplified generalizations concerning pornography and its status in the contemporary mediascape while insisting on the necessity contextualization. While discussions on pornification are carried out across national borders, they involve different tones and political investments. Debates on porn in Finland, for example, become understandable in relation to Nordic histories of the production and distribution of porn, generally permissive public opinion on commercial sex, the semi-celebrity status of domestic porn stars, subdued conservative Christian perspectives in the media, as well as a history of equality feminism in which the 'sex wars' never took fire (Paasonen 2007a; Nikunen and Paasonen 2007; Kulick 2005 on the Swedish context). In India, again, where media censorship and sexual representation are topics of intense debate, state regulation connects to a variety of issues from Hindu nationalist politics to the history of colonialism and resistance towards Western cultural dominance (Bose 2006; Ghosh 2005; Bose 2005). In these debates, 'The word "pornography" has rarely been used to denote the *genre* of pornography, that is, sexually explicit material produced specifically for sexual arousal. It has been used to describe material that *connotes* sex, like film songs, advertisements, cover girls, rape sequences, consensual sex and even beauty pageants.' (Ghosh 2006: 273) Meanwhile, the 'porn laws' recently debated in Indonesia have less to do with pornography and more with the regulation of individual – particularly female – clothing and demeanour, such as public displays of affection (Lim 2006).

As anecdotal as these examples are, they do make evident that what pornography means and what is understood as pornification internationally is not reducible to some 'general' framework. Debates on pornography – academic and not – have nevertheless been dominated by North American conceptions and political divisions in ways that help to render such differences invisible. Although certain global trends are recognizable, questions of regulation, policy and public opinion should not be generalized.

From Antiporn to Porn Studies

In the United States, debates on pornography have been both polarized and polemical for the past three decades. Discussants seem forced to choose sides either for or against pornography, which is telling of the continuing influence of the 'sex wars' of the 1970s and 1980s. Antipornography feminists from Gloria Steinem (1983), Susan Griffin (1981) and Robin Morgan (1980) to Andrea Dworkin (1989) and Catharine MacKinnon (Dworkin and MacKinnon 1988) defined pornography as degradation of and violence against women. Postulating a causal link between porn and violence – in accordance with the famous slogan coined by Morgan, 'porn is the theory, rape is the practice' – antiporn activists protested against commercial sex and aimed at banning it. While the stances of individual antiporn feminists towards censorship and sexuality varied, they shared the view of porn as an industry oppressing women and reproducing male hegemony. Porn was seen as made by men for men and representative of violent masculine sexuality. Assuming porn to be enjoyed by straight men, antiporn perspectives did not engage with female and non-heterosexual fascinations as other than expressions of pornography's general objectifying ideological function.

The theoretical and political shortcomings of antipornography feminism have since been addressed at length. Critics have pointed out that antiporn feminism relied on ephemeral definitions of the pornographic, the oppressive and the obscene while simplifying questions of representation, desire and fantasy (Rubin 1995; Duggan and Hunter 1995; Warner 2000). The problems of censorship have become evident especially in cases where regulative actions have been taken against lesbian and gay porn – tellingly, also antiporn materials have been censored (Kipnis 1996: 189). Drawing on radical feminist gynocentric tradition, antiporn feminism postulated a fundamental, binary gender division in which porn was equated with male sexuality, and patriarchal oppression was located in the realm of the embodied, the personal and the sexual. Antiporn feminism relied on ideological readings of porn and sexuality as operations of power and female oppression. While ultimately simplifying – and disempowering in terms of encounters with different kinds of pornographies – antiporn feminism, as presented in the writings of the late Andrea Dworkin, aimed at denaturalizing porn and questioning its gendered power dynamics.

Countering antiporn feminism, anti-antiporn writings of the 1990s laid emphasis on sexual differences, radical sex and the dangers of censorship as acts of normative normalization. Anti-antiporn authors conceptualized gender and sexuality as social and cultural constructions while opposing the reduction of sexuality and desire into binary models (e.g. Califia 1994; Hunter and Duggan 1995; Rubin 1995; Kipnis 1996). In other words, anti-antiporn authors also made evident the normativity inherent in antiporn feminist writings. The essential aim of anti-antiporn feminism was to support sexual freedom and diversity, especially to defend queer representation. As the titles anti- and anti-antiporn already imply, these debates have been founded on the principle of writing against. Both camps have tended to regard the other as monolithic while short-circuiting some of the more difficult questions: Antiporn feminism has steered clear of issues of porn as site of self-expression, diverse representations or subcultural productions. Anti-antiporn feminism, again, has emphasized the radical potential and imagery of pornography while omitting potential problems involved in its production or representational conventions.

The 1990s saw a wave of academic studies of porn, from Linda Williams's *Hard Core* (1989), a study of the genre of porn films, to anthologies such as *Sex Exposed* (Segal and McIntosh 1993) and *Dirty Looks* (Gibson and Gibson 1993). While distancing themselves from the binary logic of the porn debates to date, these studies built on anti-antipornography perspectives, aiming both to question the notions of gendered power relationships associated with porn and to theorize questions of desire, fantasy and sexuality. In the 1990s, pornography was introduced in academic curricula in cinema studies, women's studies and cultural studies, primarily in the USA and some European countries. In the following decade, 'porn studies' has been further established as an arena of interdisciplinary investigation in anthologies (Williams 2004a; Gibson 2004; Lehman 2006), journal special issues (recently *M/C*, *The Velvet Light Trap*, *Texte zur Kunst*), conferences, as well as articles addressing ways of teaching porn in the university classroom (Driver 2004; Jenkins 2004; Reading 2005). This 'third phase' of porn debates – by no means a synthesis of the two previous – has focused on questions of genre, interpretation, heteronormativity, taste and style. Porn studies has examined subcultural and countercultural representations, highlighting the playful and queer dimensions of porn with case studies ranging from lesbian, gay and avant-garde porn to amateur productions (Williams 2004a). Such investigations successfully illuminate the heterogeneity of pornography and question any generalizations concerning the field – yet, in doing so, they risk downplaying the continuing popularity, visibility, tenacity and economic dominance of mainstream heteroporn. In their focus on the departure from the norm, they may support the view of mainstream porn as undeserving of serious analysis, or even as something disgusting, as suggested in antiporn writings (cf. Cramer 2006).

Despite the growth in studies of porn, certain areas remain little researched: studies have been most focused on specific texts and their distribution while far less attention has been paid to the practices of their production and consumption. Porn production remains under-researched and, as Pamela Church Gibson (2004) states, the question of global sex markets tends to be a source of uneasiness and ambivalence within porn studies. In a global perspective, pornography is difficult to tell apart from other fields of commercial sex: porn production is interlaced with sex clubs as well as the international movement of (female) workforce, neo-liberal labour politics and geopolitical transformations. Pornography concerns material practices, economic and embodied ones alike. In terms of usage, porn is inseparable from physical sensations and acts (be these auto-erotic or other). There are, however, as few empirical studies of the reception and use of porn as there are of its production. As pointed out by Alan McKee (2006), the perspectives of consumers have been virtually effaced from considerations of pornography in the academia, policy-making and journalism.

From Porn Histories to Porn Futures

This volume can be seen as part and parcel of the 'academization' of porn studies. Stepping away from (the largely North American) debates over censorship and freedom of speech, as well as ones concerning child protection, *Pornification* addresses the flux between the pornographic and the mainstream while stressing the contingency of porn as a genre and category.

The anthology opens with the section *Porn Histories* that offers historical perspectives on the twentieth-century mainstreaming of pornography while also considering texts that look back in time and cast nostalgic and ironic gazes towards previous porn productions. Susanna Paasonen and Laura Saarenmaa address contemporary popular films reminiscing the 'golden age' of porn cinema of the 1970s, and the kinds of effacements that they accomplish. Framing the era as one of innocence and anti-censorship struggle, they depict the hardcore porn of the 1970s as avant-garde and radical while re-enacting its making with neat and well-shaved bodies – as inevitably mainstream and soft-core. Theatre releases in the 1970s opened the mainstream markets for hardcore porn but it was home video technology that truly facilitated the expansion of porn film audiences. In her chapter, Mireille Miller-Young investigates the development of interracial video as a specialized market category during this 'silver age' of pornography. Articulating the racial desires of their primarily white male producers, directors and writers, the films mythologized black women as sources of both fetishist fascination and disgust. As Miller-Young points out, the flipside of the democratic potential of hardcore porn is the repetition of cultural stereotypes sustaining social inequality, which, however, does not mean that their meanings would be fixed. Audiences produce their own interpretations and interventions and imageries and generic conventions are open to change as they travel from one text to another. This is also noted by Nathan Scott Epley in his chapter on the soft-core aesthetics and the contemporary resurgence of the pin-up. The idealized and sexualized classic pin-up iconography of the 1940s and 1950s has become increasingly popular and is consumed ironically as part of the retro culture of the 'hipsters', well-educated members of Generation X. As both Miller-Young and Epley illustrate, pornification does not only concern the politics of representation and circulation but also those of consumption.

The second section, *Porn Cultures*, addresses the shifting boundaries between porn, art, commercial media and practices of everyday life. Analysing the largest British gay male website Gaydar, Sharif Mowlabocus notes how categories familiar from porn are circulated as points of identification and self-definition to the degree that porn is written into the codes of gay men's everyday lives. Mowlabocus considers the position of mainstream gay porn in relation to mainstream heteroporn, illuminating both the role of pornography in gay male cultures as well as the normative functions of its ubiquitous presence. The question of porn as an element of everyday life, as well as a site of sexual learning and conflict, is also addressed by Kaarina Nikunen. Investigating the online discussion forum of the Finnish *Cosmopolitan* magazine, Nikunen shows how online sex talk makes use of pornography as reference material for sexual techniques, defining it as casual and fun but also as a disturbing presence in heterosexual relationships. Both Mowlabocus and Nikunen analyse pornification as the blurring of the boundaries of sex and porn. Reading the uses of pornography in photographic works by Thomas Ruff and Ann-Mie Van Kerckhoven, Kerstin May emphasizes the significance of context for separating the pornographic from the non-pornographic in the realm of the visual arts. Works referencing pornographic imageries can be seen as capturing the ongoing cultural negotiations on what is considered highbrow or mainstream and that which is considered obscene, low or belonging elsewhere than the art gallery. In their chapter on the intertwining of amateur pornography and celebrity culture, Kevin Esch and Vicki Mayer address the reappraisal of porn aesthetics in mainstream media culture. Drawing on research conducted at the Adult Video News (AVN) Expo, Esch and Mayer consider the history of amateur porn and its commodification, as well as its relationships to celebrity culture.

The third section of the book, *Porn Media*, considers both the position of porn in mainstream commercial media and hardcore porn as a media cultural field. Music videos, and hip-hop videos in particular, are often used as reference when describing the penetration of pornographic imageries – or at least ones connoting commercial sex – in popular culture. Reading two different versions of Khia's video 'My Neck, My Back (Lick It)', Diane Railton and Paul Watson consider pornification as concrete choices that redefine female, sexed authorship and the meaning of the song in question. Rather than generalizing on the basis of pornification, as implied in Khia's video, the authors claim that it is not the removal of clothes but rather the removal of agency that one should be concerned about when considering the politics of sexual representation. In her chapter on street advertising, Leena-Maija Rossi explores how porno chic is put in use in a Christmas campaign by H&M as gestures and postures ultimately promoting heteronormativity. Rossi discusses the possibilities of queer feminist engagement and intervention with pornified imageries, framing porno chic as an issue of standardization rather than democratization of sexuality.

The two other chapters in the section look at hardcore pornography as different kinds of 'education of desire'. Jenny Kangasvuo analyses depictions of bisexuality in porn magazines. While women labelled as bisexual support the familiar porn trope of insatiable female sexuality, bisexual men pose a challenge to normative heterosexuality: in porn, female desire must be fluid but male desire fixed. Hence potentially bisexual men are categorized as closeted homosexuals desperately trying to deny their desires. Porn magazines support the vernacular notion of bisexuality as hypersexuality whereas Michelle Carnes's reading of anal sex videos for women considers the possibilities of porn educating its viewers to think and act in novel ways. Simultaneously de-mystifying anal sex as something messy and painful, and re-mystifying it as an ultimate pleasure, the three video series discussed by Carnes encourage their female viewers to find the joys of anal sex while redefining the categories of sex education, women's porn and couples' videos.

In the concluding chapter, Susanna Paasonen addresses the Internet as a site of alternative pornographies as well as one of envisioned porn futures. Considering the porous categories of the mainstream and the alternative, old and new media, the conclusion argues against simplified readings of technological development or pornification as a media cultural trend.

Part I
Porn Histories

The Golden Age of Porn: Nostalgia and History in Cinema

Susanna Paasonen and Laura Saarenmaa

The mainstreaming of pornography is indebted to the success of feature-length hardcore films of the 1970s. Shot on 35 mm film, productions such as *Deep Throat* (1972), *Behind the Green Door* (1972), *The Devil in Miss Jones* (1973), *The Opening of Misty Beethoven* (1976) and *Debbie Does Dallas* (1978) were widely screened both in the USA and internationally. These films have since been established as classics (Buscombe 2004: 30) and milestones in both scholarly and popular porn historiographies. While some identify the so-called 'golden age of porn' through North American legislation and as ranging from 1957 to 1973 (Lane 2000: 22–3), it was in the 1970s and early 1980s that porn shifted towards the mainstream. In a trend titled by the *New York Times* as *porno chic*, pornography became fashionable, gained mainstream publicity and popularity (McNair 2002: 62–3; Schaefer 2004: 371; Wyatt 1999).

During the past decade, this golden age has been reminisced in films such as *People Vs. Larry Flynt* (1996), *Boogie Nights* (1997) and *Rated X* (2000), numerous documentaries – including the critically acclaimed *Inside Deep Throat* (2005) – and books.[1] This body of popular porn historiography depicts the decade as one of quality films with real stories, personal performers and talented directors, in contrast to the 1980s of video distribution, inflation of the porn industry, rise of AIDS and conservative backlash. With notable exceptions such as the French *Le pornographe* (2001) and the Spanish–Danish co-production *Torremolinos 73* (2003), European histories have not been reminisced to the same degree.

In what follows, we investigate what the 1970s as a decade and pornography as a genre and industry are made to stand for in American films reminiscing porno chic – how this golden age is constructed and for what ends it is remembered. Firstly, we argue that the 1970s are framed as an era of innocence, authenticity and struggle for freedom of speech while structuring out perspectives not fitting in the narrative. These selective framings are intimately tied to our second question concerning the role of nostalgia in films depicting the 1970s. Thirdly, we address the meaning of temporal distance in porn histories. Films produced some three

Figure 2.1 A selection of DVD classics in a Finnish department store, 2007. Photograph by Susanna Paasonen.

decades ago are categorized as classics in ways that further the selective styles of remembering and narrating porn histories. Shot on 35 mm film, as opposed to 8 mm film or video, these productions are identifiable through their producers, actors and directors whose biographies have been central material for films remembering the 1970s.

Popular Porn Historiography

As diverse as the films *Boogie Nights*, *Rated X* or *Inside Deep Throat* may be, they share certain common traits as popular porn historiography. *Boogie Nights* depicts the rise and drug-inflicted fall of porn star Dirk Diggler (Mark Wahlberg), inspired by the real-life character of John Holmes.[2] The biopic *Rated X* depicts the rise of the Mitchell brothers Jim and Artie, known as the creators of *Behind the Green Door*, and their fall due to drugs and alcohol. The documentary *Inside Deep Throat*, again, aims to cover the story of *Deep Throat* and its makers, the cultural impact and legacy of the film, as well as moral norms and censorship practices in the United States.

The films tell stories of male authors rising to fame and fortune while struggling for freedom of speech. These are stories of rise and fall: the rise of films, actors, producers and directors and their downfall caused by drugs, censorship or financial problems. From the film directors Gerard Damiano (of *Deep Throat*) and the Mitchell brothers to the porn stars Holmes and Harry Reems (of *Deep Throat*), these are decidedly male tragedies of fun gone sour.[3] The rise and fall of the porn decade is depicted in metonymical – and decidedly gendered – terms through male erection: in *Boogie Nights*, Diggler loses his erection due to heavy use of cocaine and as Jim Mitchell of *Rated X* admits having been unable to 'get it up' with an eighteen-year-old stripper, the viewers realize that the end is nigh. Behind these tragic figures, female actors perform supporting roles as girlfriends, wives, mothers and born-to-be porn stars.

The foregrounding of straight male tragedies leaves little room for the kinds of stories recounted by Linda Lovelace, the star of *Deep Throat*, who has proven particularly problematic in terms of popular porn history. Lovelace (alias Boreman, Traynor, Marchiano), along with Marilyn Chambers of *Behind the Green Door,* was the first female porn performer to gain mainstream fame. She gave a face and name to porno chic and was widely interviewed as a spokesperson for free and casual sex. Following the extraordinary popularity of *Deep Throat*, Lovelace's biography *Inside Linda Lovelace* (1974) detailed the joys of pornography for a broad readership. As Lovelace started disclosing her abusive relationship with husband and manager Chuck Traynor and how she was forced into a career in porn, this fitted ill with the figure of sexual liberation she was seen to present. With the aim of countering the story authored by her then husband, and cautioned by the publisher that a depressing story would not sell, she published *The Intimate Diary of Linda Lovelace* (1974), which balanced her figure of insatiable sexuality with the story of marital abuse and degradation. She has since published two radically grimmer autobiographics, *Ordeal* (2006/1980) and *Out of Bondage* (1986), and testified for the Reagan administration's Meese Commission on the harms of pornography. Allying herself with the well-known antiporn feminists Gloria Steinem, Andrea Dworkin and Catharine MacKinnon, Lovelace identified her career in pornography as abuse and even compared her films to rape. In her accounts, *Deep Throat*, the film elevated into the symbol of the golden age of porn, is an outcome and symbol of marital abuse.

Interestingly enough, the documentary film *Inside Deep Throat* largely dismisses Lovelace's arguments and frames her as both gullible and misguided. The film frames 1970s' feminist critiques of pornography through the lens of censorship and a reactionary turn toward moral conservatism. Rendering other possible feminist agendas and arguments invisible, the film sets the stage for *Playboy* publisher Hugh Hefner and former *Cosmopolitan* editor Helen Gurley Brown to disclose their views on *Deep Throat* as a landmark of sexual revolution. The effacement of feminist argumentation is striking yet necessary in terms of the film's elevation of *Deep Throat* into a symbol of free sex and free speech. The documentary evidently cannot risk the inclusion of perspectives complicating and questioning this line of argumentation.

The silencing of Lovelace and the tendency to simplify feminist perspectives is part and parcel of the dichotomous porn debate characteristic of the United States.

Focused on questions of freedom of speech versus censorship, this debate has, since the early 1980s, tended to efface complexities, ambiguities and diversities within pornography. Division for or against remains evident in North American studies of pornography and is also influential on an international scale. Meanwhile, their specific context seems easily forgotten. North American debates and political battle lines tell little of porn histories or productions elsewhere, yet the American history has, through numerous acts of retelling, come to stand for *the* history of pornography with its mythical golden age of the 1970s.

Nostalgia and Loss

The 1970s have inspired a range of North American and European cultural texts since the 1990s, from the films *The Last Days of Disco* (1998), *54* (1998) and *Velvet Goldmine* (1998) to the television series *That '70s Show* (1998–2006), numerous film remakes, re-runs and Abba revivals. Retro-fictions have resulted in an assemblage of texts that frame the 1970s as a decade of excess in terms of fashion, drugs, hedonism and sex, sandwiched between the radical 1960s and the yuppie 1980s (Inness 2003: 3). The 1970s tend to be remembered through popular culture in a selective process also identified as the 'Abbafication' of history (Haslam 2005). Although cinematic fictions featuring fashion styles, disco beats, unprotected heterosex and casual drug use may suggest otherwise, the decade was one of significant social change during which the civil rights, gay rights and women's movements all had broad social impact. The neat packaging and labelling of different decades (as radical, yuppie or excessive) works to mask the diversity of cultural trends and forces at any given time. As each decade is made to represent and stand for certain things, they become fixed as symbols (Sickels 2002). All this involves as much forgetting as it does remembering.

Porn historiographies depict a decade of parties finally ending in the hangover of the 1980s. Characterized by the rise of AIDS, cocaine, violence, greed and conservatism of the Reagan era, the 1980s surface as the end of optimism in the films *Boogie Nights*, *Inside Deep Throat* and *Rated X*, and the end of an era is encapsulated in the phrase 'party is over' (Breeden and Carroll 2002: 102; Sickels 2002).[4] Depictions of the 1970s as a lost decade of fun, experimentation and innocence work to frame history in terms of decline – a golden age can, after all, only be constructed in relation to something less golden. Such stories of loss of 'simplicity, personal authenticity and emotional spontaneity' are characteristic of nostalgia, as analysed by Brian S. Turner (1987: 151; Koivunen 2003: 66).[5] Rather than considering nostalgia as false pseudo-historicism while (nostalgically) longing for more truthful and authentic representations of history, we are interested in how porn histories envision the 1970s, the rising porn industry and its agents, and how they make use of nostalgia in the process. The films create nostalgic historiography by situating the events in the past and by referring to actual people. Juxtaposed with the following decades, the 1970s function as a safe zone for addressing porn while maintaining distance to the more recent incarnations of the porn industry. Meanwhile, past fashions and styles provide the films with a groovy retro-gloss. The clothing and hairstyles of the 1970s signify temporal distance: they imply that whether good or bad, these are definitely days gone by.

Although the films discussed in this chapter are heavy in representations of loss, this is by no means the only framing for nostalgia towards the 1970s. In his discussion of the commodification of nostalgia in the United States, Paul Grainge (2000) distinguishes between nostalgia as a mood and a mode. Whereas nostalgic mood characterizes experiences of loss and longing, mode is a question of representation and style that does not necessitate emotional investment. Hence nostalgia has been disjoined from any specific temporal references in the past and 'cannot be explained through any master narrative of decline, longing, or loss' (Grainge 2000: 32). The proliferation of retro-aesthetics in contemporary media calls for a rethinking of nostalgia and representation as not automatically connected to sentiment, and the uses of nostalgia – from mood to mode and back – are certainly variable also in the fictions discussed in this chapter. *Boogie Nights*, for example, makes use of both. Future porn star Diggler's teenage room is filled with sports gear and film posters (pin-ups, Bruce Lee, Al Pacino in *Serpico*): the film binds together iconic products of popular culture with those of the emerging porn industry in the creation of a *boyish*, nerdish and ultimately sympathetic character. In addition to the boyish, porn performers are depicted as trendy. The first scenes of the film are located in a club booming with disco beats where the trendiest people work in the porn industry. These are examples of nostalgia as a mode whereas nostalgia as a mood is prevalent in the film's depiction of the expanding porn industry of the 1980s.

Porn historiography characterizes the 1970s as an era of sexual, and even artistic, exploration unhinged by AIDS, and of adult film-making undisturbed by video technology or the economical dictates of the porn industry. As Cindy Patton states, the 1970s were about the convergence of independent art film-makers and pornographers. The artistic avant-garde saw porn as a means to explicitly critique sexual mores, while pornographers saw the possibility of attracting liberal mainstream audiences through artful films (Patton 2000: 258; also Wyatt 1999). This convergence, depicted as one adventure and exploration, is central to the creation of the golden age. Journalist Peter Bart interviewed in *Inside Deep Throat* explains that 'for that brief moment porn was part of discovery, curiosity, change. Today, it's different.'

Today, films like *Behind the Green Door*, *Opening of Misty Beethoven* or *The Devil in Miss Jones* are references and material for cultural theory (Patton 2000), and valued in terms of artistry, extraordinariness of atmosphere and story content seldom seen today.[6] In DVD reviews, the ten-minute montage sequence of optically printed and solarized cum shots of *The Green Door* is ironically compared to Leni Riefenstahl's bombastic aesthetics while *Misty Beethoven* is situated in the classical literary tradition as a parody of George Bernard Shaw's play *Pygmalion* (1916). These reviews interpret the films as brainchildren of *auteurs,* visionary and uncompromising author-directors.[7] Auteurism and references to high culture support the films' cult status. According to Matt Hills (2002: 197), cult is marked by an interest in inappropriate or low cultural forms that draws its own highs and lows in the devalued detritus of popular culture. For Hills (2002: 131–4), media cult text is, paradoxically, both 'found' (consisting of textual qualities and properties) and 'created' (by the audience and media). The present cult status of the 1970s' porn films is partially created by young film critics and enthusiasts who maintain their *connoisseur* status through familiarity with the roots and classics of the genre. These ways of remembering have more to do with acknowledging (or even name dropping) than analysis: 1970s' films are often used as points of reference when attacking the hollowness of contemporary porn but more rarely investigated at any length themselves.

Viewing the porn films of the 1970s considered as the classics of the genre, differences in style and approach to the more recent films reminiscing their creation are evident. Rather than disco, their music scores feature progressive rock, blues and jazzy tones. Films like *Boogie Nights, Inside Deep Throat* and *Rated X* tell stories of personal struggle and loss whereas the films of the 1970s are rich in gags and comedy: in *Misty Beethoven*, airplane travel evokes questions such as 'Sex or No Sex seats?' while the plotline of the *Deep Throat* is famously about a young woman with a clitoris in her throat. In a contrary affective range, the opening scenes of *The Devil in Miss Jones* feature a middle-aged woman with black fingernails desperately masturbating in prison-like surroundings and a woman slitting her wrists in a bathtub. Such scenes may evoke repulsion of the kind lacking from contemporary mainstream pornography as well as the films reminiscing 1970s' porn. Films produced since the 1990s are selective in their aesthetic remembrance. While faithfully replicating the hairstyles and sideburns of the bygone decade, they do not do so with the hairy backs, armpits and crotches which abound in the productions of the 1970s. Their tragic stories mainly involve tanned and well-groomed people.

Fixated on Film

In *Inside Deep Throat*, Gerard Damiano, the director of *Deep Throat* and *The Devil in Miss Jones*, describes the effects of video production and distribution, accompanied by melancholic background music:

> With the advent of the video camera it got to be so easy to shoot X-rated video that everybody could do it ... They were nothing. It was just one sex scene after another ...

I couldn't make that kind of film because there was no reason to … It was over. You didn't need filmmakers any more.

Damiano is next seen walking down a white wooden pier, surrounded by swirling seagulls. The sky is cloudy and summer seems to be over as he raises his arms in a gesture of helpless surrender. Damiano is shown as a tragic character whose aspirations and visions were crushed by VHS – even if he continued making hardcore films well into the 1990s. American film critic Robert Ebert (1997) titles Damiano the best hardcore director who 'went through a period of believing he could make art films about sex'. This comment is difficult to balance with Ebert's own zero-star rating of *Deep Throat*, as well as with Damiano's own oeuvre of well over forty films, including such less well-known works as *Enema Bandit* (1977) and *Young Girls in Tight Jeans* (1989).

The main tragic character of the documentary is nevertheless Harry Reems who faced trial for his performance in *Deep Throat*. An unwilling martyr of freedom of speech, Reems's desire to shift to mainstream film remained unfulfilled and he developed alcohol and drug addiction: 'I lost my home. I lost my career. I lost my friends. And ended literally panhandling in the streets of Sunset Boulevard', Reems recounts. *Inside Deep Throat* reiterates stories of loss: loss of personal career, loss of an art form and its unfulfilled possibilities. Damiano mourns the fall of art and craft for the hegemony of financial profit, and is certainly not alone in doing so. Author Normal Mailer encapsulates the shift as one 'from art to money'. If the viewer is experiencing déjà vu, this may be due to strong similarities to *Boogie Nights* and its character of the producer Jack Horner (Burt Reynolds) Horner, like Damiano, has ambitions of creating 'real' feature films with hardcore action: films with a story, proper editing and performers who act. These artistic ambitions are crushed by the introduction of home video. Enabling high profits but limited by low image and sound quality, video represents a collapse in quality and ambition, and ultimately marks the end of the golden age of semi-amateurs, enthusiasm and experimentation. In other words, the 'quality' of 1970s' porn comes into being only at the very moment when it is seen as lost.

The popularity and critical acclaim of *Boogie Nights* has given it a status of a metanarrative concerning the shift from 1970s to the 1980s, from film to video and art to money (cf. Kleinhans 2006: 152). The juxtaposition of 'art' and 'money' as production motives obscures the fact that financial motives were hardly alien to porn productions during, or preceding, the so-called golden age: *Deep Throat* and *Green Door* are often celebrated as the most profitable films ever made in respect to their production costs. Furthermore, the end of the golden age actually signified the radical expansion of the industry. Video multiplied the sales of porn films (Sickels 2002: 55; Miller-Young in this volume) and the business has since merely increased its profitability in DVD and online distribution (Lane 2001).

The narrative of loss, as expressed in *Inside Deep Throat* and *Boogie Nights*, mainly makes sense in terms of 35 mm film as a medium. Cinema distribution is missed while narrative feature film is positioned as the formal norm and ideal for pornographic representation – even if the overwhelming majority of pornographic films produced during the past century have been episodic ones and far less concerned with narrative development than the display of sexual acts and genitalia. All in all, porn films consist of sexual scenes that are not necessarily tied together by narrative. The format of film – be this 8 mm, 16 mm or 35 mm – or the existence of narrative is by no means a guarantee of quality in pornography. Nevertheless, narrative seems to become a criterion for separating bad porn films from better ones, and the medium of film gains fetish status in the process. In the words of adult film-maker Ed Peroo, 'Film had soul; video has nothing … It flows like water, but film had a texture, a feeling, something you could grab onto and feel' (in McNeil and Osborne 2005: 369; also Kleinhans 2006: 155).

Jack Horner wants to make 'real films' and resists cheap video productions. Damiano, venerated by his colleagues as the Bergman and Fellini of porn (McNeil and Osborne 2005: 53, 130–1), mourns the decline of film profession and emphasizes the centrality of authorial vision and control. These are explicitly stories of male auteurs: their ambitions cover more than financial profit; they find themselves in conflict with the rising porn industry; and their passion is first and foremost towards cinema construed as a lost object. Cinema figures similarly in European feature films remembering the avant-garde days of the 1970s. The French *Le pornographe* juxtaposes contemporary pornography with the artistic experiments of the late 1960s and early 1970s. Slow in tempo, it focuses on a veteran porn director Jacques Laurent – played by the French new wave icon Jean-Pierre Léaud – and his reflections on relationships, life, cinema and generational revolt. *Le pornographe* is saturated with nostalgia as a mood (sense of loss and bygone futures) but is void of representations of the 1970s (in Grainge's terms, nostalgia as a mode). The Spanish *Torremolinos 73* operates with an inverted logic. Entirely embedded in beige colours and less trendy 1970s' styles, the film is set in the last years of Franco's fascist regime during which the couple Alfredo and Carmen Lopez (Javier Cámara and Candela Peña) produce 'educational' 8 mm sex films for the Scandinavian market. Learning cinematographic practice, Alfredo is inspired by Bergman and ultimately realizes an existentialist – and rather absurd – feature hardcore film in homage to the auteur. While the film frames the period as one of innocence and experimentation in terms of pornography, cinematic and sexual representation like other fictions discussed in this chapter, it is not depicted as any golden age worth longing for.

Le pornographe and *Torremolinos 73* tell stories of independent productions and aesthetic experimentation. However, unlike popular North American porn historiography, they are not concerned with the juxtaposition of the 1970s with the 1980s, and the era they address is partly a different creature altogether (consider, for example, the differences between the late Falangist regime and the United States during the Watergate scandal). *Boogie Nights* depicts porn as a challenge to masculine performance, dividing men to those who 'can' and those who 'cannot' perform sexual acts in front of the camera. In these two European films, the main challenge lies in coping with the emotional blandness and banality of porn. Acting porn is easy – tolerating it is the difficult part.[8] While these films also make use of nostalgia, they cannot be conflated with the metanarrative recognizable in the films discussed above.

The Workings of Time

Deep Throat, The Devil in Miss Jones, Behind the Green Door and *Opening of Misty Beethoven* have been elevated into classics, landmarks in the American struggle for freedom of speech and experiments in a new kind of artful pornography. Temporal distance has helped to mark them apart from contemporary porn. Hence soon after the cinema premiere of *Inside Deep Throat* in Finland, *Deep Throat* DVDs were on sale at a local department store under the category of classics, in an eclectic selection also featuring Bing Crosby films and *Titanic*.

Porn from the 1970s has enjoyed an afterlife in video and DVD distribution, popular historiography and scholarly analyses of porn: these films are remembered. Studies of porn have drawn largely on theoretical and conceptual tools of film studies – including identification, desire, voyeurism, fetishism and a general interest in genre and narrative. Rather unsurprisingly, films, encompassing ones shot on video, have been staple objects of analysis (see Williams 2004a; Lehman 2006). While the success of VHS certainly explains some of this focus, the more recent transformations in the distribution of porn necessitate departure from both the dominance of films as objects of study and film studies as discipline. The focus on narrative both enables and necessitates a selective look at pornography (on films rather than still images; on certain kinds of films over others). It also seems to result in a general turn towards past pornographies, such as the canonized, pre-VHS and pre-AIDS classics of the 1970s.

The attraction of the 1970s is evident also in younger generations' interest in a time they have not personally experienced (Waldrep 2000). The story of a lost golden age is narrated not only by porn veterans, but also by people *born* in the 1970s, such as *Boogie Nights* writer and director Paul Thomas Anderson. The figure of the hedonistic, excessive, experimental and innocent decade has cross-generational appeal that is maintained through the stylized ways of reminiscing it. Historical distancing facilitates depictions of porn whereas the contemporary porn industry remains something of a taboo. It would be more difficult to imagine emotionally compelling drama featuring major stars and depicting the American porn industry of today.

In the television documentary *Desperately Seeking Seka* (2002), former porn star Veronica Hart detaches the films of the golden age from markers of skill or quality and emphasizes later improvements in work safety, technical skill and professionalism. Like porn star Seka, the main subject of the documentary, Hart depicts the golden age as fun enough but a golden one only in inverted commas. Such questioning voices tend to be subdued in popular porn historiographies, as are women's stories in general. No fictions based on the lives of Linda Lovelace or Marilyn Chambers have been produced, although director Ron Howard has apparently acquired the rights to *Ordeal*. Films like *Boogie Nights* or *Rated X* envision a homosocial golden age of men, boys and brothers brought to screens by filmmakers of different generations. Porn is represented as 'guy stuff' inherited from the older generation, which is circulated, produced and consumed among – and culturally belongs to – heterosexual men. The homosocial framework does not accommodate the voices of either women or gay men. This is noteworthy since post-Stonewall metropolitan gay male cultures probably best encapsulated the sexual abundance and excess associated with the 1970s: according to AIDS activist Rodger McFarnale in the documentary film *Gay Sex in the 70s* (2005), gay life '*was* a pornographic movie'.

Ways of reminiscing the 1970s work a domestication and de-politicization of both pornography and sex. Along with feminist voices, gay male cultures are effaced from view while white, American heterosexual men working in and developing the porn industry are left with the task of narrating the story of 'the wild decade'. Similar effacement has also taken place in the ways of remembering disco and its origins in black and gay urban cultures (Kooijman 2005). Domestication is accomplished by the display of sympathetic personalities, pop music and sideburns, 'bright images of Abba, purple flares over dangerously high platform shoes' (Graham, Kaloski, Neilson and Robertson 2003:7). Embellishing the pornographic imagery and avoiding scenes of actual porn, the films stress artistic ambition and vision while, on the other hand, depicting these as past concerns. Doing this, popular porn historiography both pays homage to 1970s' pornography and hides it from view.

–3–

Let Me Tell Ya 'Bout Black Chicks: Interracial Desire and Black Women in 1980s' Video Pornography

Mireille Miller-Young

The 1980s' 'video revolution' in the American pornography industry prompted a vast increase and change in the production and distribution of hardcore films, establishing adult entertainment as a dominant United States media industry.[1] The proliferation of diverse material stimulated the development of specialized markets for interracial (usually constructed as black and white) and all-black videos. Highly charged racial fantasies now allowed the growing consumer audience access to previously private and illicit desires. In these genres, the industry's engagement with black women, both as sex objects and sex workers, was reorganized; the production and consumption of racialized sexual desire spread on a massive capitalist scale. Porn's role as a socially transgressive sexual culture has often allowed space for multiple subjectivities, pleasures and desires to be explored, including the desires of women, queers, people of colour, the disabled and the disenfranchised.[2] However, black women's specific history of exploitation and coercion plays out in these racial fantasies in ways that are far less than transgressive. These women were ambivalently mythologized as sources of both fascination and disgust within a system organized around the marking and marketing of their absolute difference.

In these videos, often produced by white men and designed around their sexual gaze, tropes of black women as hypersexual, hyper-available, deviant and degraded – all of which dominate racialized sexual discourses in the United States historically – were made explicit.[3] Implicit in this media was the absolute disavowal of black women's bodies as loci of desire, even while white masculinity (re)produced multiple anatomies and applications for their consumption. Moreover, black women were typically situated in a bifurcated representational system as either assimilative to whiteness or totally degraded as the Other, and this paradigm is ever reiterated and consumed in the sexual marketplace. This essay explores the way in which early appearances of black women in video porn both replicate and depart from previous hardcore representations as well as the critical role video technology has occupied in pornography's location as the primary site for dissemination of heteronormative racial desire.

The Silver Age

The glamour of 'porno chic' and the golden age of theatrical film pornography came to a close with the ascendance of home video in the late 1970s. Pornography in the video era animated multiple social desires and transgressions; video technology prompted the massive extension of hardcore media as a primary economy of desire, with very intimate effects. The porn business was on the forefront of exploiting the cost-effective new technology, transferring its popular film productions to videocassette. 'In this way,' argues Laurence O'Toole, 'pornography was performing its regular duty as a key driver for the economic emergence of a new technology' (1999: 104). 'The thing that changed everything was the development of the home video industry', adult industry historian and critic Jim Holliday suggests: 'A whole new market was open to sexploitation films' (1987: 15). The adult industry's use of VHS made a range of taboo sexual interests newly accessible, vitally transforming the viewer's relationship with pornography. Rather than join the 'raincoaters' in the tawdry sex cinemas and peep shows of the nation's red light districts, video brought hardcore into the private spaces of the home, where, as Constance Penley observes, viewers could 'find out what their own fantasies [were] and what [were] the limits of their fantasies' (*History* 2000).

The gendered effect of video technology was profoundly significant, as men could indulge in an expanding variety of phallocentric fantasies and women, who might have been less inclined to frequent the adult theatres of the 1970s' porn film era, became an important growing sector of the hardcore video consumers and viewers. Whether alone, with friends, or with their male or female sexual partners, women viewers could enjoy unprecedented access to material that had previously been available only within the masculine spaces of fraternal clubs and adult theatres. Consumers could now rent or purchase videos from local retailers or through the mail catalogues, including 'classics' like *Deep Throat* (AFV 1972), *The Devil in Ms. Jones* (VCX 1972) and *Debbie Does Dallas* (VCX 1978). These prodigious transformations in the modes by which consumers accessed porn also altered the adult entertainment industry's economic structure. In 1979 VCRs were a specialist item for the tech-savvy middle class; they were found in less than 1 per cent of American homes. Ten years later, more than half of American homes had VCRs, and adult video played a substantial role in the widespread engagement with this new technology (*History* 2000).[4] In fact, because the 'majority of early cassettes were pornographic', producers of the hardcore genre actually defined the trajectory of the technology (Van Scoy 2000: 64). Although there is no data as to how consumption during this period was racialized, it is clear that the widespread dissemination of erotic materials through video allowed whites and people of colour, men as well as women, greater access to pornography. Prompting the formation of a mass audience for the mass cultural spectacle of modern pornography, the industry exploited the increased domestic availability of pornography by creating and marketing new categories of sexuality in thousands of videos.

These technological and economic transformations in the business of pornography are implicated in the development of black and interracial video as a specialized market. Video allowed racial difference to be imagined, produced, marketed, consumed, and surveilled in new and thoroughly sexual ways even while it reproduced racial (and gender) hierarchies. A powerful fascination with racial difference as sexual performance underlines how pornography acts as, like Laura Kipnis points out, a form of 'political theater' where social and cultural ideologies of desire and taboo are staged and manipulated, as sexual norms and categories are simultaneously upheld and transgressed (Kipnis 1999: 164). Because pornography functions as a 'festival of social infractions', its 'allegories of transgression reveal, in the most visceral ways, not only our culture's edges, but how intricately our own identities are bound up in all of these quite unspoken, but relentless, cultural dictates' (Kipnis 1999: 167). Race in the USA, acutely wedded to our cultural and individual psychic histories, is archived in the patrolled borders of our sexualities. It penetrates and organizes multiple levels of power in ways that are at once subtle and extreme, covert and overt, and thoroughly bound to a historical imaginary of the desire for and taboo of interracial desire.

A Specialized Market

Modern video pornography continued and made the production and specialization of erotic images of black women that reflect racial, gender, and sexual tropes of difference, availability and submission even more private and accessible to a wide audience. Mirroring the old, and newly updated, racial and sexual stereotypes of deviance, exoticism and submission, black women's roles in the racial theatre of video porn mainly included roles as subservient maids, cheap prostitutes, exotic whores and seductive witches, as black men performed roles as studs, coons, criminals, pimps and giant talking phalluses.[5] Articulations of the racial desires of primarily white male producers, directors and writers, these roles anxiously reiterated the profoundly taboo nature of desire for black bodies within a historically white supremacist society. They revealed a crisis in representation and sexual economy, for how exactly should the dark secrets of racial desire be reproduced and marketed in the context of a post-civil rights social order where such stereotypes were being contested in social life?[6]

Manufacturers, distributors, retailers and adult industry experts were captivated with the development of interracial and black 'product' as a lucrative arm of the porn economy and took up the massive industrialization of these racial types as consumer sexual preferences. Black product would consist of all-black casts while interracial product usually consisted of black and white performers, highlighting pairings between black men and white women, and white men and black women. During the 1960s and 1970s, prior to the creation of this specialized market for interracial and all-black videos, black actors were marginal to the theatrical releases, with maybe only one black man and/or black woman, and sometimes one Latina (Vanessa Del Rio) or Asian woman (Linda Wong) cast in a white-dominated film, such as in *Behind the Green Door* (Mitchell Bros. 1972) and *Sex World* (Essex 1977).

Starting in 1984, adult entertainment companies began to bring black characters from the sidelines to the fore with all-black cast and interracial black and white cast videos. Suddenly, with the release of *Hot Chocolate* (Essex 1984), *Black Taboo* (VCA 1984) and *Black Jail Bait* (LA Video 1984), white desire for black sexuality in porno became newly visualized. Writer and co-director of *Hot Chocolate* and *Black Taboo*, Bill Margold was clear about his intentions: 'When I make a movie about black people, I project *my* fantasies, *not* theirs.'[7] Such fantasies were amazingly lucrative: by 1985 it was reported that the 'genre of all-black adult tapes is extremely popular,' and that they were 'very saleable' ('Black' 1985: 13). But the broad interest among whites (across age, region, class) in media centring on hyper-explicit black/interracial sex had to be maintained as a secret, sustained to protect the freedom of white men to consume the racial Other without having to expose their fetishistic desires. For example, industry insiders instructed hardcore retailers to market black sexuality as a distinct specialized genre so as to provide white male customers easy and private access to their fetishes: 'Keep all these tapes in one section and if possible, at one sale price … Remember that with any specialty adult item, a customer may be hesitant to ask for tapes with black performers. However, if they are all together, he can pick and choose discreetly' (Fishbein 1985: 18).

This protective orientation of the prurient interests of white male spectators was not new, though, as during the illicit trade in pornography in the decades prior to the liberalization of pornography in the USA in the 1970s, 'stag films' and 'blue movies' were shown in settings such as fraternal clubs and other male-only gatherings.[8] The existence of numerous stag films featuring black actors and white actors in coitus suggests that white men were interested in consuming these materials, yet the fact that these materials were much less popular than all-white films suggests either that interracial sex would be seen as less marketable or it could suggest that certain types of cross-racial desire were too policed to allow the public demand for them in these collective white male gatherings. Decades later, home video allowed for the proliferation of porn displaying interracial sex for white spectators in ways that were previously impermissible within the strict economy of racial segregation. The modern adult video industry constantly wrestled with how to address the growing, overwhelmingly white male spectator's interest in people of colour's sexuality and the problematic of interracial fantasy as always subversive of the policed racial/sexual border. Ambivalence framed the genre as a risky, if lucrative, market for pornographers: 'Everyone is afraid of [the videos]. For the few companies that have the guts to make them, black tapes have always done well. But no one will put any money into it' (Fishbein 1985: 18). Yet, despite the historic public denial of white male desire for black women's bodies, 'We all know', *Adult Video News* (*AVN*) writer Thomas McMahon noted, that the interracial fantasy market was 'very popular' (1986: 14).

By June 1985, *AVN* declared in their review of *Black Bun Busters*, the first all-black cast anal sex tape, 'The genre of all-black tapes is extremely popular' ('Black' 1985: 13). One month later, Paul Fishbein, then editor at *AVN*, was so impressed with the growth of the genre that he formulated an action plan for manufacturers, distributors and retailers on 'How to Sell Adult Tapes: Marketing All-Black or Interracial Cassettes':

> Let's start by saying that the all-black and interracial adult videotapes that are currently on the market are among the easiest sell-through items … what has flooded the market are average-quality tapes, produced solely to exploit a new genre … However, that hasn't prevented manufacturers from selling big numbers. The market is definitely there and exploitable. (Fishbein 1985: 18)

Acknowledging the profitability of the black and interracial video genres, Fishbein's article established several key issues to the manufacture and distribution of racial difference as a specialized fetish in hardcore media. First, black sexuality is desired by whites and blacks and is thus highly exploitable in the sexual marketplace. Next, while desired, black sexuality remains taboo, hardcore media featuring blacks is consequently marginalized as a 'specialty' item. Finally, the market was saturated by 'average' videos with lower quality scripts, sets and modes of production than most mainstream, white, heterosexual porn films of the era.[9] The appropriation of black sexuality as a fetish market, its institutionalization as a specialized economy of desire consumed by a mainly white masculine and increasingly black masculine gaze, and its degraded iteration as a profitable but devalued commodity are significant here.

Feminist writer Susie Bright's groundbreaking exposé of 'The Image of the Black in Adult Video', appearing in *AVN*'s April 1987 issue, critiqued the racial fetish market for its problematic lack of care for productions with black actors. She wrote: 'Obviously interracial tapes are not a labor of love, and it shows in the quality. Few have received critical acclaim, and the ability of some of the black performers often seems wasted in the typical script environment' (Bright 1987: 56). Bright takes the industry to task for its racist exploitation of interracial sexuality in tacky, poor quality images, sloppy editing and sound, uncreative sets and simple plots that do not reflect the range or depth of black sexual subjectivities or talent. She chides adult producers for using anachronistic cultural ideologies of black sexuality in cheap, seedy productions to satiate white male consumers and attract black audiences desirous of images of black hardcore sex. Bright notes that 'black audiences will continue to have a special loyalty to black performers, and this mandate will allow producers to go on spending next to nothing, care even less and still make a bundle' (1987: 64).

Dark Imaginations

The most popular production team of the 1980s' video age was the Dark Brothers, two white men who specialized in interracial video productions. Former New York University film student Greg Dark led the direction and vision of their productions, while Walter Dark handled the business of manufacturing and distribution for videos like *New Wave Hookers* (VCA 1985) and *Black Throat* (VCA 1985). Greg Dark explained his interest in making interracial genre films that reflected a particular approach to representing Black subjectivity: 'I put Black people in my films as caricatures,' Dark explained, 'like street graffiti, almost' (quoted in Irving 1985: 53). That Dark framed his black characters as 'caricatures' and as 'street graffiti' is actually profoundly illuminating of the spectatorship, appropriation and consumption of black culture by whites in hardcore. In his videos Dark produced caricatures of blacks that imitate an imagined 'blackness' – to, in his words, 'push things as far as they can go in an outrageous fashion' – in figurations that were, in fact, true to the definition of 'caricature': distorted, inferior and ludicrous presentations (Brooks-King 2007). Laura Kipnis argues that all porn deals in caricature, the fantastical, and allegorical that tickle the underbelly of our social mores, the 'roots of our culture at the deepest corners of the self' (1999: 161). Indeed, the spectacle of black people as sexualized freaks defines the boundaries of normality and deviance, and pleasure and danger for spectators. The long history of exhibiting black peoples as sexualized objects for consumption informs pornography's racialized characterizations, ones that are inevitably 'mythical and hyperbolic' (Kipnis 1999: 163). Yet, what is fascinating in the case of early interracial video vis-à-vis the Dark Brothers is how these fantasies serve as racial political theatre. Their films perpetuate the subordination of black bodies as spectacles for appropriation and consumption, even as they illuminate the profound anxiousness of cross-racial desire.

Mobilizing the anxieties of shame and desire, the Dark Brothers' films delve into the deep mythologies of black sexuality as hyper-visible, hyper-available and hypersexual. Their film *Let Me Tell Ya 'Bout White Chicks* (VCA 1984), which advertises being 'The Original Interracial Classic' on the box cover, exploited historical stereotypes of black men as always desirous of sexually possessing white women. In the video, a group of black men, including a pimp (Jack Baker), sit in a bedroom recounting their sexual exploits with white women. One man (Tony El-Ay) emphatically resists the group's suggestions that sex with white women is better than with black women. The plot line rests with the group convincing him through their stories about extreme pleasure with white women that he should embrace interracial sex with white women in order to 'really be a man'. The opening song, a kind of rap about the merits of 'White Chicks', overlays the introductory credits and is followed by Jack Baker's (as the pimp) solo rap, which stages the film as primarily about black men's insatiable desire for white women and dismissal of what Siobhan Brooks-King terms black women's 'erotic capital':

> I like to jam and I like to jive but there's nothing better than a little white hide/There's nothing better to make a black man right than little white ass on a hot summer night/Ten only black women I would pass just to touch some sweet white chick's ass/Sho bop a dee shoo bop a doo I like white chicks and so will you/I said Sho bop a dee shoo bop a doo I like white chicks and so will you! Hey!

As in most white female/black male interracial hardcore, the plot follows a historical discourse that defines black masculinity in relationship to the big black phallus. Black male subjectivity cannot be disaggregated from the spectacle of their alleged penetrative prowess. As I have argued above, white men are the primary consumers of interracial video during this period, which means that the performance of white women as totally receptive and desirous of black men, and black men as aggressive, deviant and consumed with the possession of white women is constructed as providing pleasure for the white masculine gaze.

Most of the characters in the *White Chicks* narrate their trysts with white women as being initiated when they broke into or connived their way into a white woman's home in order to burglarize and seduce her. They are criminals posing as telephone service workers or lurking behind and climbing into windows. Others somehow use their black masculine charm to have white women invite them into their homes, and the sex is often in intimate spaces that occupy the 'white home' such as the kitchen, dining room and the bedroom. Scenes are marked by white men's absence (it's usually suggested he's at work or on a business trip) and white women's longing to break out of the confines of their normative domestic realm; a generic strategy in pornography from early stag films to the present. In this film, black men are like foxes in the hen house, but the hens have invited the foxes in. The one black man who resists the pressure to worship the sexual superiority of white women over black women during the course of the film is eventually convinced of his error when the pimp magically produces a white woman for him and the doubting man to share while the other men watch. While the black men are figured as deviant, good-for-nothing criminals who illicitly seduce white patriarchy's most prized possession – white womanhood – they actually do a great deal of labour for white manhood. Here, white masculinity, vis-à-vis the spectator, can be titillated by the operations of cultural transgression in this racialized political theatre, but is nonetheless maintained as dominant by its authority as producers and privileged consumers of these far from transgressive texts.

The constant reproduction of interracial sex as both subversive and hegemonic in this genre is really about the sexual desires of white men. This dialectic is illustrated in the Dark Brothers next video *Let Me Tell Ya 'Bout Black Chicks* (VCA 1985), a take-off of the successful *Let Me Tell Ya 'Bout White Chicks*.[10] In the video, which is no longer available and was thought by some scholars to be lost, a group of four black women maids sit around a hotel room that they are meant to be cleaning, enjoying a juicy conversation about their taboo sexual encounters with white men. Rather than follow the format of *White Chicks* by constructing a narrative whereby white men disclose their fantasies and experiences with black women, *Black Chicks* is organized around the black women maids' narratives, which become flashback scenes where the video's sexual performances occur (in a child's room, a bathroom, a kitchen and a bedroom), so that in both films it is black characters that reminisce about the pleasures of sex with white characters. This paradigm allows white men to never explicitly disclose their desires to consume or participate in interracial sex between whites and blacks. In this film, the black women's articulation of interracial sex as integral to their desires allows white male characters to be figured as merely passively responding to black women's powerful longings for interracial sex. It is black women who are the instigators of such socially illicit acts – as always, they are the ones asking for it.

Like *White Chicks*, the producers use a rap song in the introductory credits to set the stage of desire and desirability: 'Black chicks! Black chicks!/Let me tell ya 'bout Black chicks!/Black chicks love big dicks, and everybody loves … Black chicks!' The opening scene presents a disordered hotel room where our four narrators languidly rest on the two double beds. They are maids, played by Sahara, Lady Stephanie, Purple Passion and Cherri Lei-Me. Each wears a sexy 'French Maid' uniform in black satin and white lace trim with feather-trimmed high-heeled shoes. Although we do not learn all their names, they are each marked by a different colour – their feather dusters, hair clips and ankle socks coordinate in either hot pink (Lady Stephanie), aqua blue (Purple Passion), bright yellow (Sahara) or lime green (Cheri Lei-Me). In contrast to the stiff dialogue characteristic of most porn films, these actresses convincingly perform the stereotypical 'black girl' cadence and affectation – lots of rhyming, 'Oh, Honeys!', 'Mmmm Hmmms!' and 'Giiiirls!', and there is ample eye rolling, teeth sucking and hands on the hips. Their conversation begins with one commenting on the mess left in the room by a presumed white guest, and another, conveniently named Sapphire[11] for her aggressive demeanour, says she thinks the slovenly guest must have been a black man:

Blue   What's wrong with you, Sapphire, you think whitey wouldn't make no mess? As a matter of fact … [puts hand on hips for a moment] … he *knows* we're going to be here cleaning up. So he makes the *biggest* mess he can!

Yellow   No shit, if he didn't make no mess, we wouldn't have no jobs, honey!

Green   You know you don't have to be no maid cause you can *always* be a ho' because whitey *loves* us for that dick food.

Pink   Fuck all that! I rather be collecting whitey's welfare!

Green   What's wrong with you, Sapphire? Don't you know the good Lord gave us the ability to be maids *or* whores? So it's a sin for you to be sitting on your ass all day collecting welfare.

Yellow   Well, I rather be sitting on a white boy's dick all day long, you know what I mean? Those white boys, they are *clean*, honey! Now a brother, I can take his dick and put it in the corner and it would stand up by itself, it's so funky!

Blue   Mmmm humm! But you know, the whole time she's sitting on his dick she'd be trying to steal his El Dorado Cadillac! Ha ha!

Pink   Don't be talking about our fine Black brotherhood like that. Anyway, you show me just one whitey with a dick half the size of a brother's, just *half* the size.

Green   Hush up, Negro! What *you* know about white boys? Have you ever let one eat your cunt or stick his alabaster pole in your hole?

Pink   Hell no! White ass goat. Just like I said, they got little dicks.

Blue   Well, let me tell you something about that. I was working as a maid for this rich white family, and one day …

This short opening scene establishes that black women's sexualities are embedded in their labour, and this labour is simultaneously invisible and dependent upon white men. The scene frames the maids 'sitting around' talking about sex instead of working, reinforcing their representation as caricatures rather than workers. Yet, unlike black men as burglars and pimps who must break into white homes in *White Chicks*, black maids exist as workers already present in white intimate spaces. The black female body is always already a labouring body and we do not need to *see* her work to understand that as her fundamental role. Her position is dependent on white male desire, authority and control. A contradictory stereotype emerges: black women are lazy *and* they do menial labour. Without white men making a mess, black women 'wouldn't have no jobs'. Here black women exist for white men, and they are both pathologized through a racist heteropatriarchal sublimated desire and fetishized in the closest spaces of intimacy. Furthermore, the film conceptualizes black women as only fit to be domestic servants *and/or* whores for white men, and in both capacities they are 'service workers' fulfilling menial labour normalized as 'women's work' and historically represented specifically as 'black women's work.'

African American women were situated as maids in this video and so many others in the 1980s and 1990s, more often than they appear as wives, girlfriends, bosses or business partners. The eroticization of black women's historical location in domestic work, with its attendant symbolics of subservience, backbreaking labour and sexual vulnerability, comfortably normalizes the cross-racial sexual transgression taking place in the film. Black women's portrayal of the maid figure in interracial adult video represents their difference through tropes of hyper-sexuality, hyper-availability and servitude. Made vulnerable and submissive in this racialized and sexualized fantasy, they are enjoined to occupy the most intimate spaces of white patriarchy. White men are figured as masculine ideals of power, potency and mobility within this mythologized world where black men are glaringly absent. In a media genre where all subjectivities lack realism, black subjectivities are strikingly hollow. Black women's sexuality is once again defined by a politics of access to their bodies, constructed as black women's own insatiable drive for sexual and commodity consumption. Indeed, for white male viewers, the collective fantasy or historical memory of the black maid is focused upon the erotics of their domestic labour as a site of nurturing and physical intimacy. The desire for the imaginary of nurturing and intimacy with the black maid of course erases the vast history of violence against black women slaves, particularly in their role as servants to white men.

Most striking about the introductory scene in *Black Chicks* is the Dark Brothers' signification of contemporary racialized and gendered debates about welfare in their framing of black women's choices between work (their god-given ability to choose between being maids or whores) or 'whitey's welfare'. The discourse of poverty and welfare framed poor black women, who were already signified as the 'bad black mother' or 'matriarch' by the 1965 Moynihan Report, as the embodiment of the stigmatized 'Welfare Queen' in the 1980s. According to this powerful and politically useful stereotype, poor black women were essentialized as unforgivingly manipulative and lazy. This trope of black women's social redundancy in the discourse of the 1980s clearly seeps into the field of pornography. As Cheri Lei-Me tells Sapphire, 'it's a sin for you to be sitting on your ass all day collecting welfare.' For these women 'whitey's welfare' was something of white people's to raid and exploit rather than an entitlement, a right of all citizens in need. The Welfare Queen, whose stereotypical persona is also defined by black teen pregnancy, crack-baby birth rates and inner-city cultures of criminality and poverty, represented the coming together of multiple discourses on race, gender, sexuality and class in one powerful yet despised figure – the black woman. As Wahneema Lubiano describes, the Welfare Queen has functioned as an ideological vessel for these complex discourses of social deviance and political and economic degeneration; all the bad things about the ghetto emerge from and are immersed in her 'culture of poverty' (1992: 339). The hypersexual Welfare Queen is seen as belonging to the domain of black men and occupying space as a vector of disease, deviance and illegitimacy. Further, her non-labouring body is both a redundancy and an impossibility, her independence irreconcilable. The Welfare Queen is pathological because she does not work and, therefore, does not operate in white male spaces of desire that focus on intimacy and access, nurturing and servitude, sexual labour and control for black women. She is the shadow haunting the borders of white masculinist shame and fear of black woman's sexuality in their pornographic interracial fantasy. She marks the limits of cross-racial transgression and the inextricability of historical archives of race to the modern political theatre of pornography.

Repressive Power of Interracial Performances

Video pornography of the 1980s emerged as a powerful media for the dissemination of a multitude of subversive fantasies, including interracial sexuality, which at that time was specifically located as a play between racialized and sexualized black and white bodies. The genre highlights the anxieties, envies and repulsions of interracial sexuality and its perceived threat to the dominant social order as they are produced through histories of racist domination, violence, exploitation, surveillance and segregation of black bodies in relationship to white bodies in the US context. Historically, policing of cross-racial desire between blacks and whites in the USA has been essential to the normative social order, and this fact infuses representations of whiteness and blackness in pornography constantly, in both subtle and extreme ways. Considering this legacy of tightly controlled racial and sexual boundaries, it is the very proximity of black and white bodies in sexual tension that renders interracial eroticism so taboo, and thus apropos for the subversive work of pornography as political theatre where society's prohibitions and proprieties, secrets and shames, and pleasures and dangers are played out. The adult video industry developed an elaborate strategy to produce and market interracial sexuality as a niche product to mainly white male consumers, but increasingly to men of colour as well. In the years following the emergence of black and interracial video, industry producers would exploit technological and cultural trends to create video and digital hardcore for a broadening audience who would consume a multitude of sexual themes categorized as distinct niche markets.

The Dark Brothers' films *Let Me Tell Ya 'Bout White Chicks* and *Let Me Tell Ya 'Bout Black Chicks* present performances of black characters as manifestations of white male produced fantasies of power. The films construct and reify discourses of black men as inevitably and aggressively obsessed with white women (and derisive of black women), and black women as inescapably subordinate and desirous of white men (and derisive of black men). Portraying a mythology that is less about the political subversiveness of cross-racial desire and more concerned with situating blacks as invariably subordinate to whiteness, an elaborate mechanism of Othering through stereotype obscures a vast obsession by whites with the taboo realm of black sexuality even while racial/sexual boundaries remain absolutely defined. The films elide the real troubling issues that interracial desire as it is made a spectacle, appropriated and consumed presents for white men: that they are subject to their own racist policing of sex, which leaves both black bodies and their desire for them as deviant and dangerous. It is important to read the anxious performances enacted in this genre as part of the productivity of repressive power over unstable racial and sexual lines that are being created, managed and deployed by a conservative sexual, racial and gendered culture in the USA.

Yet, what remains to be explored are the ways in which black men and women have also been both performers in and consumers of pornography with their own readings of cross-racial desire and modes of consumption and subversion. Imagining spectatorship and consumption of these film texts by blacks and other people of colour, women and queers would certainly force us to rethink how the subverted gaze might alter the politics of cross-racial/gender/sexual desire and pleasure in consuming 'oneself'. Indeed, when we consider the progressive development people of colour as a target consumer audience for black and interracial pornography from the late 1980s forward, new theorizations of desire and subjectivity become necessary. With the rise of amateur and corporate interracial porn, 'ghetto porn', 'hip-hop porn', and its dissemination via digital media to millions of consumers became newly visible, mobile and consumable. As pornography becomes part of mainstream culture, black women's bodies, from soft-core hip-hop music videos to hardcore hip-hop porn videos, perform a negotiation of the shifting terrain of sexual life in modern capitalism.

Acknowledgements

I would like to thank Nicole Starosielski, Rebecca Wanzo, Xavier Livermon, Marlon M. Bailey, Matt Richardson, Amber Wallace, Lisa Duggan, Robin Kelley, Simone Weil Davis, Barbara Krauthamer, Walter Johnson, Jane Haladay, Francisca James and the editors for their instrumental and generous feedback on various drafts of this essay.

–4–

Pin-ups, Retro-chic and the Consumption of Irony

Nathan Scott Epley

Pin-ups have always been mainstream. If the recent popularity of classical pin-up iconography in the United States can accurately be called a 'resurgence', it is because the classical illustrated pin-up of the 1940s and 1950s largely disappeared during the 1970s and 1980s, victim simultaneously to the increasing explicitness of sexual images (epitomized by the appearance of pubic hair in *Playboy* and, later, its removal) and the success of antipornography activism in stigmatizing public display of objectified women's bodies (epitomized by the banishment of the girly calendar from garages and shop floors through sexual harassment policies). Of course, the term pin-up is used broadly to describe almost any purportedly sexy still image offered for visual consumption, and infamous photographic pin-ups over the years include everyone from Rita Hayworth to Farrah Fawcett to Tom Selleck to Pamela Anderson. Still, 'pin-up' most commonly recalls the idealized illustrations of women ubiquitous in the popular culture of mid-century America. Emblazoned as 'nose art' on US bombers and on billboards for US based products like Coca-Cola, the illustrated pin-up remains particularly American. Outside the USA, pin-ups never achieved the same sort of vital symbolic value nor received the same sort of stigma of sexism.[1]

Historians traditionally trace the origins of pin-ups to the explosion in magazine publishing before the turn of the twentieth century and, specifically, the Gibson Girl of Charles Dana Gibson, whose illustrations became the first centrefolds in *Life* and *Colliers* magazines (Martignette and Meisel 1996). Developed by art deco artists in advertising images in the 1910s and featuring flappers prominently through the 1920s, the form achieved its greatest popularity during the Second World War and immediately afterwards, when pin-up illustrations and photographs could be found in numerous magazines both mainstream (*Life*, *Look*) and not-so-mainstream (*Flirt, Beauty Parade, Inside Detective)*, all sorts of advertisements (Coca-Cola, Rigid Tools, Old Gold Cigarettes), and plenty of pulp fiction covers (*Just Like a Doll,* 1948, *Gang Moll*, 1953). Of all pin-up artists, Alberto Vargas is credited with most developing the form, painting for Broadway's Ziegfeld Follies in the 1920s, prominent Hollywood studios in the 1930s, *Esquire* magazine in the 1940s (creating the 'Varga Girls') and for *Playboy* into the 1970s (Martignette and Meisel 1996: 282). Pin-up calendars were particularly popular, famously as published by *Esquire*, but perhaps more prominently as what industry leader Brown and Bigelow called 'remembrance advertising', the stereotypical pin-up calendar printed with a business's name and logo (Martignette and Meisel 1996: 24). In a related practice, pin-ups also found their way onto countless pieces of advertising swag such as matchbooks, ashtrays, playing cards and key chains. Conventionally, the classic illustrated pin-up featured an idealized female form, usually a full body, overtly sexual without explicitness, often arranged in improbable positions: backs are predictably arched while the lower legs achieve what Susie Bright (2003: 69) calls 'porno toes' as the figure flexes the arches of her feet to simulate the look of extreme high heels.

At the beginning of this century, the iconography of the classic pin-up was back – increasingly common as both reprints and reconsiderations of the original art and in contemporary neo-pin-ups that mimicked and recuperated vintage pin-up styles. My research begins to put contemporary pin-ups in context by taking up one of the challenges of Laura Kipnis's influential work on pornography and attending to the class address, class-based patterns of consumption and class politics of the pin-up resurgence (1996: see especially the chapter on *Hustler* magazine). Today pin-ups take part in the retro style privileged by urban hipsters of Generation X. Referencing Pierre Bourdieu's work on class and taste, I connect pin-ups' popularity to the habitus of what I call the 'hipster' class fraction, specifically as it informs its members' knowing, and therefore quintessentially ironic, consumption of kitsch. Class fractions are, in large part, produced in and through performances of taste. Hipster consumers appreciate these lowbrow, mass-produced and unavoidably sexist remnants of 1940s' and 1950s' culture despite, and even, *because*, they know better. I conclude by suggesting that their ironic consumption is better understood as fundamentally cynical, using Peter Sloterdijk's theorization of politically disempowering contemporary cynicism.

Cheesecake Factories

I started to notice the resurgence of pin-up iconography in early 2002. I remember the specific ad, a full-page magazine layout for Skyy Vodka called 'Starlet': a young model with a retro dress and even more retro hairstyle kneels on a plush white rug (bearskin?), one hand cradling the lens of a 16mm Bolex camera while the other grasps the striped necktie of the off-screen photographer. Sets, costume, props are all borrowed from classic pin-up illustrations, but the photograph also presents a certain posed-ness typical of the genre. The photo seems retouched to emphasize the shadows and folds of the model's dress, making it appear more like an illustration. 'Starlet' was one of a series of Skyy ads, appearing as early as 1998, that evoked the retro 'cocktail culture'. A number of these ads quoted classic pin-ups explicitly. During the same period, RJReynolds built entire marketing campaigns for its Camel brands around pin-ups. Pin-up girls – especially cigarette girls, complete with pillbox hats – figured especially prominently in ads for the nostalgic brand, Red Kamel. Targeted to chic 'urban sophisticates' (Physicians 2006; Suicide Girls 2006), the brand was launched not in convenience stores but in 'trendy bars and nightclubs' in major North American Cities (Bloomberg Business News 1996). The illustrated pin-ups in ads for Camel's line of flavoured cigarettes (including Warm Winter Lime and Kauai Kolada) were targeted to the same hip demographic: the pin-ups deviated from classic mode only in the addition small tattoos and piercings.

Pin-ups may be generically mainstream and commercial, but they are appropriated in advertising or as commodities themselves or as inspiration for new DIY art in very different contexts. The advertising images of cocktails and cigarettes mentioned above are significant in this study because they suggest how retro-pin-ups in North America target the young, urban and hip, an alternative subculture conveniently overdetermined as 'alternative' and 'subcultural' by both its members and the marketers who hope to sell stuff to them (Fig. 4.1). I specify this connection differently, in terms of habitus and class fractions rather than subcultures or advertising industry demographics. Pin-ups and retro themes more generally are back in plenty of venues not at all associated with urban hipsters, such as *TV Guide's* June 2003 set of four collectible covers promoting the new season of *Sex and the City*. Interestingly, although the four images almost seem to copy specific Gil Elvgren pin-ups from the 1960s, the similarity instead demonstrates how utterly conventional and repetitive classic pin-ups were.[2]

In addition to these sorts of commercial appropriations of pin-up iconography, actual pin-ups from the past have reappeared in diverse settings. Many websites, from Pinupfiles.com to Amazon, feature and sell prints of the classic illustrations and several others sell access to new photos that reproduce, without noticeable irony or comment, the classic pin-ups style. Restaurants, such as the retro-themed family-style chain Maggiano's, prominently display Vargas prints in specific locations (Fig. 4.2). Since the mid-1990s, numerous successful coffee-table books featuring pin-ups and pin-up artists have appeared, several of which are published by Taschen, a relatively young German publisher with a catalogue that features equally prominently books on art and books on sex.[3] Countless gifts and collectibles available today also feature pin-ups (Fig. 4.3). Classic pin-up art graces auto air-fresheners, T-shirts, totes, plates, hairpins, tiepins, lighters, money clips, beer bottles, glassware, blouses, purses and pillows. Such items are for sale all over the Web. Significantly, they are featured prominently in jewellery, clothing and gift stores that specialize in kitsch and cater to the young, the urban and the hip. (Most bricks-and-mortar kitsch

Figure 4.1 Pin-ups adorn microbrews and bar coasters. Photograph by author.

retailers are local and independent, with only Urban Outfitters becoming an international chain.)

The pin-up resurgence is most extensive on the commercial Web and in niche magazine publishing. Websites and zines that feature classic style pin-ups usually participate in one or more 'alternative' subcultures that, with more irony than nostalgia, appropriate mid-twentieth-century cultural styles. Pin-ups have been central to retro culture/swing culture/cocktail culture/lounge culture/tiki culture revivals in North America.[4] One important element of the retro revival has been burlesque shows pin-up put-ons that purport to challenge sexist ideologies within an aesthetic of female display. I call them 'neo-pin-ups', and they explicitly reject the 'mainstream'. Typical of the genre is *Varla* magazine, a national alt-music and culture glossy that regularly features tattooed, pierced and glamorous pin-ups purportedly challenging traditional femininity. According to Varla.com, 'Varla Girls are the girls who make heads turn everywhere they go, be it the grocery store or a punk show. We're not talking about the cookie-cutter bubble-heads like in those other men's magazines, we're talking about fierce women who have cutting edge style, fierce personalities, and ferocious sexuality. Feminine redefined'.

Figure 4.2 Vargas pinups on display at Magianno's restaurant, Durham, North Carolina, USA. Photograph by author.

The possibility for liberating, performative display of the female body is one of the hallmarks of third-wave feminism. Maria Elena Buszek, whose work thoroughly documents historic connections between feminism and the pin-up, points out that many young feminists have adopted pin-ups as mascots: 'the "girlie" pictures of the pin-up genre have become symbolic of the "grrrl-style revolution", as a way for younger feminists to continue to simultaneously associate with and disavow the feminist culture that preceded them.... [approaching] the pin-up with a simultaneous dose of criticism and affection that seems to have emerged as a defining trait of the third wave itself' (2006: 347–48). These third-wavers take up kitsch as a critique of traditional gender and sexuality. As Debbie Stoller suggests in *Bust* magazine, which published some of the most trenchant statements about

Figure 4.3 Photo collage by author.

third-wave style, 'many of us made pilgrimages to our local Salvation Army, buying up 50s dresses that made a pointed statement about just how different we were from prefeminist housewives, and vampy 40s gowns that allowed us to camp it up in our new role as feminist fatales' (1999: 45).

Recuperation of pin-up iconography is, of course, part of the broader feminist project of reclaiming role models.[5] According to Susie Bright, one of the founders of the influential lesbian magazine *On Our Backs*, which published its own neo-pin-ups in the 1980s, 'rebellious' feminists recognized the heady confidence and transgressive sexual power of pin-up women (2003: 73). However, this discourse of female empowerment though performative display is also taken up by alt porn producers, including media-favourite Suicidegirls.com. The business's co-founder and public face, Missy Suicide (Selena Mooney), emphasizes how she was inspired by classic pin-ups (Marshall 2005; see also *HBO's Real Sex* 2003; Physicians 2006; Suicide 2004; and Suicide Girls 2006). Crucial to the stated ethos of the site is that the models are themselves the artists, in control of their posted images and accompanying blog entries.[6] Coming full circle, then, a significant subset of alt porn embraces retro style while claiming a politics of female empowerment.

Classic pin-ups iconography's current popularity includes multiple articulated practices: mainstream as well as demographically targeted advertising, mass-produced kitsch decor, niche publishing and a range of vernacular cultural production that is, to one degree or another, for hipsters/by hipsters. This last category of DIY production, particularly when articulated to a feminist politics, takes up kitsch in refusal of dominant pop tastes and traditional gendered representations. There is something classically amateur about the retro and pin-up resurgences in how the adored style and artefacts conventionally converge with the most commercial of enterprises. When the world's largest adult video company, Vivid, recently established a new alt porn imprint, it chose Octavio 'Winkitiki' Arizala, previously known for his proudly amateur tiki-lounge themed pin-up website, to direct its first feature (the rockabilly-themed *Rebelle Rousers*).[7] Certainly neo-pin-ups on alt porn websites like Suicide Girls (and its many, many imitators[8]) also fit too easily into the commodifying sexism of the membership-based pay-for-porn Internet industry. The politics of contemporary pin-up production and reproduction are hard to disentangle, but they emerge more clearly when considering the practices and contexts of their consumption.

Having one's Cheesecake and Eating it too

Most pin-up iconography is conventionally sexist in its representations of female subordination. Plenty of pin-ups tell a more complex story, but more tell a dramatically conventional one of objects to-be-looked-at and available for consumption. I suggest that the recent popularity of pin-ups is not in spite of their conventional sexism, but because of it. Interest in the reappearance of pin-ups in the USA led me to understand the complicatedness of their consumption as indicative of how a knowing, artistically inclined, often geographically specific class fraction engages ironically with popular culture.

In order to get at articulations between certain labour, political and popular culture practices, I understand the unity of this class fraction through Bourdieu's concept of *habitus*.[9] Habitus generates distinct and distinctive practices and is also a classificatory system that makes distinctions between what is good and bad – in other words, different tastes (Bourdieu 1998: 8). A 'class fraction' is organized in and organizes social space through different habitus. A class fraction is not a subculture, in the sense of a group of people who self-consciously identify with specific cultural artefacts (and with each other). Habitus denotes, rather, a constellation of practices – economic, social, cultural – that cuts across subcultural identities. Bourdieu's theories permit classification of articulated practices based on empirical observation and discursive analysis – the danger of this method lies in seeming to reify this classification or pigeonhole a group of individuals. As predictive as this analysis may be of 'encounters, affinities, sympathies, or even desires' within a class of agents, these *theoretical* class fractions do not constitute *real* classes or groups (Bourdieu 1998: 11).[10] Bourdieu writes, 'One moves from the class-on-paper to the "real" class only at the price of a political work of mobilization' (1998:

11). In other words, specific articulations of class identity and class politics must be performed for a Bourdieuian class or class fraction to resemble 'social class' as traditionally understood.

Although habitus resembles little the sort of subcultural identities we are used to talking about (punk, hip-hop, etc.), I want to choose a vague subcultural category as a placeholder for the class fraction most implicated in the pin-up resurgence: 'hipsters'. Hipsters might include a range of 'alternative' North American subcultures that overlap – some Goths, the sort of bikers who ride Vespas, chic geeks and vintage divas, those who proudly don clunky shoes and clunkier glasses. 'Hip' fits well enough the class fraction I describe, although, in this essay, my analysis cannot take up what are arguably the two most central elements in the story of American hip: race and sexuality.[11] Looking at pin-ups and looking for the politics of consuming kitsch ultimately led me to more narrow issues of class and the aesthetics of everyday life. As I will suggest, hipsters have recognizably hip tastes – thus their ironic embrace of the pin-up – but they also congregate in hip places, have hip jobs and take a critically hip stance towards the rest of the tragically un-hip world.

The hip have always gravitated towards bohemian neighbourhoods where rents are relatively low, and this is still the case for neo-bohemians of the late-twentieth-century USA. The hipster renaissance in urban neighbourhoods like New York's Williamsburg, San Francisco's SoMa and Chicago's Wicker Park, however, also depended on government policy – such as city zoning ordinances designed to promote gentrification – and specific local shifts in capitalist modes of production (Ross 2004; Ross 2003; Lloyd 2005). Embracing and expanding the DIY movement, hipsters of these neo-bohemians produced and patronized plenty of independent art exhibits, punk concerts, burlesque shows, theatre festivals, film festivals, street festivals – but these same artists and art enthusiasts also provided no-collar labour to knowledge industries (stereotypically commercial Internet companies) located in the same neighbourhoods. Hip, at the turn of the twenty-first century, had its own geography, and the hipsters who lived in these neighbourhoods formed the vanguard of the flexible artisan labour new capitalist industries required.[12]

The hipster habitus articulates no-collar labour practices to cultural practices of taste. Robert Lanham is very much on the mark when he insists, again and again throughout his comedic 'Hipster Handbook' that hipsters have highly refined taste. Possessing a self-conscious style that sets them apart from the masses, they embody cool as they consume cool things.[13] In particular, hipsters have a taste for freedom, generally expressed as nonconformity. Since tastes are always most salient as distastes, hipsters perform a critical sensibility that places their culture above and apart from the masses and their mainstream crap (like all counter-/alternative-/sub-cultural styles, hipster taste can be profoundly conformist in its refusal of 'the mainstream'). Hip also sells and, as Thomas Frank (1997) points out, rebellion against mainstream conformity has been the favourite pose of American mar-keters for half a century. Ubiquitous 'hip consumerism', Frank argues, accelerates consumption as a remedy for alienation and boredom at work and even for the banality of everyday consumption itself: 'The countercultural style has become a permanent fixture on the American scene ... because it so conveniently and effi-ciently transforms the myriad petty tyrannies of economic life – all the complaints about conformity, oppression, bureaucracy, meaninglessness and the disappear-ance of individualism that became virtually a national obsession during [and since] the 1950s – into rationales for consuming' (Frank 1997: 31). The conformist main-stream is an imaginary adversary; still, on the surface, the contemporary hipster's style is broadly anti-bourgeois. Each wave of immigrants to neo-bohemia disdains the poseurs who follow, and all decry the selling out that accompanies each neigh-bourhood's increasing prosperity (Lloyd, 2005: 238). Hipsters are also known to favour pre-gentrification working-class bars, where they order working-class drinks like Pabst Blue Ribbon beer. They embrace mass-produced commodities discarded by their parents and grandparents, especially items that retain the patina of working-class aspirations. Played out on the streets of 'transitional' neighbour-hoods, hipsters' slumming reinforces, as Andrew Ross notes, their sense of freedom: 'For the temporary bohemian, voluntary poverty [evokes] freedom, to be enjoyed among low-class residents whose involuntary poverty, by contrast, con-strained their freedoms' (Ross 2004: 156).

Hipsters' idealization of urban working-class culture is part of what distin-guishes this habitus from a broader retro 'movement'. Theirs is not the generic retro of Disney's theme parks, Cracker Barrel 'Old Country Store' restaurants or Past Times shops and catalogues (see Brown 1999). The retro hipster engages in productive consumption (e.g. promoting retro lifestyle in online zines) and active pastiche (e.g. assembling wardrobes from thrift store cast-offs). This DIY spirit within hipster retro culture accompanies, of course, countless targeted marketing campaigns through which products like the Honda Element and New Beetle are hip while the equally retro Chrysler PT Cruiser is anything but. In the service of brand identification, the cultural capital of hipness is rendered varyingly as authen-ticity, quality, creativity or originality, but besides this sort of strategic niche mar-keting, hipster nostalgia also articulates to their no collar jobs and the geography of neo-bohemia. Moreover, presumptions about hipsters' postmodern mood of longing or cultural amnesia inadequately explain their nostalgic practices.[14] Hipsters haven't forgotten their history; in fact, they consume kitsch because of its history. Their recuperation of kitsch is not naïve, but knowing (Grainge 2000: 29). Hipsters put their recycled culture in quotations marks, and a significant part of their pleasure in this consumption lies in the active performance of these quotation marks.

In other words, what is different about the consumption practices of this class fraction lies less in what is consumed than in how things are consumed. Rebellious consumption depends on irony. If, as John Leland insists, 'hip is a form of enlightenment' that flourishes in periods of rapid technological change (2004: 61), then hipsters' ironic orientation towards the commodities they consume – not to mention their jobs – depends specifically on their sense of superior knowledge. Hipsters, in other words, *get it*. Irony is the key to their superior poses – for hipsters, Lanhem asserts, 'irony has more resonance than reason'.

Irony exploits and exposes the gaps among the expected, the expressed and the 'real'. Whether verbal or structural, irony also reinforces existing 'discursive communities' – which, for purposes of this analysis, can be considered homologous to Bourdieuian class fractions – excluding those who don't get the ironist's intentions (Hutcheon 1994: 17).[15] Irony in this sense also lies at the heart of camp sensibilities: as Susan Sontag points out in her influential 'Notes on Camp', camp has always been 'esoteric – something of a private code, a badge of identity even, among small urban cliques' (1964b: 53). For Bourdieu, taste is constitutive, productive and reflective of *habitus*, and the shared sensibility called camp is taste in the fullest sense of the term – taste in people, in objects, in emotions, in thoughts (Sontag 1964b: 53).

Recuperation of retro-kitsch by third-wave feminists and hipsters more generally takes up camp's ironic stance toward popular culture. Classic pin-up iconography, in particular, engages what Sontag calls camp's 'essence': its 'love of the unnatural: of artifice and exaggeration', including 'the exaggeration of sexual characteristics' (1964b: 53, 56). Both Bright and Buszek appreciate the Second World War era illustrations of Alberto Vargas, finding sexual ambiguity not only in many of the figures' masculine costumes and 'don't-give-a-damn' postures, but also in their irreconcilable pin-up bodies: improbably large and buoyant breasts and porno toes compete with strong arms and shoulders and boyish hips (Bright 2003: 71; Buszek 2006: 186).[16] Buszek also praises the pin-ups of Bettie Page whose 'brazen, over-the-top poses and pointedly light-hearted approach to performing as a pin-up served to expose the very construction of the genre, revealing both its artificiality and performative nature, as well as its potential as an expressive medium for the women so represented' (2006: 247). As noted above, similar perspectives lie behind the neo-pin-ups of *Varla* and Suicide Girls. Such camp readings and renderings of pin-ups, however, tend to emphasize certain artists and images that diverge from dominant conventions of the genre. Buszek argues persuasively that 'the genre has … represented the sexualized woman as self-aware, assertive, strong, and independent', but she also allows that 'many pin-ups are indeed silly caricatures of women that mean to construct their humiliation and passivity as turn-ons' (2006: 8). In classic pin-ups, for every image of a sexually self-determining woman, there are at least as many where the figure is explicitly caught unaware, subject to an objectifying gaze, embarrassed or even terrified as her dress blows awry or her panties fall to her ankles.[17]

Camp taste refuses both mass and elite culture aesthetics. Irony's evaluative edge critiques the clichéd and conventional. Still, there are no political guarantees when it comes to ironic re-appropriation. As Linda Hutcheon insists, irony can be 'both political *and* apolitical, both conservative *and* radical, both repressive and democratizing' (1994: 34).[18] The politics of camp are similarly unstable – or, rather, unavailable. Sontag, in the second of her fifty-six points about camp, suggests that 'it goes without saying that the Camp sensibility is disengaged, depoliticized – or at least apolitical' (1964b: 54). Something happens to camp, moreover, when it encounters the logic of the commodity. Its affect, indeed its affection for kitsch objects (its amateurism), entangles with consumption practices that generate more and more consumption.

It is the hipster's camp sensibility and ironic pose that makes consuming pin-ups OK: the logic is that yes, I know it is sexist and because I know, I can enjoy these representations guilt-free. Closely related to this logic is a progressive-sounding (but really closer to libertarian) politics of personal freedom that refuses to tell anyone (much less legislate) what her pleasures and fantasies should or shouldn't be, a perspective that is not exactly pro-pornography, but is distinctly anti-antiporn. This perspective unintentionally revises the old saw of the old sexual revolution – if it feels good, do it – into it does not matter what I consume as long as it gets me off. (After all, I am not responsible for the patriarchal sexual politics and practices I have inherited.) Hipsters' embracing of the pin-up is not disavowal of the politics of representation, but merely permission to consume in spite of *and because of* those well-worn politics. You can consume how you want and still hold on to your values. You can offer up your body for visual consumption without compromising 'what really matters'. In a more complicated sense, you can find pleasure in an almost circular process of consumption in which you consume your own susceptibility and resistance to the pin-up representations.[19] Thus, the resurgence of pin-ups is, in practice, not just ironic consumption but also the consumption of irony. Such circular irony seems almost self-perpetuating: it provides permission to consume apolitically; to consume cynically; to consume more and more, period.

Liberating Cynicism

When articulated to consumption, irony serves a politics more appropriately called 'cynical', a term I use specifically in reference to Peter Sloterdijk's *Critique of Cynical Reason* (1987). Sloterdijk's conception of cynicism resembles little the common-sense understanding of contemporary pundits whose repetitive application of the label 'cynical' to any opponents' policy has hollowed the term almost completely. Neither does Sloterdijk see cynicism as something new, one element of a distinctly postmodern consciousness. Rather, he perceives the roots of contemporary cynicism in Enlightenment rationality and the critical penetrations of ideology that today represent the values of thoughtfulness, insight and intelligence.

Traditional understandings of ideology and ideological critique suggest that people are duped, that they can't perceive the real conditions of their existence because they suffer under *false consciousness*. With hard work, so the story goes, the avant-garde who sees through ideology may lead the misguided masses to the truth. But these days, we are all critics and our false consciousness is highly enlightened. In Sloterdijk's words, modern cynics evince 'a sophisticated knowledge accumulated in informed, intelligent minds, a knowledge that moves elegantly back and forth between naked facts and conventional facades.... . [a] radical, ironic treatment of ethics and of social conventions, as if universal laws existed only for the stupid, while that fatally clever smile plays on the lips of those in the know' (1987: 4). With their cynical investment in kitsch objects like pin-ups, hipsters take pleasure in their own interpellation: 'I know I am being had, isn't it fun?' In its most pervasive forms, cynicism precludes utopian thinking, making it increasingly difficult to imagine how things might be different. Rich with understanding, full of appreciation (like camp) for the multiple layers of artifice, cynical irony starts to become 'a sort of surrogate for actual resistance and opposition' (Hutcheon 1994: 27). Hipsters certainly 'get it' – they perform every day the sort of critical distance, the refined taste at the heart of our humanistic academic practice – but the cynical critique at the heart of their habitus is an impoverished criticism, an understanding divorced from almost any agency outside of the commodity system.

Cynicism is not merely the mode of our everyday consumer practices but also helps rationalize mobilized, flexible labour practices. Consuming irony itself, members of the hipster class fraction also put irony to work, such that conditions like temporary work, subcontractor status, lack of pensions and health insurance and stock options in lieu of real wages all feel like freedom. But as feminist neo-pin-ups suggest, cynicism is not the necessary end of the pin-up resurgence. 'True' camp is passionate and 'close' to its adored objects (Sontag 1964b: 59). To combat cynicism, Sloterdijk also privileges an intimate, self-reflexive and definitely *ironic* treatment of culture, achieved not through 'elevated, distanced critique that achieves grand overviews but [in] a space of extreme closeness' (1987: xxxiii, 292). Irony can be empowered by its intimacy with dominant discourses. By mimicking these discourses, using their own signifiers, ironic performance appropriates some of their power, undermines, or at least 'relativizes', their authority, and disguises its own subversive potential until it is (often inadvertently) consumed (Hutcheon 1994: 29). What resistance may be in all these ironic, campy pin-up recuperations depends on their very intimacy with the sexist conventions of the form. Rather than camp, then, the potential of neo-pin-ups is better understood as drag: 'In much the same way that Judith Butler has argued that drag cross-dressing can mime, rework, and resignify the external signs and stability of gender ideals, so too [can] the pin-up mine, rework, and resignify the signs and stability of specifically female sexual ideals' (Buszek 2006: 12). In their excessive idealization of femininity, pin-ups display women in drag as girls – or, rather, the impossible dream girls of industrial popular culture. The secret is in the mix, the pastiche of familiar conventions of female beauty – classic pin-up iconography – combined with elements taboo to dominant ideologies of gender and sexuality.

Part II

Porn Cultures

–5–

Gay Men and the Pornification of Everyday Life

Sharif Mowlabocus

Whether the focus be on its history, its representation, its media or its politics, even the briefest analysis is enough to demonstrate that pornography permeates British gay male subculture, together with the identities and practices that it frames. Pornography is written into the code of gay men's everyday lives and it continues to shape understandings of the Self and Other in increasingly powerful ways. Of course pornography and everyday life are rarely separate spheres, interacting with one another on multiple levels and often in contradictory ways. Yet it should be noted that while collisions between the pornographic and the non-pornographic occur throughout British culture, some subcultures have developed specific relationships with pornographies that deliver different outcomes to those found elsewhere. In other words, neither pornography, nor society should be treated as singular concepts but rather as a constellation of diverse and divergent forms that are loosely grouped together in what are often unstable and highly subjective categories.

While there may well be similarities between all pornographies, the cultural politics surrounding the contexts of its production and consumption means that 'mainstream' gay pornography has a unique and specific relationship with the subculture that it caters to. In this chapter I shall briefly sketch out the development of this relationship before discussing how Internet-based practices are changing its dynamics through an illustrative case study of Gaydar.co.uk, Britain's most popular gay male website. In doing so, I shall demonstrate how key structuring devices found within archetypal gay pornography have become increasingly integral to self-representation in many gay online spaces, and consider the implications that this has both for those that conform and for those who 'fail' to fit the typology promoted on the website.

I make three caveats before I continue. Firstly, my case study focuses on a British-based website, and therefore the findings will, to some extent, be culturally specific. However, while Gaydar.co.uk has a British bias (with profiles organized according to geographical region), the website welcomes non-British users.

Secondly, in exploring this online space, I am neither suggesting that all British gay men use Gaydar, nor that Gaydar and the practices that are contained within this site are solely the domain of British gay men. While the analysis that follows should be understood as taking place within the context of British gay subculture it should be noted that, in this instance, the culturally specific may be illustrative of wider trends found in gay cultures elsewhere.

Finally, from here on I shall use the truncated term 'gay-porn' as a means of identifying and referring to the mass-distributed commercial pornography produced by professional adult entertainment studios in America and Europe for consumption by gay and bisexual men, and which is the most successful form of gay male pornography. This type of pornography is both lauded and criticized for its use of toned, often hairless, well-endowed actors, its hammy narratives and (somewhat ironically) its promotion of an 'all-American' ideology of hegemonic masculinity, which serves to (re)inscribe the gender binary onto homosexual practices. In this chapter I use 'gay-porn' as opposed to 'gay male pornography' in order to differentiate this commercially successful form from the wider grouping of sexually explicit texts produced for consumption by gay men, which includes more 'marginal' pornographies such as amateur/home-made pornography and alternative pornographies – 'alt porn'. As with heterosexual pornography, gay pornography is not a singular entity; using the term 'gay-porn' allows me to provide a short-hand reference to this observation, while identifying the specific type of gay male pornography I am referring to in my discussion.

Developing Relationships

In Britain and the United States, the production of (retrospectively) gay male pornography prefigures the formation of what Alan Sinfield has termed a 'metropolitan' gay culture (1998: 6). The term 'metropolitan' here refers to the most stable, socially recognized, politically assimilated and economically productive expression of homosexuality to be found in the West today. Metropolitan gay culture is *physical*; it refers to the gay village, and the proliferation of clubs and bars of shops and cafes that cater to urban gay men. But it is also a *lifestyle*, a way of *being* and a way of being seen as gay. Yet even prior to the emergence and sedimentation of this post-liberation (and in Britain, post-legalization) commercial culture, homosexual pornography was being produced and distributed with homoerotic porn loops being made available to the 'discerning few' as early as the 1950s (O'Toole 1999: 64). Indeed the homosexual print media of the 1960s, relied on 'slightly risqué, discreetly naked pics' of young men to attract its audience (Weeks 1990: 180) and later, the construction of an out gay identity in the 1970s coincided with a sudden increase in the amount of gay pornography produced (McNair 1996: 16). The result of this was that pornography catering to this emerging subculture

became readily available and offered a representation – and by extension a validation – of the desires and experiences of this culture.

Such validation can be attributed to the multiple functions pornography has
served this minority group. For many men, gay-porn may be their primary link
between a non-urban, isolated existence and an otherwise remote and inaccessible
gay culture (Burger 1995) and while many gay men may not have regular physical
access to metropolitan gay culture, the representation/validation of that culture
through gay-porn has communicated specific discourses surrounding masculinity,
body shape and sexual practice to those living in the 'queer diaspora'. Richard
Dyer (1992) has noted the political potential of gay male pornography, particularly
the sense of empowerment inherent in such texts, where the 'deviant' homosexual
act is reorganized as both positive and life-affirming; something that is rarely promoted by the hegemony.

Of course acknowledging the centrality of pornography to British gay culture
should not entail promoting it as a wholly positive phenomenon. Many have prob-
lematized this relationship, identifying both the potential pitfalls as well as the
benefits of such an association. For example, pornography seriously undermined
the tense and fragile bond between second-wave feminism and the emerging gay
rights movement during the 1970s. Many feminists during this period viewed all
pornography – gay and straight – as misogynist, articulating and validating the
power inequalities of the gender system through sexual representation (see
Stoltenberg 1991; Dworkin 2000; and MacKinnon 2000). Gay men responded to
this criticism by reclaiming gay pornography as a culturally important form that
should not be bracketed together with 'straight' or mainstream versions (see Clark
1991; Dyer 1992; and Edwards 1994).

Such battles reveal the relations of power often at work both within and outside
of the pornographic text. The power of pornography extends beyond the producer,
actor(s) and consumer, operating at a wider, cultural level via multiple methods
and often in paradoxical ways. In the decade following the 'sex wars', for instance,
pornography became an effective tool in a different battle, this time against HIV
transmission. In both Europe and the United States, HIV/AIDS interventions
exploited culturally resonant 'pornographic vernaculars' (Patton 1991: 45) in order
to produce and validate safer sex messages within gay male communities. This co-
opting by HIV/AIDS interventionists illustrates the dynamic power of pornography and it is this dynamism that has lately been realized through digital
technologies of production and consumption. Through a range of new technologies
and technical processes pornography has been subjected to a remapping and redefinition (O'Toole 1999: 179–81) and most recently these processes have converged
within the virtual environments created by the Internet. Pornography continues to
be cited as one of the biggest winners in the dot.com industry (Beaver 2000:
374–5) and the recent cultural and technological convergences occurring within
the porn industry mean that today there is more pornography, made more readily

accessible, to an ever-increasing demographic, than ever before.

At the beginning of the second media age (Poster 1995) gay culture finds itself at a critical crossroads similar to that of the 1970s. This juncture serves to delineate the different routes along which gay men's future relationship with pornography can traverse. Linda Williams (1992: 262) has hypothesized that pornography produced by, and featuring, sexual minorities, could provide a political response to the misogynist and aggressive pornography of the mainstream market, offering a platform for the discussion of non-oppressive sexual practices and identities. Today the Internet gives this claim a potentiality that it hitherto lacked. Where previously the consumption of pornography involved purchasing material located within a specific genre, and often within a specific space, the availability of different pornographies, together with the way in which these pornographies can now be collected together (for instance via TGP listings and links pages) means that the consumer can access non-normative pornographies with unparalleled ease and comparatively little investment (and when I talk of investment I mean not only at the material-economic level, but also on the moral, psychological and political planes).

This engagement may be proactive, or reactive, the inaccuracy of many listings resulting in exposure to pornographies completely different to what the consumer anticipated. Such accidental slippages provide but one example of how Williams's (admittedly utopian) prophecy could be realized. Perhaps it is too much to expect of pornography that it undermine and dismantle the binaries of homo/hetero, male/female and active/passive, but the possibility at least is there, and the Internet has made this possibility far more tangible.

Metropolitan gay male culture, however, appears unwilling to transgress such boundaries, choosing instead to avoid the path of political discussion in favour of a multiplication of texts based largely on existing systems of representation. This is not to say that digital porn is simply a reworking of print and video-based forms. I have elsewhere identified the importance of the Internet to the production of new pornographic discourses and sexual practices such as barebacking (Mowlabocus 2007). A variety of fetish subcultures (bukkake, BDSM, intergenerational, plushies) have similarly exploited the communicative power of the Web in order to disseminate – and promote – their pornographies and, by extension, their cultures.

But metropolitan gay culture is also involved with web-based pornography at a level beyond the representational. Indeed, the amalgamation of ICTs with the structures of gay-porn has proven to be a shaping force within contemporary urban gay culture, not only signifying gay male sexuality, but increasingly providing a cultural framework through which sexual identity is produced, negotiated and maintained. This framework is most easily identified in the user profiles found on dating and community websites such as Gaydar.co.uk. The user profile is a self-authored web text that has become the most common form of self-representation amongst gay men in contemporary Britain and through a close reading of this new cultural form, changes in the relationship between gay culture and gay-porn that I alluded to above can be identified and critically evaluated.

Gaydar.co.uk

While by no means an exclusively gay format, the user profile appears to be central to the production, maintenance and communication of identity in gay web spaces. At the heart of the Gaydar dating website is a database of profiles that users can access, once they themselves have created an account and authored a profile. The profile is the principal method of communication on Gaydar and all searches on the website utilize profiles as reservoirs of information that can be accessed according to the desires of the browser. In line with Manuel Castells's (1996) definition of the information economy, this harnessing of data has a material underpinning, and if the primary purpose of Gaydar is to bring gay men together, the secondary purpose is to transform them into an identifiable demographic.

This secondary function is perhaps not visible on the site itself though it is made abundantly clear on the website of the company that runs Gaydar.co.uk (Fig. 5.1) Describing themselves as a 'network of complimentary new media', QSoft Consulting confidently state that 'QSoft IS the gay market' (QSoft Consulting) positioning Gaydar as a tool through which the hitherto elusive demographic of high-earning, high-spending gay consumers can be targeted. This duality has been labelled 'Janus-faced' by John E. Campbell, in his work on gay affinity portals (2005: 665). While Gaydar is not a portal, its commercial underpinnings and representational styles are similar to those identified by Campbell, making it another example of this trend within gay cyberspace. The commercial facet of the profile is perhaps unsurprising considering the origins of the form, which lie in market research and commercial data analysis. But the profile has since evolved beyond this field and is now commonly used to create an online representation of the embodied user through which s/he can communicate. As such, the profile can best be described as 'the creation of a digital persona, which represents an individual and is used as a management tool in fashioning interactions with the individual' (Phillips 2002: 418). Profiles are central to interactions on Gaydar and when entering a chat room or sending a message users are identified by their handle, which provides a link back to the profile and allows other users to 'see' them. As such the profile renders the subject culturally legible within this space and should therefore be understood not as a practice of disembodiment but in fact one of (re)embodiment.

Allucquère Rosanne Stone asserts that the body is always articulated and regulated through 'textual productions' and that society employs these productions in order to 'produce physical bodies that it recognizes [*sic*] as members' (2000: 524). On Gaydar the user profile not only represents the gay male subject in cyberspace, it operates as a medium through which subjectivity is produced and rendered legible, echoing Amelia Jones's assertion that 'technology not only mediates but produces subjectivities in the contemporary world' (2002: 250). The multiple acts of self-identification invoked by the Gaydar user profile have previously been identified (Mowlabocus 2005) and there is little doubt that such processes of identification are potentially empowering for a minority group who have historically been characterized as *invisible*.

The brutal and violent acts of investigation, oppression and extermination that gay men have been subjected to during the twentieth century are a direct result of this invisibility and the ability to pass among the power holding group, to move through its most intimate spaces and share in its hegemonic dominance, remains a driving force behind the judicial and extra-judicial aggression meted out upon the body of the homosexual man. As illustrated by some of the most systematic forms of oppression (the pink triangle of Hitler's Final Solution; the witch-hunts of McCarthyism), the *identification* of the homosexual male has been a key stage within his suppression. It is therefore unsurprising that during the first half of the twentieth century invisibility was an integral facet of Western homosexual subcultures, or, by contrast, that gay political activism, together with the foundations of gay male culture, have been predicated upon notions of visibility and identification. From Pride parades to rainbow flags, to civil partnerships, to the coming-out 'imperative', visibility has become ingrained within metropolitan gay culture. Often this visibility is expressed corporeally, through fashion (e.g. the clone's leather wear) through body marking (such as tattooing and piercing) and through body manipulation (including the hyper-muscularity of the 'Muscle Mary') serving to code particular bodies as gay, and in doing so, countering the invisibility of homosexuality. Such acts are exercises in authorship as gay men make themselves culturally legible through these processes of self-identification. Gaydar continues this process of authorship providing what Thomas Foster (2001: 449) has termed a 'spectacularized gayness' previously unavailable to this invisible minority.

Within the context of heteronormative hegemonic society, such acts are undeniably powerful and have the potential to be politically beneficial at both an individual and collective level. However, they may also result in outcomes that are more ambiguous than perhaps first imagined. The discourses that frame and permeate the Gaydar profile mean that this visibility is subject to specific structures of representation that may in fact restrain gay subjectivity at the point at which it is revealed online. Twinned with the commercial underpinnings of Gaydar, the acts of browsing, searching and categorizing that occur in this web space serve to fragment identity and reduce it to a series of data points, which are evaluated against the corporeal benchmarks of looks, body size, type and sexual role. And, as I shall now demonstrate, it is at this point that Gaydar culture becomes intertwined with the structuring devices and aesthetics of commercial gay-porn.

Sex Factor

In December 2004 Gaydar launched *Sex Factor*, a peer-rating system that allows users to 'vote for your favourite guys on the site – or to enter yourself' (Gaydar). Winners are announced monthly and, while there are no prizes for winning (other than having your profile advertised on the leader board), the contest has become extremely popular amongst the Gaydar community; over 30,000 entrants and more than 6.5 million votes were cast in the first five days of the competition alone. There are currently sixteen categories in which to vote and these can be roughly divided into three genres; clothing/fetishwear (leather, rubber, uniform, sports gear), age (young guys 18–21, young guys 22+ and older guys) and body type (bears, cubs, skins and punks, muscle). Some categories (Hip, Alternative, Guy Next Door) straddle genres, though 'Hip' and 'Guy Next Door' certainly suggest a particular age, body shape and clothing preference. These categories have been chosen by Gaydar and it is clear from the examples listed above that the focus on the visual is intense; certain profiles win because the user fits the 'look' that a particular category promotes.

While Gaydar has chosen these specific categories they are not in any way new, but instead draw on genres already established in gay-porn. In utilizing these genres *Sex Factor* celebrates what we might call a pornographic typology of metropolitan gay culture. In doing so, the website serves to perpetuate the notion that these distinctions and categories are not only valid but in some sense fundamental to British gay identities. We need only bear in mind the immense popularity of the competition to validate such an assertion. The swift acceptance of *Sex Factor* by the Gaydar community demonstrates the underlying significance of such systems of classification circulating in contemporary British gay culture. At the same time it reveals the practices of embodiment, commodification and consumption that are involved in mediating subjectivity in gay male cyberspaces.

Furthermore, while the categories at first appear to separate and distinguish bodies, subjectivities and practices, a closer investigation exposes a level of slippage between the different 'types' suggesting, somewhat paradoxically, both an ambiguity as to the meaning of these categories, and the establishment of a specifically metropolitan 'look', which Gaydar inevitably promotes above all other possible identities. For example, many in the 'Hip' category look as though they could also qualify for the 'Muscle 18–30' category. Similarly, some of the users in the 'older men' group could also be classed as 'bears'. There are no guidelines as to what these categories mean: it appears that users are supposed to know a priori what the conventions of each category are. This would suggest that while there is a level of classification that fragments gay culture into multiple identities, underpinning all of these is a homogenizing gay aesthetic – a particular masculinity – commonly found in gay-porn and now cultivated on Gaydar.

Finally, considering we are dealing with bodies and subjects that inhabit spaces both on and offline, this cultivation is also occurring within the 'real' world of contemporary gay male culture. Age appears to be an important factor but surpassing this is body shape, many of the top profiles featuring men with remarkably similar bodies; toned and developed muscles, even tans and (save for the bears and cubs) minimal body hair. These bodies also resemble one another in terms of the pose struck by the user and though it would be wrong to label this pose as 'butch' (in the same way that Tom of Finland characters could be called butch), it does represent the performance of a specific masculinity, namely the 'straight-acting' or 'regular' masculinity often found within the narratives of gay-porn.

Peter Horne and Reina Lewis have discussed the heightened investment Western gay cultures have in visual representation, including representations of the body (1997: 104–5) and the term 'body fascist' is often used in criticisms of gay culture's obsession with the corporeal. The 'no fats, no femmes' ethos of urban gay culture is neither new (nor indeed specifically gay), but the integration of new media technologies into this subculture marks a definite re-inscription of this obsession, together with the boundaries of what is (and therefore also what is not) acceptable. By linking processes of visibility with signification practices, *Sex Factor* integrates gay men into a specific mode of self-representation, illustrating the proliferation of a specific 'brand' of gay lifestyle and identity, namely the metropolitan gay lifestyle, that (as has already been identified) online. From tanning to depilation to muscle-growth to posture, the gay male body is simultaneously 'seen' in cyberspace and *controlled* via the practices that construct it online. As a result, gay men are instructed to (re)negotiate their relationship with their bodies at a physical, mental and cultural level.

Following Stone's argument then, *Sex Factor* illustrates the processes of legibility that occur on Gaydar and reveals the pitfalls of non-conformity, as failure to adhere to pornographic conventions renders the subject unreadable and invisible once more. If the categories validated by *Sex Factor* borrow from pre-existing pornographic categories then, as Table 5.1 illustrates, almost every category available on *Sex Factor* is mirrored by contemporary gay-porn genres and can be identified in recent pornographic releases. One could argue that this is simply a case of art reflecting life; however the relationship between pornography and gay male culture is far more complex. If anything, the relationship is that of life reflecting art with *Sex Factor* utilizing pornographic genres in order to categorize – and in turn, construct – the identities that inhabit Gaydar.

This investment in the structuring devices of gay-porn serves to inscribe a new narrative onto the subject, a new framework within which he must operate in order to be recognized. While the overweight, the disabled and the non-Caucasian can and do inhabit Gaydar, their inability – their 'failure' – to conform to these pornographic ideals renders them 'illegible'; lacking access to the methods of understanding promoted in this space. Meanwhile, those who *do* fit this constrained narration of the self are subjected to what I term a discourse of 'cybercarnality',

Table 5.1 The pornification of gay male culture becomes clear when we compare *Sex Factor* categories with those currently used in commercial pornography.

Sex Factor *Categories*	*Gay-porn Genres*	*Recent Gay-porn Releases*
Leather	Leather	*Open Trench* (Zipper – unknown)
Rubber	N/A	*Gay Latex Dreams* (Canamax – unknown)
Uniform	Uniform/Uniform Twinks /Military Men/Cops	*Top Secret* (Men of Odyssey – Douglas, J.)
Sports Gear	Sports/Sports Twinks/ Twink Gym Guys	*Football Orgy 2* (Triga – unknown)
Muscle (all ages)	Studs/Muscle Men/Young Studs Muscle Fuck (Triga)	
Bears/Cubs Bears	Manimal (Legend – Dior, K.)	
Young Guys/Guys Next Door	Twinks/First Timers	*Beachboy* (Eurocreme – Lincoln, M.)
Guys Next Door (31+)	Studs	*Straight Men Fuck* (Triga – unknown)
Older Guys	Daddies	*In Gear* (Channel 1 – LaRue C.)
Hip/Alternative	N/A	*SkaterBoy* (Eurocreme – Lincoln, M.)

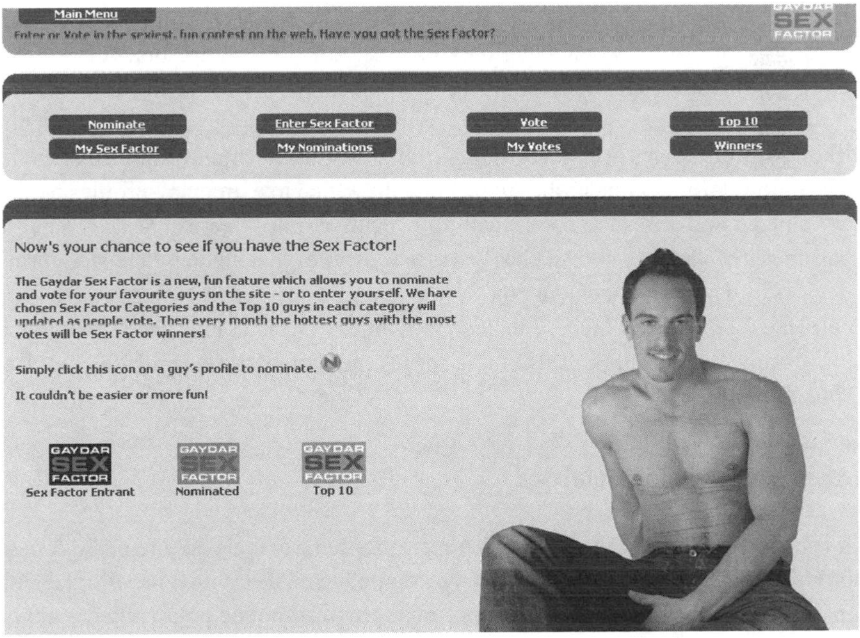

Figure 5.1 Gaydar.com.uk. Photograph courtesy of Gaydar.com.uk.

which I identify as the primary discourse through which the gay male body is rendered visible and available for consumption in online spaces.

I employ the term cybercarnality here as a means of recognizing the specific forms of knowledge at work within the formation and maintenance of gay subjectivity online. Gaydar allows men to represent themselves via the medium of the profile but this method of representation simultaneously serves as a technique of surveillance. In authoring a profile, which then becomes his online persona, the gay man subjects himself to a discursive machinery that fragments, analyses, codifies and evaluates him. This surveillance apparatus is a knowledge machine and its aim is to *identify* the gay male subject through a specifically erotic knowledge established within the arena of commercial gay male pornography. The 'newbie' may not necessarily conform to the categories of *Sex Factor*, but if he is to 'fit in' – that is, if he is to function, be understood and be found within search engines – and, perhaps most importantly, if he is to attract attention from other users, then he must submit to the conventions of this cybercarnality.

To repeat myself, this is not to say that those who do not fit neatly into a category offered by *Sex Factor* cannot 'exist' on Gaydar. Just as you can place a contact advert in a magazine that does not fit with an identifiable 'type', so you can create a profile that does not conform to the categories outlined above. However, such a profile inevitably exists *in relation* to these categories. That is, individual subjectivity is defined against pre-existing classifications and is judged against such classifications. I may not fit into any of these categories but I am comprehensible – that is to say legible – only in relation to certain age brackets, certain body types and certain fetishes.

Cybercarnality is central to the Gaydar user profile and the text and images utilized by users to construct their online selves regularly employs the language of gay-porn in order to render the subject legible. Of course, in many profiles bodies are clothed and poses are not sexually provocative, but if we use *Sex Factor* as a barometer of success, we can clearly see that profiles that abide by the structuring devices of gay-porn – including the aesthetic codes specific to each category – are celebrated on Gaydar, literally hailed as 'winners' for matching the unwritten by universally recognized (at least in this space) requirements demanded of the classification process.

Approaching Conformity

It is almost impossible to imagine that metropolitan gay male culture could, would or indeed should extricate itself from the composite relationship it has formed with mainstream gay pornography. Such pornography may not be politically correct (it regularly employs racist, sexist and even homophobic discourse in its narratives) but to wholly condemn it would be to ignore the complex and subtle bond that many gay men have developed with this form of representation. Indeed, within the context of heteronormative society gay-porn is always counter-hegemonic, though whether this subversive imperative is ever fully realized is, at best, questionable. As gay men integrate new media technologies into their everyday interactions, forming new cultural practices online, so their relationship with the pornographic has also developed. The creation of digital representations of the self are perhaps most profoundly felt, and most politically useful to a minority group who continue to remain invisible until they choose to risk violence, humiliation and rejection by identifying themselves as sexually dissident. However, such identifications are heavily influenced by pornography and the problematic politics inherent in such discourse. If the representation of homosexuality has made 'life bearable for countless millions of gay men' (Dyer 1992: 123), it is playing an increasingly central role in defining – and policing – understandings of what it means to be a gay man in Britain today.

The consequences of this will no doubt be most powerfully experienced by those bodies that do not 'fit' the categories promoted by Gaydar but who still wish to stake a claim within gay culture. Gay male pornography may well have the potential to break down sexual boundaries, to usurp the primacy of heterosexuality and to open up sexuality beyond the rigid binary of gender difference. But while we wait for this great revolution, the exact opposite is occurring in gay cyberspace. Gay-porn is securing the perimeters of gay identity, forming ever more impenetrable boundaries and validating a set of identifications and practices at the expense of all others. If the potential of homosexual pornographies is to *queer* reality, then the reality of gay-porn serves to condense homosexuality into to a single overarching identity; one that does little to challenge hegemonic norms or to liberate sexuality.

Websites

Gaydar [Online], http://www.gaydar.co.uk

Gaydar – Sex Factor, http://www.gaydar.co.uk/sexfactor (accessed 21 December 2004)

Gay DVD SEX Videos, online store and reviews, http://www.gaydvdsexvideos.com/dvd-genres.html (accessed 12 February 2005)

Hitwise Real-Time Competitive Intelligence, http://www.hitwise.co.uk/ (accessed July 2002)

QSoft Consulting, http://www.qsoft.co.uk/frames/middle1.asp?link=/media-pack/platforms.html (accessed 22 June 2005)

Vidshop.com, http://www.vidshop.com/main.php (accessed 12 February 2005)

–6–

Cosmo Girls Talk: Blurring Boundaries of Porn and Sex

Kaarina Nikunen

Contemporary media publicity is characterized by increased interest in sexual behaviour: intimate encounters of politicians, celebrities and ordinary people are reported in explicit detail. Such 'sex talk' is not produced only by media professionals but increasingly by media audiences turned active participants in various online spaces. Discussion forums and chat rooms with easy access and a high degree of anonymity offer ideal spaces for anonymous sex talk and confessions that might otherwise be too risky to reveal (Wood and Smith 2001).

This chapter examines young women's discussions (and definitions) of sexuality and pornography in the semi-public realm of *Cosmopolitan* magazine's online discussion forum. It addresses the meanings of their sex talk with a focus on the role of pornography in everyday life, as well as the various tactics of negotiation and/or resistance assumed by the members of the forum in relation to consumer culture and the porn industry. Internet sex talk is hardly pornographic as such but, due to its straightforward nature, may well serve pornographic functions in the sense of giving rise to bodily sensations and arousing its readers and writers alike (cf. Dyer 1985).

Cosmopolitan and Female Sexual Agency

Cosmopolitan has been described as a magazine promoting sex as empowering to women (Machin and Thornborrow 2006). Published in forty-four versions around the world, *Cosmopolitan* is a well-established brand. The magazine sells more than just something to read – it provides a set of values related to power, independence and entertainment targeted at women in their twenties. In to addition the magazine, these values are expressed and circulated also via television, cosmetics, books and fashion (Machin and Thornborrow 2003). *Cosmopolitan* is famous for its focus on sex, realized in first-person narratives, expert perspectives and an infinite number of tests. The role of sex is emphasized in such spin-off products as *Cosmo Kama Sutra* and *Cosmo Bedside Quiz*.

The success of *Cosmopolitan* lies in its ability to address a global audience. It has been argued that its lure owes to the use of abstracted and sensual imaginary that helps to overcome any barriers created by real, local worlds (Machin and Thornborrow 2003). Women in *Cosmopolitan* represent the hegemonic heteronormative idea of feminine female beauty as coded in short skirts, red lipstick, high heels, long hair, revealing tops or hemline. With this coding, *Cosmopolitan* follows the general trend of women's magazines to offer difference without diversity (Eggins and Iedema 1997) and, doing this, it exercises the performative function of ritualized reiteration of gender norms. In the1960s, *Cosmopolitan* followed the same cue of sexual liberation as *Playboy* by offering new, playful sexiness to urban liberal young adults. However, while *Playboy* celebrated its version of 'natural' male sexual drive complemented by innocent girls next door happy and willing to please men, *Cosmopolitan* stressed the role of female sexual knowledge in keeping a man. (Dyer 1986: 31–2; Radner 1993). Many readers may view the magazine as trivial due to its playful tone (Hermes 1995). The ideology of *Cosmopolitan* can nevertheless be recognized as a broader cultural trend evident in television series (*Sex and the City, Ally McBeal*), advertising (Attwood 2005; Rossi in this volume) and urban nightlife (singles bars, women's events). Cosmopolitan magazine could be described as part and parcel of postfeminist discourse that produces 'a new feminism geared toward female sexual activity' (Negra 2004; also Projansky 2001).

The attitude of in-your-face postfeminism can be read from various articles and stories offering routes to sexual confidence. Sexual power in *Cosmopolitan* is harnessed to consumerist ideology, framing sexualities and lifestyles as issues of choice and freedom. In the case of *Cosmopolitan*, postfeminism encompasses a mix of active female sexual agency and dependency on (heterosexual) relationships ('how to get and keep a man'). Thus its technology of sexiness refers to certain 'marriagability' (Radner 1993: 59) based on sexual expertise. As Hilary Radner (1993) argues in her analysis of the new heterosexual contract coined by *Cosmopolitan* in the 1960s, the goal still was for a single girl to marry. However, unlike in the 1950s, her capital was now increased by sexual knowledge. The Cosmo brand has developed in tandem with cultural transformations in the rights, employment and education of women that have contributed to their increased independence, as well as increased interest toward their sexual power.

Making Sense of Virtual Intimacy

As more and more women began using the Internet in the 1990s, content producers awoke to addressing female users and providing services for them. As Paasonen (2002) has pointed out, commercial websites for women tended to define their target audience through the use of pastel colours, round shapes and italic fonts. Such sites were rarely deconstructive in terms of gender but tended to promote

family and friends. This is telling of the dual standing of sex in society: it is ubiquitous in public images and texts, yet something protected in private lives. This contradiction may cause heightened expectations and aspirations concerning sex since there is no actual knowledge of 'the average'. The most recent study of sexual behaviour in Finland (Kontula and Haavio-Mannila 2001) shows that while appreciation of sex has increased, dissatisfaction also seems to grow. This potential paradox may have to do with high expectations owing to the increased visibility of representations of sexuality in popular culture. As a public site for disclosing sexual information and experiences, the Cosmo forum participates in the definition of successful and plentiful sex as a central aspiration for young women. Like many other Internet forums, Cosmo is one of shared curiosity, counselling and peer advice. Members ask questions that are replied to with carefully phrased, detailed advice and information following the style of advice-giving online forums (Morrow 2006). The forum also functions as a site for gathering capital on sexual knowledge.

Postings are mostly straightforward and graphic. There is no beating around the bush when introducing new issues, nor are euphemisms or other periphrases in use. The tone of the discussion is nevertheless quite matter-of-fact, thorough and even friendly. Threads usually start with a question concerning either a personal problem or a listing/vote/questionnaire of some sort. Consequently, listings and peer guidance form the majority of postings. The supportive style of Cosmo works to affirm a sense of community and is recognizable also on other sites designed for women (Cooks, Castaneda and Scharrer 2002; also Laukkanen 2004). Cosmo differs from other Finnish sex forums targeted at women in its friendly style and fairly homogeneous community. The sex discussions on the online forums of *Vauva* magazine ('Baby-magazine', targeted at mothers and pregnant women) and Ellit (a lifestyle portal for women), for example, are fairly aggressive. Their disputes over preferred penis size or the tightness of vagina – to which both male and female users participate – are regular and brusque. Discussions include provocative remarks and jokes rather than actual questions or sexual dilemmas, as on the Cosmo forum. In many cases, male pseudonyms dominate the discussions. Differences from Cosmo are quite striking and can be at least partly explained by the fact that the latter has nine moderators in comparison to the more modest resources of the other forums (on moderators, see Edwards 2002).

Cosmo sex discussions involve the celebration of sexuality: users' enthusiasm over exciting positions and the discovery of new techniques speak of joyful, diverse sex lives. There is no trace of the coyness or shame that usually accompanies public discussions of sex. In spite of this celebration of sexuality, there are certain norms limiting its conditions and possibilities. The most dominant of these involves an underlying normativity of the couple. Members refer repeatedly to their boyfriends and relationships. Expressions such as 'us', 'our bedroom' or 'we like it' help to frame sexuality in terms of stable relationships. However, as the

Finnish term for he/she ('hän') makes no distinction in terms of gender, the gender of the partner remains occasionally unclear. What is not said is equally illuminating: if some of the female members are in a relationship with women, this is not articulated in any way to others. Recently a new thread on group sex has appeared on the forum in which one of the members enquires whether others have had group sex together with their boyfriends. Sex with women is not, then, ruled out but anchored in the heterosexual relationship. The ideal relationship is constructed as sexually active: failure, reluctance, impotence or the lack of sex do not usually amount as topics. Sex talk is characterized by an emphasis on the technical: sex is largely defined in terms of positions and techniques as supposed to emotional aspects. In many ways sex is constructed as a taste culture dividing and binding users according to their likings.

The act of writing sex makes users into authors recounting their private desires and sexual behaviour – and constructing narratives of their sexual lives. This, as well as the possibility of reading similar stories coined by others, may also serve as a source of pleasure – even if the tone of the messages is quite neutral and void of the suggestive air of fantasy. Popular topics such as sexual preferences, pubic hair or oral sex circulate also in other *Cosmopolitan* web discussions. As a frame of reference, the *Cosmopolitan* magazine offers topics for discussion (such as multiple orgasms addressed in the magazine in the time of writing). The topics discussed are not isolated but linked with certain shifts in cultural practices and ways in which bodies are culturally marked. Susan Bordo (1993: 246) refers to this constant rearrangement of body as cultural plastic. The increasing popularity of cosmetic surgery, body shaping and moulding is present in the messages referring to 'disgusting' body hair or the best body parts for piercing.

Look, Learn and Swallow

Offering peer guidance on sexuality, the forum also takes part in shaping the grounds of 'good sex', and good heterosex in particular (Warner 2000). In this guidance, pornography is usually referred to as a source of sexual techniques. Cosmo forum makes evident the conflation of pornography and sex: porn is used as instructional material, as if echoing the legitimizing of pornographic representations as sexual education (Arthurs 2004: 40). Promising to deepen women's knowledge of sex, the forum follows the *Cosmopolitan* ideology of advancing female sexual agency and contributing to the sexual education of women (Nead 1988; Oullette 1999). However, whether pornography (films, online porn) always offers good advice or not is not something agreed on by the members of the forum. Porn divides opinions, as a discussion on oral sex illustrates.

> So my problem is that I don't know how to do a blow job. How do you do that?? Please explain in as much detail as you can!!!

The message received over a hundred replies explaining the art of oral sex in detail. The replies were quite practical and paid attention to 'not taking the penis in too deep' and 'being careful of the teeth'. Some replies referred to porn films as practical guides, causing minor disagreement on the possibility of learning sexual skills from porn:

> Hey, I don't think anyone their right mind would advise someone 'to look and learn from porn films'.
> Everything is pretentious and exaggerated in porn films, at least that's what I think. You'd rather ask the man you're handling what he likes.

A separate discussion, this time on the taste of sperm, included collective reasoning over the inflated expectations concerning sex, which were associated with the contents and effects of porn.

> I'm just thinking that young girls have such strong pressures of being like porn stars and having to do what they do etc. I mean pressures that you have to do things you don't want to.
> I've noticed those delusions myself of having to perform like a porn star and then thinking I'm nothing cause I'm not naughty enough.
> Those who don't have experiences of sex read or watch porn and think that this is something you have to do like swallow sperm even though you don't want to. You think it's only good when you swallow. Well then I think it is bad thing if you have to do it against your will or under pressure.

There is concern over the pressure young women may experience after watching porn films and attempting to perform like porn stars in order to please their partners. Members agree that porn films seem to create false expectations of sex and are hence particularly harmful if taken as realistic examples. It is noteworthy that access to porn is taken for granted when discussing sexual pressures. The discussion eventually turns to women's experiences of men performing cunnilingus on them and whether it is possible to do it 'right' or 'wrong'. There are various examples of bad experiences and inability to reach orgasm during oral sex. These messages speak of the imperfect moments of sex that disclose sex as practices to be learned (Warner 2000: 177). The final postings on the thread deal with the details of fellatio. Two members describe feeling nauseated by the mere thought of sperm. One of them has created a technique in order to avoid the taste:

> It's quite handy to take the sperm under your tongue so you don't taste it and feel it …
> And I've heard or read from somewhere that you can do it so that the guy is wearing a condom. It probably feels less then but still some. That's something to try. And then there's just getting use to it.
> Yeah, maybe I just have to grin and bear it. Anything for my baby.

The acceptance of discomfort illuminates the power of cultural ideals in heterosexual relationships. Some techniques, acts and practices seem to be more 'must' than others. This, however, spurs a reaction from other members who strongly advise women not to bear everything or do things they do not enjoy. The concern over pleasing without deriving pleasure from it seems to resurface in the discussions – echoing a feminist principle of standing up for your sexual rights. The overt interest in sexual techniques suggests that female sexual competence equals skilful performance for the purpose of male pleasure. Indeed, there is a sense of pride in messages disclosing the capability of satisfying a male partner. This is not to say that women's own sexual pleasure would be absent. Female pleasure is frequently referred to but it seems intertwined with the ability of giving pleasure and performing well.

Moments of shame and embarrassment, again, involve inability or ignorance concerning sexual techniques. Questions such as 'how is a blow job actually done?' are framed with apologies and blushing smileys. It seems that sexual activity and knowledge form such an ideal on the Cosmo forum that ignorance and innocence require apologies. The silence over passive or non-existent sex lives equally suggests the norm of active female sexual agency conforming to the Cosmo brand. This is evident in postings where users, while disclosing their problems, make reference to their otherwise 'healthy sex life' or 'sex on a daily basis'. Problems in sex seem less related to one's relationships than the lack of necessary skill or sex toys. Consequently, toys are often seen as a solution to sexual problems. As Jane Juffer (2004) notes, sex toys have become mainstream merchandise sold within the heteronormative confines of 'normal' sex. Toys carry sexual meanings (that may be challenged) related to particular kinds of sexual behaviour. Information about dildos, vibrators and gels circulates on the forum, signalling their frequent use. In this sense, the forum serves as a platform for distributing information on available merchandise and events (such as the annual 'sExhibition' fairs that include various professional and amateur shows, displays, rewards and markets for sex-related merchandise) and for promoting commercial sex. Some discussions are however polemic, especially the one concerning sExhibition. The possibility of attending the event and watching female striptease spurs strong objections. The lines of 'normal' sexuality are drawn particularly in such moments of vocal disgust. Merchandise such as dildos and outfits are welcomed, whereas live performances are considered more problematic and evaluated through the discourses of female oppression and victimization (Dworkin 1979; cf. Attwood 2004) – but also through affective bursts of homophobia.

Virtual Porn Between Us

Recurrent references to commercial sex on the Cosmo forum suggest that porn is present in everyday life and referred to as a source of sexual skill and knowledge

– interestingly enough, among young women. Porn is usually seen as something consumed by male audiences, in spite of porn also being produced with female consumers in mind (Juffer 2004). Feona Attwood (2005) points out that the marketing of sex products for women focuses strongly on toys and clothing whereas pornography remains more problematic. Indeed sex markets for women emphasize the contemporary ideal of femininity associated with style, fashion and self-expression, thus implying an increasing chasm between the male and female markets. The default porn user remains male while 'porn for women' often postulates a special genre emphasizing active male sexuality and romantic female sexuality (Fig. 6.2). In opposition to such notions of female sexuality, the tone of the Cosmo forum is far from romantic. Yet pornography can remain a controversial topic. When introduced as a problem, pornography usually has something to do with a boyfriend. Cosmo users repeatedly describe having caught their boyfriends viewing porn or finding porn on their computer. Members describe their anguish over the 'discovery' and ask advice on what to do.

> One of the problems that keep coming up is my boyfriend's habit of watching porn. He watches porn almost everyday either on the Internet or on TV. And I know a little too

Figure 6.2 Sex markets for female consumers in Tampere, Finland. Photograph by Laura Saarenmaa.

well the kind of women he tends to choose from the selection of porn sites (dark/blond big tits old/young etc.) These types don't resemble me at all.

Response is supportive:

> By accident I noticed some time ago that there was some porn again on the computer. I try to think that well he can watch it when I am not at home or if I am not in the mood (he probably doesn't know of me knowing). The hardest thing for me is that they all seem to be those young girls masturbating. And women who look very different from me ... After the first shock I decided that if he watches I'll watch too. But I definitely won't be watching girls masturbating, yuck. I have to look for something for myself some day. It does feel bad to think that he has watched porn but I can't just forbid it. Well, so far he has watched so I wouldn't know had I not accidentally found out so it's all good.

Here the main problem seems not to be the boyfriends' habit of watching porn inasmuch as women's inability to accept it. Unable to remove porn from their relationships, Cosmo women accuse themselves of not having enough self-confidence to accept their partners' hobby. The question of self-esteem relates to the tanned, fit, surgically enhanced female bodies featured in mainstream porn. The thread continues:

> I understand you completely and I agree. Exactly because of that I never watch porn (although it is fun etc.) You don't have to accept your boyfriend's doings.

Since the forum is dedicated to sex talk it requires a permissive attitude towards various forms of sexuality, as is evident in the way that members try to convince others of not being against pornography: that 'porn is porn' and 'porn is fun after all'. Another thread discussed whether cybersex should be considered cheating. The majority of replies (altogether sixteen) concluded that cybersex equals cheating whereas viewing porn does not, since the former involves two parties in reciprocal action while the latter concerns commodities produced for the purpose of arousal. This thread did not consider porn threatening although the examples discussed above spoke differently. This may reflect shifts in cultural attitudes towards pornography as mere entertainment or illuminate the specificity of the Finnish context. Unlike in the United States, Finnish debates on pornography have been fairly moderate and public discussion more or less liberal, if not positive towards porn.[2] Especially in the early 1990s, public debates on commercial sex emphasized liberal politics and a move towards a new and more permissive post-socialist Europe. Framing pornography as fun is something almost to be expected in the Finnish context. This makes porn a difficult target for critique and leads Cosmo members to undermine their discomfort towards porn:

It just feels so bad to deny something from the other, and it really doesn't affect our sex life. He's told me that he'd stop if I'd ask but also said that it would be foolish to deny something like that. Because of this I have also watched some porn. And well, part of it is exciting. I've watched it by myself couple of times, which helps to understand my boyfriends' view (realising how minor thing it actually is). But yes, quite a lot of the stuff is categorizing and so yuck, uh.

But then we decided to try something new and bought a porn film and agreed that we'll watch it only together and we'll throw it away if we'll fight ... maybe you should try the same.

We have it the other way around. I like to watch but my honey doesn't like the habit at all. He doesn't like to watch even with me.

I'm not bothered at all by the fact that my boyfriend watches porn – although he doesn't do that very often. I think it's a good idea to watch porn together – I did with my boyfriend the other day. But I must say that in many parts I had to close my eyes or look away because I felt so embarrassed.

In practice, then, experiences of porn may be awkward and disturbing, yet the women feel the need to accept it in spite of their discomfort. Some of the discomfort seems to be caused by the knowledge – or assumption – that porn caters to male desires. Especially looking at female performers is defined as disturbing. The porn in question may not be as decidedly 'male' as the discussion implies, yet the ways in which women discuss porn marks them as outsiders that seem to desire some other kind of porn that would better take them in consideration as a target group.

Porn does not merely add spice to sex life (although it is introduced as such) but seems to influence and constitute more fundamental understandings of sexual practices, their limits and possibilities. Mainstream heterosexual porn contributes to relationships and the crafting of sexual practices while also giving rise to conflicts and moments of contestation. In the Cosmo forum, porn is discussed on a very general level, rather than by mentioning specific films or video titles. This implies an understanding of porn as a bulk of repetitious imagery, as 'more of the same'.

A similar tendency to abstract porn is recognizable in the culture at large. Almost anyone can say something about pornography without reference to specific genres or texts. Pornography, it seems, does not require similar expertise as prime time television shows or Hollywood films. Lack of specificity speaks of porn's cultural position as the low, yet recognizable and contested.

Discourses of Porn

Cosmo forum constructs an apparently liberal, celebratory space for sex talk. Celebration of female sexuality echoes the women's liberation movement of the

1960s, which linked gender equality with greater sexual confidence. Liberalism was followed by voices of sexual conservatism drawing on behaviourist sexology and hierarchical biological divisions between men and women, hence polarizing notions of male and female sexuality. Seeing women as victims and men as violators, this trait has been particularly influential in political campaigns over sexual rights and regulation (Segal 2004; cf. Dworkin 1979). Cosmo forum clearly challenges such views of women as less sexually active. Instead, women's attitudes towards sex seem straightforward and 'technical'. Cosmo forum cherishes sexuality in its various forms, but this celebratory space is not without its limits. The sex discussed may sometimes stretch the boundaries of heterosexuality but straight relationships remain the default starting point. Although the discussions involve strong sexual activity and pleasure, there is a sense of conformity and submission as the boundaries of the relationships are tested. The ability to perform and please a boyfriend seems to override personal reluctance or even disgust. Thus success in sex is not merely about getting off but centrally about getting the boyfriend off.

The discussions contain various discourses of porn. First of all, there's the discourse of porn as education: watching porn in order to learn new techniques. This discourse refers to pornography being increasingly a source and site of sexual advice (Mason-Grant 2004: 148). Besides being a site of learning, pornography seems to be more and more related to mainstream media and entertainment. This is illuminated in the discourse of porn as fun that draws on the liberal view of porn as enjoyable and harmless, as something that is easily accessed and present in everyday life. The discourse of porn as pressure, on the other hand, emphasizes the demanding ideals that porn imagery sets for young girls and women, drawing on feminist and antiporn discourses. This discourse speaks of the way the female body, recognized as flawed, is related to discomfort rather than pleasure (Attwood 2005). Interestingly, the ideals are not challenged as such; rather, individuals are left with the task of resolving the pressures.

Although most of the discussions are written in a matter-of-fact style, the discourse of porn as disgusting appears emotional. Since disgust is difficult to explain, it is rationalized by using antiporn rhetoric of subordination and categorizing of the female body. Interestingly the argument in antiporn rhetoric, however rational it may appear, tends to lean on underlining the sensation of filth and disgust, as pointed out by Michael Warner (2000: 181). Discourse of disgust is also used to emphasize borders of 'the normal' and to deny any signs of lesbian desire. Porn is in many cases discussed as self-evidently made for men. The discourse of porn as something for the boys does not question the naturalized male interest in porn, but finds no place for the female gaze. This discourse refers to the potential and problem of the female porn markets (Attwood 2005) and assumes pronounced gender differences in the understandings of sexuality.

The discussions of young women point to pornification as the presence of porn in everyday life: porn functions as a resource of sexual techniques and pleasures but its presence can also be disturbing. The Cosmo forum adds to the sexual knowledge of its users – as does pornography. Such proliferating knowledge does invite women to explore new sexual categories and horizons, yet quotidian porn and straight sex talk may equally well work together to create new kinds of norms concerning desire, sex and sexuality.

–7–

Making Porn into Art

Kerstin Mey

A woman – half sitting, half kneeling on what looks to be an upholstered stool – is captured in a closed-off interior situation. She inhabits and slightly exceeds the life-size portrait format of the photograph. While her head is facing the viewer directly, her body is turned slightly to the left. In the somehow blurred colour image the viewer can make out that her legs, which are awkwardly spread apart, give some limited sight of her sex. She is dressed in black stockings held up by suspenders. The outfit is completed with a tight and skimpy black corset that finishes beneath the breasts, buttressing them, as well as extreme knee-high and high-heeled boots in white. They are the kind of boots that are a standard requisite in the sex business. The hazily veiled picture still allows the viewer to recognize that the woman's head is subject to some kind of gagging. Her eye, nose and neck regions are covered up with black material. Closer inspection shows her arms are tied to the side of her body and her slim legs held in a rather strenuous position by straps that are fastened around her waist and ankles (Mey 2006: 129).

The totality of this performative arrangement appears to display a pronounced fetishist obsession and tamed/sublimated yet confident SM desire. The woman oscillates between luring agent and attractive focal point of such want. With her exhibitionist glamour, she calculatingly invites the voyeuristic gaze and imaginative interaction with her, which also nourishes and affirms her proposition. The image is directed at a socially integrative optics of voyeurism, that is to derive sexual stimulation or satisfaction from watching secretly the undress and/or sexual engagement of others. It emulates the love of looking, the pornographic curiosity and affective deferral inherent in Western consumerist society.

This bondage image looks strangely familiar – a photographic scene that may have been encountered many times before in the pages of porn magazines or similar Internet sites. Yet, this particular photograph is a unique, large-scale print by contemporary German artist Thomas Ruff. Skilfully mounted, it can be encountered in an art exhibition as part of his series *Nudes* (1999–2000). Likewise it can be found on the glossy pages of a large-format art book of the same title and accompanied by a preface written by the acclaimed French author Michel Houellebecq (Ruff and Houellebecq 2003).

Ruff's venturing into the pornographic is by no means a provocative exception in the contemporary art scene – quite the opposite. Much of current art is concerned with the more or less explicit representation of sex, or as John Waters and Bruce Hainley (2003: 7) state in *Art – A Sex Book*: 'Contemporary art is sex ... it's all about sex.' And not just contemporary art. Western art throughout its history has been connected to the exploration of sexual relationships and the display of human sexuality – in more or less explicit ways, guided by conventions and standards of beauty.

However, in terms of aesthetic classification, value hierarchies and cultural acceptance, there exists a fine and yet fluid dividing line between pornographic depiction and what has been called erotic arts. Both categories of representation aim at the arousal of the flesh. They seek to titillate and seduce. They intimate or flaunt sexual wish-fulfilment, pose as a substitute for real human sexual transactions. Yet, the attribute 'erotic' denotes the agreed or established permissibility of such sexual representation. The label 'art' attests aesthetic quality to the depiction and gives credence to a complex formal repertoire and symbolic meaning that appears measured and appealing to the mind. Pornography is commonly regarded as the negative other: the non-aesthetic and excessive, the mere carnal stimulant, the simple and lowbrow, the smutty and ultimately deplorable. The pornographic is that which should not be paraded publicly, which should, if produced at all, remain off-stage, off-scene – hence, its convergence with the category of the obscene. It should be noted here that although pornography and obscenity are habitually used synonymously, obscenity represents a more general concept that incorporates explicitly and excessively violent and other indecent and non-aesthetic expressions.

The demarcation between erotic and pornographic representation is closely interconnected with aesthetic, moral and legal standards of the time, with institutional frameworks and specific circuits of dissemination and parameters of discourse. It is firmly embedded in the broader economic, political and cultural conditions and historical circumstances of society. In other words, what is seen as art and what as pornographic is based on value judgements and can vary from period to period and from culture to culture. Notions of the pornographic are inflected by class, gender, race and generation and are intimately intertwined with shifting taboo zones.

Not only has pornography become noticeably more popular in recent times, it has also provided a prevalent reference point for contemporary artists like Robert Mapplethorpe, Paul McCarthy, Marlene Dumas, Sue Williams, Natacha Merritt and many others. This begs the question why pornographic displays generate such interest among mainstream art practitioners? And when does porn become art? This chapter will consider these questions by drawing on recent work by Thomas Ruff and the contemporary Belgian artist Anne-Mie Van Kerckhoven.

Both artists operate with digitally manipulated photographic images. It can be argued that the invention of technologies of mass reproduction such as photography, video and digital imaging has propelled not only the production and thus the availability and accessibility of pornographic material. It has also fuelled the fluidity and cross-fertilization between what is considered highbrow or mainstream art, including erotic art, and what is judged to be obscene and perceived or condemned to linger at the margins of dominant cultural values and domains.

Thomas Ruff: Nudes

Ruff has selected and downloaded the raw material for his series of nudes from the vast number of Internet sites that circulate sexually explicit photographic material. The images were taken from the economy of online pornography, much if not most of it independently produced. Numerous claims have been made for the impact of digital information and communication technologies on cultural assumptions, consumer attitudes and behaviour, on the ways knowledge is produced, distributed and accessed, and on the ways reality is symbolically represented. These claims have been closely linked to the argument that one of the drivers for the development of the means of mass or global communication and information is the quest for higher degrees of immediacy. Each new text, imaging and sound recording technology, from the early photographic camera to the digital video camera, from the mechanical music box to the home entertainment system, from the book to the computer, all of those interventions have sought to reduce the media interface of representation. Technology has aimed to transcend the book page, the television screen or computer display. The desired and attempted eradication of these mediation interfaces between the actual event or real object and the viewer holds the promise of achieving a more 'direct encounter' with reality, a greater 'transparent' immediacy and authenticity (Bolter and Grusin 1999: 51). Porn has been regarded as the ultimate test case for immediacy, which is the desire to move beyond the limits of representation 'and to achieve the real.... The real is defined in terms of the viewer's experience; it is that which would evoke an immediate (and therefore authentic) emotional response' (Bolter and Grusin 1999: 51). The logic of immediacy is closely interrelated with the logic of hypermediacy, as Jay David Bolter and Richard Grusin have persuasively argued. Hypermediacy means the combination of multiple media (such as a web page, a video game or a music CD-ROM or DVD) that takes its 'raw ingredients' from 'images, sound, text, animation and video in any combination' (Bolter and Grusin 1999: 31). The interplay between the logic of transparent immediacy and hypermediacy constitutes and (trans)forms practices of remediation that is the 'representation of one medium in another' (Bolter and Grusin 1999: 45).

The concept as well as the social and cultural function of pornography seems intimately linked with a desired sense of presence, of 'transparent representation of the real and the enjoyment of the opacity of media themselves' (Bolter and

Grusin 1999: 21). What could be a greater confirmation of a medium's capacity for immediacy than the witnessing of actual sex? This experience is hardly spoilt by the knowledge of the capacity of digital imaging technologies to manipulate and fake images, which has eroded photography's claim to authenticity and intensified the long-apparent crisis of representation over the past decades.

Ruff's recycled and appropriated digital *Nudes* first appeared as low-resolution, relatively small web images, commonly 72 dpi. Before he blows them up to almost life-like proportions, their file size is just large enough to fit them clearly enough on the average computer screen. The intended monumentalization would have produced individual pixels of two square-centimetres each and thus destroyed the representational quality of the image. Instead, each of the seventy-two pixels per inch is multiplied by thirty-six. This operation generates the impression of a semi-transparent veil that blurs the whole mis-en-scène, denaturalizes and depersonalizes it (Winzen 2002: 148). Based on the principles of control and chance, order and disorder, some further image manipulations out of the digital bag of tricks have been employed to soften, haze, obscure and conceal the spread, bound and copulating bodies. Movements and actions become silhouettes. This manoeuvre accentuates the performative element of the display, the staging of the body, but it does not make it more striking and distinctive. Rather, it reiterates and stresses the repetitive nature of pornographic photography, its clichéd poses, positions and props in a way that the individual picture can be hardly recalled, yet it cannot be forgotten either. There is a tacit level of communication at work in them that operates below the radar of conscious thought and remains difficult to fully elicit.

The visual material Ruff has selected for *Nudes* comprises references to the pin-up tradition. In some instances (in)sight is given of female genitalia and some phallic displays are exhibited. The images also include exaggerated French kisses, lesbian exchanges, full-blown intercourse in heterosexual as well as homosexual variations, and soft forms of sadomasochistic configurations. Most of the images would normally function as 'warm-ups for the decidedly phallic activity' that constitute the core of heteroporn (Williams 1995: 37). The online material selected appears to have been modelled on the logic of commercial, skilfully scripted and edited porn imagery. The activities put on display by Ruff are mostly an 'emblem for the erotics of the heterosexual, male viewing observer' (1995: 37).

The digital photographs subscribe to the pragmatics of arousing sexual desire. This becomes obvious in their direct references to the conventional formats and dominant gendered economy of watching sex in secrecy (i.e. voyeurism). Whilst any online display can potentially draw on the multimediality of the digital realm in which image, sound, text and animation join forces to excite their users, Ruff has restricted those staged bodies in action to visual still reproductions. As the surrounding environment becomes blurred and homogenized, other scene-setting and marketing elements, which might have been involved in the initial online exhibition, have been removed. Instead, the corporeal gestures and optical signals, which have become conventionalized in the advertisement and selling of sex, are placed centre stage. Reducing the potential of their intended seduction in favour of an investment into the cultural codes of their visual construction through a strategic emphasis on the performative character of the posing and exhibit of sexually motivated acts, he provokes active visual apprehension that moves beyond the cursory look and instantaneous image screening.

Ruff's concentration on manipulated and monumentalized still photography in an act of retroactive remediation re-invokes an old rivalry between photography and painting. What the digital online material sought to greatly lessen if not to make totally transparent in the consciousness of the user, who has become increasingly accustomed to the moving image, has been strategically stressed so that the images spell out their mediated nature. Rather than representing reality, they represent images of images of reality: simulation instead of immanence (Winzen 2000: 151).

In size and format, Ruff's sexually explicit displays have been customized for exhibition in a representative space, a public or semi-public situation: a gallery, reception area or drawing room. The extensive critical discussion in and beyond the field of experts, the institutional and discursive validation of this photographic series and its producer through dealers, art fairs, museums and private collectors anchors it firmly in the mainstream of contemporary international art.

As these untitled but numbered pictures are also available as coffee-table publications for the more or less discerning book buyer or collector, they are potentially exposed to a broader public. Thus they are lent an enhanced degree of longevity beyond any attention to the work that the exhibition circuit would have managed to achieve on its own, even with an extensive critical discourse and media coverage. The glossy book format with its pronounced durability, representative character and continued availability (or at least accessibility through public libraries and second-hand bookshops) enhances the cultural currency and status of both the publication's subject and the art's producer. The book format also differentiates the work from the economics of the Internet, with its predominant existence for the now-time (*Jetztzeit*) and instant accessibility, its accelerated wear and tear.

The case has been made that Ruff's series of *Nudes* has evolved from the artist's continuous efforts to examine the potential of both traditional and digital photography particularly in terms of their indexical function. Indexicality signifies the dimension of a sign (and photographs, as much as other cultural images, are signs) in which the signifier is not arbitrary, but is directly connected in some way to the signified. Photography as light-writing functions similarly to the footprint in the sand, as Susan Sontag (1979) observes: in the first instance, the camera can only capture the sexual for instance when it has appeared in front of its objective and is relayed to it through light. Yet the outcome is already informed by the programme of the optical apparatus and its user's choices: the actual angle of the lens, distance, focus, exposure, etc. The seized information can then be potentially manipulated

– in traditional photography through analogue processes, and within digital media in more radical ways, which undermine any notion of authenticity and immediacy (see Flusser 2000). Yet still, the notion of photography's special indexical relationship to the world, which forms the foundation of its system of representation, informs the belief and trust in the medium's capacity to document reality, including sexuality, in a factual and objective way. It is still seen to get closer to the real world than painting – the realm of imagination, fiction and heightened symbolism – would have ever been capable of. Painting always reveals itself as an aesthetically elevated and refracted mediation of the world, a kind of make-believe.

Photographs as complex cultural signs are closely connected to the issue of conventionality. They are constructed on the basis of cultural codes, which in the context of this book beg the question, 'How does one recognize a pornographic image?' The Italian philosopher and writer Umberto Eco asked a similar question in 1989 with regard to the pornographic film and argued that its typical characteristic is dead time, time in which nothing happens. In order to mark the transgression of moral (and aesthetic) norms as such and to awake an interest, the sexual interaction has to be distinguished from the everyday, from normality, from the expected (2001: 321–2). Similarly, the performances of sex depicted in pornographic photographs are conventionally situated within rather banal and often bare if not dreary environments to draw the attention to the act rather than the surroundings. The latter is usually limited to essentials and props that are necessary to make the scene (sensually) plausible for the spectator. The camera lens zooms in (almost) exclusively on the (entangled) bodies of the agents, and in particular on their primary and secondary sexual organs, as well as their (titillating and copulating) actions as a proof that real sex is taking place. The framework of a series of images may put a scant narrative overlay to such an ensemble, but not in Ruff's case. Untitled or merely numbered, they are more difficult to identify as individual or sequential art works and more akin to much of the anonymous output within the enormous and continuously expanding, profitable area of pornographic (and multimedia) imaging.

The artist has described his own motivation for this series as a reflection on the genre of nude photography, which is situated within the field of tension of social and moral values, and, in terms of its pictorial content, at the boundary between art historical precedents and mass cultural expressions. The indicative series title places the work ambivalently into the proximity of the dynamic and shifting boundaries between the mass reprographic genre and the esteemed and more exclusive realm of high art. It not only provides a descriptor of the work's content, but serves as a euphemism in both directions: Ruff's already mediated pictorial worlds reference pornographic photography, which is equally marked by professional investments as well as amateur attitude, yet always carried by a calculating, mercantile impetus. Through their format and presentation, the appropriated pictures also create a continuity within the domain of high art – a continuity that is as affirming as it is mocking. It points to the long history of Western representation of the female nude and its driving male heterosexual desire that spans from Titian, Velasquez and Goya via Courbet, Manet and Rodin, to Matisse, Picasso, Freud, Richter and Balthus and many more (Mey 2006: 136). This art form has been promoted as erotica rather than pornography through the powers and mechanisms of the art institutions and their discursive and critical circuits, as described earlier. And finally, Ruff's appropriation of Internet pornography relies on and is complicit in the economic structure on which the industry is based. As an economic sector, web pornography encompasses a diversity of approaches and practices, and in general it yields high profits. Yet its professional and amateur actors, predominantly women, are on average not that well paid, nor do they have (many) social rights in the workplace. More often than not, their creative investment is neither acknowledged nor does it generate cultural capital (status and prestige). Many of the models remain nameless. Ruff takes advantage of this unequal, exploitative power relationship. As a signature-artist he accumulates cultural prestige and profit through the appropriation of these anonymous and/or (further) anonymized works.

Ann-Mie Van Kerckhoven: Head Nurse

Ann-Mie Van Kerckhoven's visual strategies are situated in a field of tension similar to Ruff's. They too concern the mobility and dynamics of images across different cultural arenas, from mass media to the museum, from advertisement to the art gallery, from the magazine pages to the expensive art book and return. These forms of circulation are interconnected with respective conditioned cultural practices of looking, with forms of social consumption. Van Kerckhoven's increasingly layered multimedia work also deals with the female nude, but in a much more extensive and consistent way than Ruff. Photographic images of females in alluring and tantalizing poses from a wide variety of printed mass media have provided the stock for much of Van Kerckhoven's visual work especially since the mid-1990s. Her particular interest is directed at the popular pin-up format. Her main concerns rest with the objectification and commodification of women in the climate of a growing mediatization of contemporary life (Van de Sompel 1999: 84). She has been spoilt for choice as the last century and the beginning of the new millennium have been saturated with pictures of beautiful, highly desirable, yet unreachable, intangible and unattainable women (and increasingly of men too). As appetisers for the sale of consumer objects – from cars to sofas – and as pin-up merchandise themselves, they nonetheless illustrate very palpably the commodity character of the fe/male body and of sex. Much of the collated material is taken from the vernacular of everyday information and communication.

The artist compiles, orders and stores those images but also words and text fragments in digital databases. The databases are exploited to produce increasingly complex non-linear multimedia narratives consisting of overlays of image, text and video animation. They bring together pictorial fragments that oscillate between graphic design and imaginative figuration, advertisement and textbook illustration. The final outcome takes on a variety of forms: video clip, film, elaborate spatial installation, web display, still image. Mostly they are designated for public display in the gallery space.

Over the past decade, Van Kerckhoven has been committed to her extensive ongoing didactic project, *Head Nurse*. Stages of the project are based on material the artist has collected from the 'naked women press', which dates back to the pre-sexual liberation times. These mass reproduced images were 'meant to meet men's desire to look at women in different stages of "undress"' (Van de Sompel 1999: 82). Other parts of this ongoing work in progress appropriate images of women from the 1970s (and later decades), which coincided with their liberation campaign.[1]

In an early series under the *Head Nurse* umbrella, amateur photography is cited both formally and metaphorically. Here, photographic images of women have been digitally manipulated to emulate the contrast-saturated language of graphic design. Through line, schematized form and contrast they bring out those supposedly seductive gestures and attributes of the represented. Underpinned by a standard portrait format, the pictures highlight the repetitive principles of camera angle and unimaginative composition. They are accompanied by examples of technical jargon from the domain of photographic process, technology and history such as *polarization, refraction, reflection, luminescence and fluorescence*. Whilst experimenting with the parameters of the apparatus and photochemical processes, with light-sensitive material and technical equipment, the illicit and transgressive genre of pornographic photography has sustained its remarkable popularity amongst amateur photographers working behind the closed doors of the darkroom. The production of such material operates in similarly covert and complex circulation and feedback loops. They may be distributed from hand to hand or through (carefully) coded online channels. In the context of amateur photography, the pornographic images may not only serve as a kind of male trophy, but also as exploratory tools and stimulants of personal sexual desires (Jacobs 2004a).

In another complex part of *Head Nurse* including *Nursing activities, direct*; *Nursing care+timing*; and *Nursing need* (1996–9), Van Kerckhoven plays a different game with the conventions of the centrefold spread to unsettle conventionalized ways of looking. She reduces the mass-reproduced photographic images of female nudes to their outer contours and places them on to a flat, monochrome background. These images are accompanied by text integrated in the pictorial format. Not only are the chosen phrases significant, but so are the choice of styles of text. The juxtaposition of scribbled handwriting in some of the work and Courier standard print typeface pitches against each other different cultural stereotypes and systems of knowledge, power and authority. Read in conjunction with the imagery and the overarching title, *Head Nurse*, this can be understood as exposing and working through binary oppositions on which Western thought has been based for so long: mind–body, male–female, science–art, rational–emotive, subject–object, public–private; licit–illicit; formal–informal, and which mark the economy of pornography too. Van Kerckhoven's remediation and de-naturalization of the images over time and space also foregrounds the complexity and dynamic of contemporary social and cultural practices: that which is and has come out in the open and that which remains hidden away, which is marginalized and excluded. *Head Nurse* paints a complicated picture of gradually shifting boundaries between different cultural domains, including the ones between high art and popular culture, between traditional and new media towards stages and forms of hybridity.

The pin-up culture was built on the putative advertising potential of scarcely clothed or naked women with fabricated sexual personas suggested through the staged re/presentation as correlation between model, styles of codes of (un)dress, environment and target audience (Hellmann 2002). Existing in close proximity to the communication of advertising, pin-ups share a crucial characteristic with it: both are fictional rather than fictive. The (reference) question regarding truth or falsehood, which is dominant in other discourses, is suspended in favour of criteria that determine their effect, noticeability, their potential to motivate or stimulate, and thus their power of seduction. In order to be effective, they are always required to exist in the here and now; they need to appeal to the zeitgeist; they have to be in tune with the ruling fashions and predilections. In response to these criteria, aesthetic strategies are functionally employed to produce contemporary 'artefictions', which read as contemporary 'artefacts' (Schmidt 2000: 56). The constructed images have to display a developed degree of cultural plausibility and pragmatic persuasion that assures their neat fit into the pretence of a specific sociocultural mentality and reality. And yet they need to capture the attention and imagination of the onlooker through a degree of extraordinariness in exposure, suggestive narrative and formal novelty.

Van Kerckhoven's accumulation of pin-ups demonstrates vividly the cultural, stylistic and pragmatic changes that have occurred over time, as well as the continuities within the category of sex object and mass commodity in a climate where the rise of new technologies has led to an increased prominence of pornography in all spheres of cultural activity. While the technical qualities of images may have radically improved, their themes, motifs and stereotypes, have become ever more repetitive (Mey 2006: 139). She shows that the genre depends highly on processes of translation, adaptation and remediation of codes and styles to suit different cultural realities, depending, for instance, whether they seek to appeal to the respective reader of the *Sun*, *GQ*, *Hustler* or *Playboy*, or their equivalent in the realm of the Web, comic magazines, poster books and other printed erotica (Schmidt 2000: 56). In its high-art variation, this genre featured prominently in the work of photographers Helmut Newton, Bill Brandt and Irving Penn among many others. For

American Pop artist Tom Wesselman, the pin-up has also provided a recurrent motive; for instance, in his series of decorative paintings from the 1960s titled *American Nudes*.

The Address of Pin-Ups

In the pin-up genre, the body functions as a sociocultural design product: a perfect physique accomplished through a regime of diet, exercise and/or surgery; beautiful features drawn out with the help of make-up, manicure, hair and body styling or enhanced through syringe and scalpel. And as such it is naturalized. Yet, its staging in front of the camera lens (and under the influence of the airbrush) accentuates precisely the manufactured character of the performing body and the body performance as an enticing wrapper for equally manufactured and exploited human desires (Schmidt 2000: 56). The discipline that is being required and expended in attaining and maintaining a body that is regarded as flawless, perfect and thus presentable seems to be diametrically opposed to the transgression and excess that are linked with notions of pornography and sexual gratification. However, within and beyond the realm of advertising, erotically charged pin-ups as well as the increasingly explicit and daring simulations of nudes, interacting and copulating bodies, serve – undoubtedly – as energy conductors. (Kerckhoven often brings this to the fore through her choice of artistic material including lit neon tubes.) While pin-ups fuel the senses they do not hold the promise of satisfying the awakened desires of the flesh. Instead, the energy they generate is sublimated into the urge to buy, into an addiction to media consumption including pornography, or is employed for ideological propaganda – to promote the liberalism of Western society, for instance.

In order to function in this way, pin-ups have to indicate clearly who is speaking to whom, from where and when. They address in the second-person mode and indicate familiar rather than polite terms with the addressee, which equates to the '*du*' in German or the '*tu*' in French. The pretended, externalized close-up and personal delivery, the exhibition of intimacy has traditionally been the underwriting principle of this genre, as shown above. With a pronounced emphasis on titillating posing rather than the enactment of sex, their nature is erotic rather than pornographic. To maintain their full potential as emotional and bodily sublimative force, the pin-up cannot really become available. Their gesture must remain a soliloquy, an imagined gestural conversation in solitude.

The incessant de-contextualization of pin-ups through their transposition into the domain of the one-off original or limited edition artwork, the recombination and retroactive manipulation of the reproductions of women's staged bodies, transforms them from a conventionalized visual bait into a cultural anti-force. Van Kerckhoven's imaginative treatment of the visual vocabulary of unabated everyday exhibiting explores the viewers' relationship to the visual re/presentation of those objectified bodies and their underlying symbolic charges. As in the case of Ruff's work, for this strategy to be effective, the shift in the cultural context of the images' circulation, encounter and debate serves as a precondition. As analytic rather than synthetic procedure Van Kerckhoven's approach breaks down the spectator's attitude as voyeur and includes their observations as subject of the proposed cultural interrogation. Her work makes evident the constructedness of the erotically charged photograph. In the domain of high art, Ruff and Kerckhoven's strategies unearth the erotic/pornographic photographs' inherent aesthetic standards and moral codes. They thematize, if not problematize, the increasing and uncritical naturalization of commodified sex(uality) in everyday life.

–8–

How Unprofessional: the Profitable Partnership of Amateur Porn and Celebrity Culture

Kevin Esch and Vicki Mayer

The annual Adult Video News (AVN) Adult Entertainment Expo attracts international media producers, distributors and fans for the buying, selling and celebration of all things pornographic. Located in recent years in the Las Vegas Sands Convention Center, just off the famed casino strip, the AVN Expo in recent years has drawn more than 30,000 people of all genders and sexual orientations (AVN 2006). Much of the Expo programming is directed at the fans. Over the post-New Year's weekend, the fans can meet and greet their favourite porn stars, acquaint themselves with the latest bondage attire and gadgets, and pick up convention freebies, from a signed celebrity photo to sample DVDs. On the second night of the festival-like event, *AVN*, the largest trade magazine for pornography in the United States, sponsors an awards show, complete with red carpets, statuettes and the paparazzi. In these moments, the Expo illustrates the commercial imperatives and tensions within pornographic industries.

These imperatives are visualized on the floor of the convention itself. At the front doors, where fans and journalists enter, the 'porn majors' have apartment-sized stations, demonstrating their market position and trade strategies. Of these, three company booths – Vivid, *Hustler* and Club Jenna (named for its icon Jenna Jameson) – had larger-than-life portraits of their professional porn stars towering over the Expo floor. This attention towards celebrities in the business was matched only by the number of booths emphasizing new forms of distribution. Companies, such as Metro Interactive, Adult Supersource and Digital Playground presented high-tech backgrounds, new media gadgets and free literature emphasizing the accessibility of porn at home. As one moved towards the back of the centre, the spaces became less ornate and more densely packed, with special sections featuring gay erotica, ethnic women dressed as schoolgirls, and porn wardrobe options. Yet, these two themes – celebrity branding and new technologies – framed the concerns of nearly everyone in the business. That is, in a media-saturated environment, how would companies create brand names that last beyond a feature film

99

or video? Further, how would those brands be accessible and relevant to ordinary consumers? The answers to these two questions were both elusive and sources of anxiety, replicating the fears felt across media industries as a whole. Walking through the Expo in 2005, these fears filtered throughout the convention space, reaching even the sections in the least prominent parts of the centre.

Sandwiched between the sex toys, emergency exit doors and the concession stand, amateur porn producers were in the largest numbers in the least visible part of the Expo (Fig. 8.1). Lacking the high-tech monitors and celebrity guests, it was also the section most in transition. Vicki Mayer had known some of these producers from the streets of New Orleans, where many of them shot videos of public nudity at Mardi Gras, and met many others for the first time. They told her that the genre was changing, becoming more like commercial television and mainstream popular culture. These changes affected the ways they produced and distributed their products, creating challenges and many frustrations along the way.

In truth, however, genres are ever changing, as Rick Altman (1999) has argued. Traditionally, film and media studies have seen genres as fairly concrete, recognizable objects of study, even if they do change and evolve over time (as the

Figure 8.1 Fans flock to the Expo to take photographs of their favourite porn stars. AVN Expo, January 2005. Photograph courtesy of Debbie Nathan.

amateur porn producers agree). For example, *The Great Train Robbery*, a Western from 1903, or a 1960s short porn film shot on 16mm, are by this logic still generically grouped with either Clint Eastwood's *Unforgiven* (1992) or the collected works of Vivid Video. In a profound rethinking of theories of genre, Altman asks us to consider that genre is 'not the permanent *product* of a singular origin, but the temporary *by-product* of an ongoing *process*' (Altman 1999: 54, italics in original). This process is a continual negotiation, or what Altman calls 'genrification', in which multiple parties – producers, marketers, professional film critics, academics, filmgoers – participate. To return to our two examples, Altman notes that *The Great Train Robbery* has only retrospectively been dubbed a Western, at the time being identified with crime films, railway films and 'scenics'. The 16mm short, meanwhile, would have just as easily been described as part of the 'beaver' genre or even, according to a contemporary newspaper ad, an 'experimental underground film' (Schaefer 2004: 379). Different eras and different viewers produce different generic classifications.

The similarity of Altman's term 'genrification' to our anthology's topic, 'pornification', is instructive. It suggests that pornography is itself hardly a stable category, instead being defined by its constant reappraisal, both from within (e.g. amateur vs. corporate porn) and without (porn vs. 'mainstream' media). This chapter explores the relationship between amateur pornographers and the dominant porn producers, particularly in their use of celebrity performers, as a way of examining the symbiotic relationship between the porn and mainstream media industries. Although the terms 'pornographic' and 'mainstream' are slippery constructions in themselves, our point is to demonstrate how similar these industries really are in terms of their aims, needs and strategies. By looking at amateur production and producers, then, we can see who benefits from this symbiosis and who is left out. While it is hard to generalize the state of media, porn or otherwise, based on such a small sample, this chapter is meant to raise some questions that we might ask for the future.

Corporate Amateur Porn? A History of Ambiguities

Dedicated largely to soft-core imagery, home sex videos and independent webcam sites, 'amateur pornography' lies at the margins of mainstream media and pornography. Amateur pornography grew independently of either industry as an outgrowth of the video revolution of the early 1980s, when millions of people bought their first home video camera and budding film-makers decided to make their own pornography. These largely home-grown roots have made amateur porn unusual in that it still tends to be made outside of the larger media production centres. This has continually presented distribution problems for producers, because they are not part of established business networks, and recognition as a production trade category. *AVN* only began issuing awards for the best amateur pornography in the late 1980s.

In her history of amateur film, Patricia Zimmerman argues that amateurism is not simply a lack of professionalism, but in fact a means of securing and maintaining the organizing principles of the public sphere and of capitalist production. The 'methodical, controllable, and regulated' public sphere is thereby distinguished from 'the chaotic, the incoherent, and the spontaneous' spaces of our private existence (Zimmerman 1995: 11). In a capitalist film-making environment, expertise wins out over improvisation, rigid division of labour over a creative fluidity of labour, remunerated mechanical performance over authentic performance 'for the love of it'. The amateur film functions as a 'cultural reservoir for the liberal pluralist ideals' that have little place in the economic rationale of the film-making industry (Zimmerman 1995: 5).

The amateur porn genre has traditionally adhered to Zimmerman's analysis of amateur film as a whole even as corporations have begun to use the term 'amateur professional' to designate workers in many reality television genres (Mayer 2006). Aesthetically, amateur pornography has typically remained only as good as the quality that the consumer-grade video equipment allows. Grainy images, poor lighting and shaky camerawork have been standard to the look of the genre, though producers have been inventive in adapting to shooting conditions. The narratives in amateur are also a hotchpotch of individual inventions. Some amateur porn can be as simple as a couple copulating in a hotel, while other videos mimic travel documentaries or music videos. Amateur, as a genre, frequently impinges on other production categories, such as 'gonzo pornography', in which the director becomes the actor in the sex scene. Amateur can also be muddled with 'alternative porn' since much of amateur porn infers sex without showing it, much like the series of fetish videos that make up many alternative product lines. The hybridity of the genre is part of its appeal to producers, who have the independence and freedom to work across generic boundaries, and consumers, who buy in the hopes of getting a rawer, more authentic sexual product.

This authenticity was important to producers eager to define the boundaries of amateur. Specifically, many said amateur refers to the unpaid status of the performers, though a long-time director of amateur pornography noted that some form of remuneration is common, even if it doesn't compare to that of star performers. The director cited his own work as an example of classic amateur shooting.[1] For the past ten years, he has banded together with the owner of the production company to go on a boat trip at Lake Havasu, Arizona. The location, a remote party stop for swingers, offers an inexpensive set for filming uninhibited exhibitionism and sexual play. Few on screen receive much in the way of payment, except perhaps some free beer or a trip on the company boat. Even the female 'models' that this director hired for the Expo were largely volunteers, and complained to Vicki that they got free trips to Las Vegas but earned more money doing retail work in California.

The lack of big money shifted over the course of the 1990s with the introduction of the first amateur porn corporations. A seeming oxymoron, the emergence of these companies marked the wider mass commercialization of amateur, and the clarification of 'amateur' as less a production category than a generic signifier. In the USA, the largest amateur retailer, Mantra Entertainment claims to post some $10 million in profits yearly from the sales of its primary product line, the *Girls Gone Wild* video series. Shot largely in public places, from the streets of New Orleans, Louisiana to the beaches of Hawaii, the series capitalizes on the idea that ordinary women (and men, in their latest releases) will take off their clothes and release their sexual inhibitions to be part of a brand-name video series. The company's strategy relies on the convergence of media technologies that keep production costs low and distribution diversified. The company contracts camera operators, generally recently graduated film students, to shoot digital video on location across the United States and as far away as Mexico. *Girls Gone Wild* clips, as well many other varieties of amateur porn, can be found on television infomercials, purchased on pay-per-view, downloaded from the company website, and shipped daily to a personal iPod or cellular phone. In the age of media convergence, amateur porn has become as ubiquitous and diverse as its producers, hundreds of whom attend the AVN Expo yearly.

As the field for amateur filled, the emergence of branding strategies and celebrity production seemed two ways to get a product noticed. In an age when virtually anyone can launch a website in order to attract members to see public nudity, the benefits of media convergence for amateur video also seemed to be its Achilles heel. The leader for building a brand, Mantra, was not present at the Expo, eschewing altogether its association with pornography. Yet the company had introduced several marketing strategies that affected the rest of the amateurs' considerations in making and selling their products. First, Mantra most explicitly engaged in merging pornography and celebrities, contracting with music and television stars to produce *Girls Gone Wild* videos. In the early 2000s, Mantra publicized agreements with Snoop Doggy Dogg, Eminem and Doug Stanhope (host of the defunct TV series *The Man Show*) to create celebrity-hosted amateur videos. Second, the company associated the video brand with celebrities by hosting parties and club events that spotlighted Justin Timberlake and others donning hats and T-shirts with the *Girls Gone Wild* logo, photos of which were then posted to the company website and sold to tabloids. Finally, Mantra has worked to package and market the star potential of the company's CEO Joe Francis (Mayer 2005). Taking cues from porn industry giants Hugh Hefner and Larry Flynt, Francis adopts the role of party host and playboy. Company commercials show Francis inviting ordinary women to share in the opulence of his private jet and extravagant lifestyle. These strategies built upon other marketing tactics already used in the trade, such as television infomercials and web-based membership clubs, to create widespread synergies between media and entertainment industries.

Although porn distributors largely ignored the genre in its early years, today, it is a healthy part of the pornography economy with various inroads in mainstream media. The amateur category boom has itself become the subject of commentary on mainstream news programmes, talk shows, tabloid stories, and video documentaries. Corporate brands and star hosts tempered the promises of independence and authenticity within the amateur production community. While the growth of the industry has made its brands household words, bringing more investors and interested producers into the genre, it also brought the business of amateur into line with other media businesses (Fig. 8.2).

Repurposing Porn in the Age of Convergence: Market Pressures

The proliferation of pornography in popular culture today is the latest trend that references media industries' historical attempts to control their products through standardization while appealing to consumer desires for diversity and difference. Both are business imperatives under capitalism. Schematic story lines and familiar talent rosters take the guesswork out of media production, saving time and

Figure 8.2 Men pose with their favourite porn stars at the Expo. AVN Expo, January 2005. Photograph courtesy of Debbie Nathan.

resources while preserving profit streams. By the same token, media producers believe that it is the newness and difference of products that attracts everyday consumers to buy, spending their time and energies on a particular radio programme, magazine or website. This tension, between standardization and differentiation, Janet Staiger dates to the beginnings of the film industry in the early twentieth century.

> The emphasis on uniformity does not mean that a standard will not change in small ways. New technology, new products, and new models are continually put forth as alternative standards for the field… . In fact, for the film industry, change was an economic necessity. In the entertainment field, innovations in standards are also prized qualities. The economic reason is that the promotion of difference between products is a competitive method and encourages repeated consumption. (Staiger 1985: 97)

In this sense, pornography is no different from other types of media industries. Sex, whether hardcore, soft-core or just implied, helps differentiate contents across various types of standard media texts and platforms.

The history of star production, for example, proved an object lesson for media industries in how to extract value from the various ways of sexually presenting a body. Richard Dyer's classic analysis of stars as intertextual signs cites Marilyn Monroe as the paradigmatic example of this. Monroe's longevity as a sex symbol depended on her various and ambiguous productions across pin-ups, films and publicity materials – productions read as 'natural, not dirty or obscene, but rather unthreatening, vulnerable … available, on offer' (Dyer 2004:46). From an economic standpoint, her intertextuality as a star allowed more companies to use the same mediated contents as their own property. Monroe's malleable images benefited both Hollywood studios and publications, especially *Playboy*. The magazine, famed for bringing sex into the US suburbs, claimed the representation of the enigmatic nude Monroe, who posed for the camera prior to her stardom. As Monroe's value grew, so did *Playboy*'s as the exclusive owner of the images. Monroe's ambiguous iconicity furthered the magazine's agenda to cater to a youthful male comfortable with his consumerism. By consuming sexualized products, Bill Osgerby (2001) argues, men in the 1950s could be both masculine and consumers, a reversal of the feminization of shopping in the late nineteenth century. In turn, *Playboy* could straddle the line between under-the-counter porno mags and mainstream consumer publications, such as *Life*, which also benefited from promoting Monroe's celebrity. The mutual profiting from shared representations across media genres developed as a way of distinguishing a new media outlet with a sexy, though not completely determinable content.

After the 1950s, this strategy became even more prominent. Media industries used celebrity production as a means to standardize control over the production of content, while not appearing to have a monopoly over the meanings of celebrity.

Joshua Gamson (1992) demonstrates that even though in the industry, stars were considered 'merchandise', 'inventory', 'properties' and 'investments', they were presented to the public as real people whose authentic differences could only be revealed through *more and different* media texts.

With the expansion of cable, satellite and broadband channels, media industries' hunger for contents that can be used flexibly across texts and platforms has increased exponentially over the past decade. Yet these networks and stations have far fewer sources for the revenue to create their own content. Advertising expenditures on television have fallen, spread out among a far greater number of outlets and different media delivery vehicles. Syndication, the cash cow of the industry, is also threatened. With the development of new media technologies and content-ripping software, television copyright has virtually no value as amateurs and 'pirates' can lift television contents, edit and reassemble them, to sell as their own. To fight these trends, John Caldwell (2004) writes that television executives have embarked on a strategy to 'repurpose' the same content in multiple formats. The digital images from yesterday's news can be re-cut into a tabloid programme, inserted as website graphics, or added to a digital media archive. No longer tied to a particular programme, digital images can fulfil multiple duties across texts and media platforms and create potential for synergy between different products. In this desperate search to fill programming slots on an international scale, 24-hours a day, sex has historically proven to be the most malleable material money can buy.

As Maureen Orth, an entertainment writer first for *Newsweek* in the 1970s and later for *Vanity Fair*, comments, 'Overexposure is par for the course now; there's no sense that today's stars are supposed to last. A constant stream of new names is necessary to keep the wheels turning and the dollars flowing' (Orth 2004: 61). If media industries profited steadily off the continual reinvention of figures like Marilyn Monroe and Madonna, the new logic of repurposing means that reinvention operates at a far more rapid and fragmented pace. Paris Hilton is the example *par excellence* of the frenzied repurposing of porn across media. Heiress to an international hotel chain, Hilton and her former boyfriend Rick Salomon made a home sex video in 2003. The grainy and poorly lit four-minute video found its way into Internet distribution, weeks prior to Hilton's reality television debut on Rupert Murdoch's Fox Television. Followed by an hour-long version distributed by Salomon himself, the Hilton home video led to instant celebrity, complete with journalistic coverage, magazine photo shoots and, of late, an international tour to promote Guess jeans. Her brand name product lines, including perfume, jewellery and handbags, sell best in Japan, where *Vanity Fair* describes her 'as big, if not bigger than, any movie star' (Smith 2005).

Compare Hilton's case to previous examples of famous figures managing the revelation of pornographic images. In 1983, Vanessa Williams was stripped of her Miss America crown after nude photos of her appeared in *Penthouse*. Years later she reinvented herself as a singer and actress, yet the lesson remained, as feminist critic Ariel Levy writes, that 'then, being exposed in porn was something you needed to come back from. Now, being in porn is itself the comeback' (Levy 2005: 27). The notoriety surrounding two amateur sex tapes in the 1990s – *Pam and Tommy Lee: Hardcore and Uncensored* (1997) and, to a lesser degree, *Tonya and Jeff's Wedding Night* (1994) – was hardly embraced by their stars. The footage of former Olympic figure skater Tonya Harding was sold to television by her ex-husband, Jeff; while Pamela Anderson and Tommy Lee took legal action to prevent their stolen 'home movie' (as Lee called it, distinguishing it from porn) from being released (Hillyer 2004). By contrast, Hilton has parlayed her literal exposure into a self-made, highly mutable brand exposure. Despite her consistently heterosexual display, first in the publicized video and later in her tabloid-shadowed life, her sexuality remains ambiguous. In her television series, *The Simple Life*, she frequently plays the role of the bi-knowledgeable teenager, telling girls and boys alike in a baby voice how they can look 'hot'. Off-screen, she marshalled the 2005 Los Angeles Gay Pride Parade. As Naomi Wolf put it, Hilton is 'an empty signifier' that 'you can project absolutely anything onto' (quoted in Smith 2005). Media producers have lined up to reinvent her as a movie actress, an author, a pop singer and a supermodel. These small-batch productions (one film, one confessional book, one hit song and one campaign) will lead in their target markets just long enough for the next product to roll off the line.

Certainly the adage 'sex sells' is as old as media industries themselves, but the way that sex has become more pliable to the demands of a global economy is new. The need to repurpose contents allies mainstream with pornographic industries in the production of ephemeral sexual texts that both industries can shape to fit a desired time slot, page width and sponsorship without long-term commitment or repercussions. Sexual differences have become a standardized fare for marketing. Ariel Levy explains,

> If we were to acknowledge that sexuality is personal and unique, it would become unwieldy. Making sexiness into something simple and quantifiable makes it easier to explain and to market. If you remove the human factor from sex and make it about stuff: big fake boobs, bleached blonde hair, long nails, poles, thongs then you can sell it. Suddenly sex requires shopping: you need plastic surgery, peroxide, a manicure, a mall. (Levy 2006: 184)

Levy's statement at once captures the market advantages to the pornification of everyday life in media, because sex as objects is easy to repurpose. Furthermore, it points to the genrification of everyday sex, evoking Altman's semantic category of genre identification. Sex as a genre becomes associated with a particular formulaic visual vocabulary – 'big fake boobs, bleached blonde hair, long nails, poles, thongs' (Fig. 8.3) – just as the Western has come to be associated with saddles, spurs and shootouts. As the experiences of amateur porn makers belie,

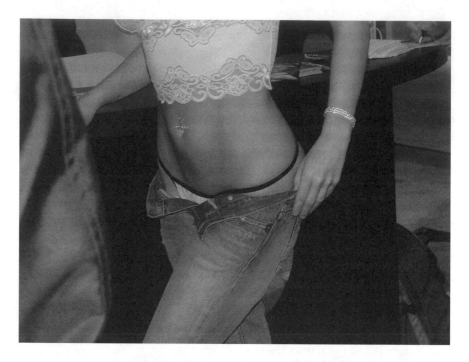

Figure 8.3 Thongs are generic signifiers in amateur porn. AVN Expo, January 2005. Photograph courtesy of Debbie Nathan.

however, not everyone benefits from the standardization that pornification requires, pushing certain differences even further to the margins of either mainstream or pornography.

The AVN Expo: The Mainstreaming of Amateur Porn

By 2005, it was clear to everyone involved in amateur porn that the genre was on the radar screens of media industries beyond pornography. The AVN award for 'Best Renting Title of the Year' and 'Best Selling Title of Year' was *One Night in Paris*, the hour-long version of the infamous home video with Paris Hilton, re-cut and repurposed as 'amateur' pornography. The tape was considered amateur because Hilton was not paid for her debut performance, but the award spoke volumes to producers about the vanishing line between amateurs and professionals in pornography. Further, the AVN 'Best Amateur Release' was a series called *Adventure Sex*, a production of Hustler LFP and distributed through HustlerTV, one of the giants in the pornography industry. The presence of big name stars and major distributors left amateur producers wondering how they might compete. 'Last year there were five booths more of this type than there are this year. And there were five more the year before that', commented Michael Hutchison, co-founder of the soft-core amateur company Buttweiser Productions. Like Hutchinson, long-time amateur Expo exhibitors noticed a strange winnowing of the field even as their contents had become more publicly accessible (Fig. 8.4).

For Frank Meyer, founder of *Wild West Videos*, the mainstream visibility of Mantra in the late 1990s had the negative effect of attracting far more people to amateur production. He himself thought that production would be a straightforward affair:

> I thought it would be a lot easier. You have no idea what you're getting into when you start and it has been very difficult. There's a lot of people in there and every year in

Figure 8.4 Amateurs or professionals? AVN Expo, January 2005. Photograph courtesy of Debbie Nathan.

Mardi Gras we meet people who think they're big time. Ninety percent of them you don't see them the next year. There's only a few companies that have a lot of staying power and really work at it and stick around year after year. Then there's me, a little, independent guy who doesn't have the big backing of money.

Like the majority of amateur producers, Meyer financed his operations with his day job, in his case, paralegal work. Other producers worked as photographers, retailers and even teachers to supplement their incomes just in order to enter the market. Once there, the stakes were high to match the standards set by the bigger companies.

Meyer's strategy, also echoed by various producers in the field, was to contract with professional talent, a line that supposedly separates amateur from all other porn forms. Meyer hired Mary Carey as a 'spokesmodel', someone who would introduce and narrate the amateur footage. A professional porn star of some repute, Carey would not be involved in the segments captured live on the streets of New Orleans, Louisiana and the public beaches of San Diego, California, but would be located on Fiesta Island, a private vacation spot in the city owned by Princess Cruise Lines. The appearance, for Carey who received $500 and a cut of sales profits, creates direct associations between pornography, a mainstream tourism corporation, as well as everyday people taking their clothes off. 'It's a win-win situation', Meyer explained, referring to both his and Carey's desires to repurpose and perhaps mainstream her image. Carey, who ran unsuccessfully for the governor of California in 2003, made no secret of her political ambitions. Similarly, the presence of Carey upped the ante for other production standards. Meyer spent his free time on the Internet searching for musical bands and graphics designers that wanted the free exposure and association with Carey as well. By triangulating synergies between celebrities, amateurs, production locales and services needed for the video, Meyer hoped to achieve the production values to sustain the interest of distributors.

If getting a porn star to host one's amateur video was relatively easy, distribution was difficult and costly. Big amateur distributors, such as International Video Distributors, American Adult Movies and Cable Entertainment Distributors, had their choice of amateur producers and preferred those with a track record. Marc Bruder, president of CED, said he did not even consider producers unless they had high production values and a series to offer. The demand for series seemed unnecessary from a television programming standpoint, as the tapes were to be used as free teasers in hotels offering pay-per-view services. Instead they functioned to limit the number of producers that distributors would have to deal with, since a series would supply the greatest amount of content for a bundled price or the lowest cost per quantity.

And that was just the beginning of distribution costs, according to Vince Rocca. Co-founder (with Michael Hutchinson) of Buttweiser Productions, Rocca tallied up the 'surprise' costs of going mainstream with an amateur budget, including boxes and packaging, legal fees, and duplication costs. Whereas DVDs cost less than VHS tapes, 'wholesalers want like a thousand copies', said Rocca, who outsourced the work through Chinese companies. Each DVD further needed a barcode, an $800 process required for online sales through companies like Amazon.com. Finally, amateur companies have had extensive legal issues to contend with. Rocca and others keep First Amendment lawyers on retainer and transformed their budding businesses into LLCs, a legal designation that hinders owners from being sued directly. All of these elements translated to more capital up front just for market entry. The hidden expenditures of mainstreaming amateur created so much anxiety for amateur producers most were not sure in what form they would be at the AVN Expo again, if at all.

To a Corporate Amateur Future

As we have shown, the existence of corporate amateur pornography is hardly oxymoronic, but rather an indication of the fluidity of a genre that retains the signifiers of amateurism even as it abandons its humble economic roots. This is only the latest development in a trend that has brought together mainstream media and pornographic industries. The introduction of celebrities, reality series and higher production values into amateur brought these pornographic industries into line with other economic models for television broadcasting, video distribution and media star production. As a result, the amateur genre has become better known to a wider range of consumers, but fewer and fewer companies dominate its creation and production.

Scholars, journalists and popular commentators have largely written the history of pornography as an industry separate from mainstream media. Yet, as this volume demonstrates, the mainstreaming of all things porn suggests that the two industries cross-pollinate each other, if not creating what John Caldwell calls 'ancillary textuality' (2004: 47): the use of film and video contents across media to generate multiple revenue streams cheaply for a single product. Caldwell specifically addresses the new economy for television in his definition, but it is easy to see that sexual texts easily find their way between media platforms and contents. As everyday people 'pornify' their personalities – displaying themselves on webcams, appearing nude in public venues   and stars reinvent their images to include sexual displays, mainstream media industries benefit from the rapid repurposing of their images, attaching them to a far greater number of products and services outside of adult entertainment industries. In this sense, 'pornification' is the media strategy that ensures not only the standardization of sex across media, but also a multiplication of possible differences. Perhaps it is in these differences that amateur producers can still create, innovate, and transform media.

Part III
Porn Media

–9–

Sexed Authorship and Pornographic Address in Music Video

Diane Railton and Paul Watson

It is now commonplace to argue that music videos are a site where women's bodies are sexualized and eroticized, that is to say, explicitly positioned within an economy of sexual desire. So, for example, Sheri Kathleen Cole proposes that 'the commodification of sexuality is central to the creation of most music videos' (1999: 1); Imani Perry critiques the sexism of hip-hop videos in which women appear 'quite explicitly as property, not unlike the luxury cars, Rolex watches, and platinum and diamond medallions that are also featured' (2003: 136); Jocelyn Cullity and Prakash Younger argue, in relation to MTV in the USA, that 'most of the video storylines are male sexual dream worlds or fantasies', and, in relation to MTV India, that, 'the female as a body is predominant in all facets of MTV India programming' (2004: 99, 200). Indeed, to some extent this exhibition of the sexualized body in music video is inevitable insofar as its primary function is to promote songs which themselves often contain narratives of romantic love, tales of sexual yearning or simply accounts of sex itself. The fact that such sexualized displays may be predictable does not, however, lessen their significance. Quite the contrary, far from neutralizing their political charge, it is the very ubiquity of music videos and the apparent inevitability of their eroticized content that makes them a particularly fertile cultural resource in the attempt to understand the link between forms of representation and the way those representations define, delimit or expand ways of being in the world. As we have argued elsewhere, the display of the sexualized body as an object of desire is crucial to music video's economies of both pleasure and profit. As such, it acts as a lens through which we can observe, and thus investigate, the ways in which contemporary culture perceives itself (Railton and Watson 2005). Simply put, the sheer quantity of sexualized images and the frequency with which they are produced and reproduced in music video is significant in itself. But perhaps more importantly, here, is the range of different ways in which the female body can be, and is, sexualized in music videos. So, even if the sexualization of women's bodies in music video is predictable, the way that this is realized in any one video is not. And the way that it is realized can produce very different ways of reading and interpreting any given video. So, while authors such as Cole and Perry take a critical stance towards what they see as the exploitation and objectification of women's bodies in music videos, a number of other writers have argued, by contrast, that music video can be a site for the subversion of normative sexed and gendered roles. In this way, Maria Shelton suggests that music video is 'a location for ideological struggle' and that despite the presence of 'sexism, racism, and classism' it also stands as 'a site for resistance' (1997: 107).

In this respect, the music videos of Madonna, in particular, have been a focus of debate about the potential for using the sexualized body as a tool with which to critique gender norms. As Sheila Whiteley asks, 'is she pandering to the typical role of women in pornography, or are there careful symbolic containment structures which define the woman as "in charge", so providing symbolic satisfaction rather than male fantasy?' (1997: 271). Her reading of Madonna's video for 'Justify My Love' (1990) is one that firmly places Madonna 'in charge' and, therefore, not simply pandering to male sexual fantasy or norms of feminine passivity. This idea that Madonna's sexual performance is rendered positive and political, and thus distanced from mere pornographic display, is both a common one and one that is predicated on Madonna's authorship, indeed ownership, of the video and its erotic content. For instance, Brian McNair argues that Madonna 'is both the object and subject of her work, directing and appearing in it with equal enthusiasm. She *deliberately* presents herself as the object of a voyeuristic look in sexually explicit images' (1996: 136, emphasis added). On this analysis, even if Madonna regularly appropriates a variety of pornographic styles and poses, the very fact that these acts of appropriation are intentional, that is to say the deliberate act of an authorial/artistic agent, serves to divest the pornographic tropes precisely of their pornography. Moreover, Madonna has been credited not only with using her video repertoire as a way of questioning and 'deconstructing' sexual stereotypes, but also with creating spaces for other female artists to portray themselves as 'self-assured sex specialists' (Gauntlett 2004: 171). Indeed, her political influence is seen to extend even further as she is also credited with teaching 'young women to be fully feminine and sexual while still exercising control over their lives' (Paglia 1993: 4). In other words, the sexualization of the female body in music video can be seen as something problematic – as an extension of the all too familiar exploitation of women and their bodies – but is something that can redeemed, and in fact welcomed, when it comes as part of a self-conscious, authored display of female power and erotic agency. One implication of this is that the display of the female body in music video is in itself neither necessarily problematic nor progressive, something to challenge or celebrate, and, as such, any universalizing moves to theorize it in this way ought to be resisted.

This latter observation becomes all the more urgent when, as is increasingly the case, the sexualized display of bodies in and through popular culture entails a suspicion of irony. Indeed, it is precisely what Linda Hutcheon calls the 'suspicion of deceit' which accompanies irony's indirections that 'when combined with the idea of power ... makes for a certain unease' (Hutcheon 1995: 9). For irony messes up neat models of communication, problematizes intentionality, complicates the discursive situation and installs ambiguity into the interpretive process. In other words, where irony is present meaning is to some extent always multivocal, unfinished, unstable and incomplete. There are two principal implications of this. Firstly, given that irony is predicated on the creation of deliberate semantic confusion then 'there is little guarantee that the views of people producing and reading the texts necessarily meet' (Paasonen 2005b). Indeed, insofar as irony self-consciously interferes with the communicative relationship between utterance and interpretation then it is inevitably a 'risky business' (Fish 1983: 176). For the creation or inference of surfeit meaning, that is to say meaning in addition to the literal, an unsaid as well as what is said, may not only be used to avoid the 'premature foreclosure' of a text by allowing the possibility of doubt (Culler 1975: 158) but can also 'function as a kind of boomerang if ironic distance is erased and things read literally' (Paasonen 2005b). The second main implication is, at least in part, a by-product of this potential for ambiguity and misunderstanding. This is the idea that irony 'can and does function tactically in the service of a wide range of political positions' (Hutcheon 1995: 10) and, as such, is 'transideological' in nature (White 1973: 38). In other words, irony can be mobilized as a conservative force to 'shore up the foundations of the established order' (Elliott 1960: 273) or as a weapon directed towards deconstructing and decentring that order. And, of course, this situation becomes further vexed when both of these ironic positions can apparently be found in the same text. So, depending on which critic one reads, the attribution of irony to Madonna's recycling and reworking of already defined feminine identities is variously seen as a feminist critique of hegemonic gender discourse or as just another manifestation of patriarchal power. Either way, however, perhaps the central critical problem that attends discussions of irony 'resides in the fact that irony can obviously be both political *and* apolitical, both conservative *and* radical, both repressive *and* democratizing' (Hutcheon 1995: 35). The ironic display of sexed bodies in music video is, therefore, neither intrinsically regressive nor necessarily radical, neither a good nor a bad thing, right or wrong. Rather, as with generalized claims that popular culture is increasingly becoming pornified, the notion that music video is now a key site through which pornographic imagery is mainstreamed must be approached with caution. For in any given instance the assimilation of pornographic codes and conventions may be progressive and to be welcomed but also may be politically dubious and worrisome. And, of course, in this situation sweeping generalizations are of little use precisely inasmuch as the political edge of sexual representation can only be grasped on a case-by-case basis. Indeed, the two different videos released to promote Khia's 'My Neck, My Back, (Lick It)'[1] (2002, 2004), in America and Europe respectively, provide stark evidence that sexualized imagery, and even such imagery which accompanies the same song, can readily take on vastly different meanings.

Authorizing Female Sexuality

David Gauntlett has suggested that there is now space within popular music for female artists to be 'unapologetically sexual agents/actors, asserting their own needs and desires, and refusing to be treated as mere sex objects by men' (2004: 170). And 'My Neck, My Back, (Lick It)' is a song in which, lyrically, Khia does just that. The way that the song is portrayed visually, however, works, in one instance, to reinforce this reading of it and, in the other, to radically undermine it. Both videos not only contain the sexually explicit lyrics of the song as part of their soundtrack but also offer a visual interpretation of those lyrics through sexualized performance and the display of the female body. However, while the lyrics remain constant, the nature of that performance and display differs considerably and does so in ways that fundamentally change the politics of its sexual address. In what follows we want to unpick the differences between these two sexualized narratives and argue that, in uncoupling the lyrical performance of the song from its author and recasting it around the fetishistic imagery and pornographic tropes of the later video, the more challenging political potential of the earlier video and, indeed, the song itself becomes short-circuited.

'My Neck, My Back (Lick It)' was first released in America in 2002 and emerged out of the genre of popular music variously known as Southern rap and Dirty South hip-hop. This is important in two related respects. Firstly, while this is not a genre normally associated with politicized lyrics, it, and the genre of hip-hop more broadly, has nevertheless provided a space in which a number of female performers, or more exactly black female performers, have addressed issues to do with the gendered politics of everyday life, and particularly of heterosexual relationships. Indeed, Shelton argues that 'female rappers *must* invert stigmas, redefine feminine subjectivity, and repossess the gaze in order to gain respect' (1997: 107, emphasis added). Secondly, the use of sexually explicit lyrics is both a common, and indeed an identifying, feature of the genre and therefore can be a key means through which these politics are articulated. Beverley Skeggs has argued that some women rappers 'use a "demand" discourse to celebrate female sexuality and autonomy, articulating what is usually a perniciously silenced sexuality … female rappers turn themselves from sexual objects into sexual subjects. In doing so they challenge the basis of the social order which seeks to contain them' (1993: 299). In other words sexually demanding lyrics are used as a means to claim subjectivity for their authors who, by speaking out, are 'disrupting the dominant scenario that posits women as passive objects of active masculine desire' (Forman 1994: 53). Indeed, the lyrics of 'My Neck, My Back (Lick It)' can be understood in this way as, like many other Dirty South rap tracks, they are sexually explicit not only in terms of their narrative content but also in terms of the (racialized) language which is used to express it. And, as Jason Haugen (2003) points out, the use of such language by women is not only more shocking than when it is used by men but shocks precisely insofar as it challenges 'hegemonic femininity'. Within this context, then, the sexual demands of Khia's lyrics which instruct her 'nigga' to 'lick my pussy and my crack' can be understood as simultaneously generic – inasmuch as such sexually direct language is a routine aspect of this category of music – and exceptional – inasmuch as the spaces available to women within popular culture to express such demands remain relatively rare. Indeed, in order for the song, and by extension the video, to be broadcast on radio and television these demands could not be made in such a sexually explicit vernacular. Crudely stated, there would be little point producing a song that, due to various legal and regulatory frameworks governing the transmission of potentially offensive material, would get little, if any, airplay. Commercial imperatives, therefore, necessitate another, reworked, version of the lyrics, one that can furnish both a cleaned-up edit suitable for transmission on radio and provide the basis for the production of a video. Two principal strategies are deployed in this clean-up operation. The first consists, to one degree or another, of rewriting and/or rephrasing the problematic content. On the whole this is achieved through supplanting potentially offensive words such as 'nigga', 'ho' and 'bitch' with more innocuous terms like 'fella', 'player' and 'girl'. The second strategy is effected by masking the word 'pussy' with a breathy sigh which in turn then becomes assimilated into the rhythmical arrangement of the song. With this much established, we shall now turn to a discussion of the earlier US version of the video, or more precisely to the ways it situates its sexual address as an authored expression of its performer, Khia.

The video is based around a single scenario – a house party at which guests are seen to variously relax in the garden and outdoor pool, eat food from the barbecue and, later in the evening, dance inside the house. Indeed, the nature of this scenario is crucial to the political reading of it insofar as it establishes a plausible, normal context in which sexual activity could both take place and be discussed. Furthermore, the normalcy of the setting is reinforced by the way the partygoers are dressed and the way they behave. They wear everyday clothes – swimsuits by the pool, and jeans or shorts with T-shirts, vest tops or bikini tops elsewhere. They swim, roll on the grass, cook on the barbecue, dance – both individually and with one another. In other words, the setting for the video is a realistic and natural one and what could be seen as pornographic lyrics are thus immediately rendered unexceptional at least in part by locating them within a logical, believable space and place. Within this setting, sexual activity becomes seen as ordinary behaviour as bodies dance in close proximity and people touch, rub against each other, caress and kiss. Moreover, the bodies in the video are not merely situated as carnal bodies but, more complexly, as bodies which are the focus for a number of pleasures, which include the sexual but also encompass other activities such as eating, drinking, dancing and sunbathing. In short, even if sexual activity is part of what is happening in the video, it is certainly not the only thing happening. And what is more, as the video makes apparent, what is happening is clearly determined by the particular wants and desires of those at the party, not by any voyeuristic fantasy of the audience. Indeed, perhaps most importantly, Khia herself is not only always in control of her own body but is also squarely located as the author of the song's sexual demands. Her body is never abstracted or fragmented and we are only invited to watch her with her knowledge and permission. For at every turn her performance acknowledges the gaze of the camera and, by implication, the audience's own gaze. Quite literally, in fact, as even when she has her back to the camera she turns her head to meet us face to face. Indeed, whether she is relaxing on a poolside lounger, dancing with the others or performing directly for the camera, easily the most frequent image in the video is of Khia lip-synching the lyrics of the song. Simply put, the video literally puts the words into Khia's mouth. And while on the one hand this is an obvious claim, on the other it is crucial to situating the video within a gendered politics. What is undoubtedly a sexually explicit song, but a song which nevertheless is predicated on the presence of postfeminist sexually liberated female agency, becomes, in the video, embodied in Khia's authorial voice and performance of in-control sexuality. For, in consistently returning our look at her and taking ownership of the lyrics, not only does Khia claim authorship of the song's graphic sexual narrative but also positions that narrative as part of a discourse of female sexual empowerment. So, although the lyrics are sexually explicit, perhaps even pornographic, the US video is not. While sex is important, it is not all-important. The video makes no attempt to arouse or titillate the audience. Nor, for that matter, does it construct a voyeuristic position from which one can contemplate an objectified and pacified female body with impunity. Rather, what is remarkable about the video is that it works as a representation of a situation in which in-control female sexual agency is not simply permitted but normal.

This reading of the US video, one which sees it as a self-conscious, clearly authored narrative of a sexually confident and assertive woman who 'knows' the politics of her own gendered position, may be interesting in itself but is especially important here just insofar that the pornification of the UK video turns precisely upon the removal of the distinctly political authorial voice. Which is not to say that this latter video adopts an any the less self-conscious approach to its own aesthetic economy. Indeed, if the US video's self-assured sexual discourse can be traced to feminist and womanist traditions of female empowerment then, by contrast, the UK video's exploitation of fetishistic imagery has its own genealogy in traditions of hardcore and soft-core pornography – traditions that, as will become apparent, can be traced back to set-piece scenarios in porn films such as *Debbie Does Dallas* (1978) through to 'softer' expressions in mainstream films such as *Cool Hand Luke* (1967), the *Bikini Carwash Company* films (1992/1993), various Playboy playmate videos and, more recently, its putative ironic rearticulation in numerous lad's mags, teen movies and adverts. So, while both videos are aware of their own aesthetic history and both know that they are, in one way or another, about sex, in the end the two videos position the viewer very differently in relation to the representation of the female body and produce starkly contrasting political possibilities. And the nature of these differences in position and politics becomes obvious from the first shot of the UK video, a video which features neither Khia herself nor the house-party scenario but is instead based around the performance of three stiletto-heeled, bikini-clad young women washing an H2 Hummer.

You Took the Words out of My Mouth

The opening sequence establishes the principal aesthetic and stylistic strategies of the video. During the song's intro the video cuts between a close-up of the three women's buttocks – which is in fact the first image we see – a low angle reverse-shot which foregrounds their crotches and navels, and a tracking shot which emphasizes the movement of their breasts as it follows them walking down the street towards the car. These shots are cut together with equally stylized images of the car arriving in the same street where the subsequent action takes place. Indeed, we are immediately invited to regard the women's bodies and the Hummer in the same way, that is to say, as fetish objects to be looked at and coveted. Moreover, both our ability to do this in the first place and the voyeuristic pleasures it implies in the last place are secured by effacing, or more accurately erasing, markers of the women's individual personality so that all that is left are differently clothed, but similar, bodies. This evacuation of personality is achieved perhaps most notably in the uniformity of their lip gloss and the obfuscation of their eyes by sunglasses, a strategy which both blocks their look and engenders ours, but is confirmed in three brief cutaway shots in which, despite individually lip-synching to the lyric 'do it', it is more or less impossible to distinguish between them. Where difference is marked, however, is across their bodies, their colour-coded swimwear and distinctive jewellery serving as the key mechanisms through which (non)identity is signalled. In this respect, the equivalence between the female body and the body of the car is further reinforced, for it too has its own colour-coded identity and embellishments. As such, this opening sequence not only sets up the video's economy of visual pleasure but also establishes that it has not three, but four, principal protagonists. This is important in the sense that as the video progresses it becomes increasingly apparent that the fourth character, the Hummer, is not simply a fetish object but is coded as male and is installed as the surrogate subject for the implied male viewer. In other words, while in this initial series of images the Hummer is itself fetishized both in relation to the women's bodies and our own gaze, it is subsequently repositioned as the recipient of the women's sexual attentions and thus functions as a proxy phallus for the viewer. For even if the remainder of the video, on a literal level, depicts the three women washing, valeting and servicing the car, on another level it is a complex collage of erotic imagery and (male) sexual fantasies culled from a range of pornographic forms and genres.

Composed principally from a master shot, which shows all three of the women washing the car in exaggerated poses, and a series of inserts,[2] which depict one or other of the women performing acts that are highly evocative of explicit sexual activity with abstracted parts of the car, the rest of the video functions as a potpourri of pornographic tropes. For instance, we are shown close-ups, in turn, of the rim of the steering wheel, the nipple-like button of an air-vent and the polished surface of a wing mirror being slowly licked. One of the women polishes the car's phallic armrest in a manner redolent of masturbation and, with a knowing look, wipes a dipstick in a similar fashion. Another is shown in the back seat of the car rubbing the pipe of a vacuum cleaner seductively over her neck and cleavage. These shots of the women, however, do not serve to restore their identity but rather work to further obscure it as they are intercut with images of fragmented and objectified bodies. So what we are presented with is a concatenation of disconnected body parts where the buttocks of one woman are replaced by the lips of another and images of hands wielding wet sponges are followed by close-ups of thighs in an unidentifiable confusion of female flesh. Moreover, subjectivity is eradicated along with identity as this display of bodies stands as a substitute for performance of the song and, thus, the lyrics of the song disappear into the background as our attention is focused on the images rather than the words. The anonymous women, therefore, never get to 'disrupt the dominant scenario' of female passivity as they are never seen to perform the 'demand lyrics' of the song. They are only ever shown lip-synching to the discrete phrases of the chorus, that is to say, the breathy sigh that replaces the word 'pussy' and, in isolation from each other, the words 'my neck, 'my back', 'lick my'. More precisely, one woman is shown mouthing the words 'my neck' while washing the door of the car, another mouths 'my back' while sponging the car's fender, yet another sighs breathily while leaning against the car and being sprayed with water. Indeed, it is in the use of fluid, or more exactly sprayed water and soapsuds, that the video finds its chief reservoir of sexual metaphor. In the first instance, as the women 'wash' the car they squeeze sponges of soapy water over their bodies so that thighs, breasts, torsos become splattered with white foam in emulation of the money shot of pornographic film-making; a shot which, as Williams argues, is both for and about the pleasure of the male participant/viewer rather than that of the female protagonist (1989: 101). And secondly, as the video progresses we are introduced to three new characters; middle-aged firemen who are seen admiring the women as they wash the car, discussing them with each other and, ultimately, spraying them with water from a hose held between their legs at crotch level. The video ends as the hose is switched off and a trickle of water leaks from the tip of the nozzle.

When Irony simply doesn't Wash

There are a number of key differences between the videos that render one available for a positive, postfeminist interpretation and link the other with certain traditions of pornographic imagery in a way that renders such a reading difficult, if not impossible. As discussed above, these differences are not only formal and stylistic, but also differences in the motivation for what we see and how we see it. Simply stated, if on the one hand the action in the US video can be said to be motivated compositionally insofar as it presents a coherent fictional world in which factors such as the setting, the clothing and the behaviour of its protagonists are congruous with both the song's lyrics and its genre, then on the other hand the imagery contained in the UK video is marked by incongruity. Abstracted from the 'real world' and situated in the fantasy world of 'lad's mags' and top-shelf magazines, the sexualized tableaux which characterize this video seem to be motivated merely by the desire to put anonymous women's bodies on display to be variously scrutinized, objectified and leered at. However, and notwithstanding the importance of these differences in themselves, it is the denial of an authorial voice, and by implication agency, in this latter video that is perhaps politically all-important. Indeed, whereas the US video puts the words of the song quite clearly in Khia's mouth, as she is shown to 'sing' it and get a response to it from the other people in the video, the UK version does not permit the women a voice at all. The disconnected words they are seen to mouth, and the sigh they are shown to make, become simply vocalized sexual responses rather than words with meaning. And it is here that the sigh takes on particular importance as it becomes detached from the rest of the lyrics, no longer simply a euphemism for the part of the body to be licked, and takes on a significance of its own as we repeatedly see images of women sighing with pleasure as they are sprayed with foam or doused with water from the firemen's hose. So, instead of being part of a request for action the sigh comes to indicate *re*action, no longer part of a call for something to be done but rather a response by the women to something that has been done to them. The demand discourse of the lyrics, where a woman is confidently and explicitly instructing her partner in ways to give her sexual pleasure, is, thus, nullified. Indeed, the notion of active female sexuality is further belied as the women themselves are shown to be the ones responding to the command to 'lick it', giving pleasure rather than receiving it.

Two videos, then, that adapt and deploy the lyrics of Khia's 'My Neck, My Back' in very different ways, and ways that have important consequences not only in terms of the representation of the female body, but also in terms of the way we might, or might not, read those representations as pornographic. And while it may be premature to use this analysis as a basis to make any broader claims concerning the putative mainstreaming of porn or the pornification of everyday life, it nevertheless remains the case that the kind of imagery which characterizes the latter,

UK, video, imagery which self-consciously hijacks the codes and conventions of porn genres for mainstream audiences, is becoming increasingly prevalent both in music video generally and popular culture per se. Indeed, the sexual linking of female bodies and fast cars, for some time a regular fantasy scenario of porn films and more recently a common feature of several paper-based and/or web-hosted 'auto' magazines such as *Max Power*, *Fast* and *MaxSpeed*, seems to be breaking out of its niche. Specifically in terms of music video, the scenario of the fetishized female body washing a car is itself the organizing principle of DJ Peran's *We Want to be Free* (2004) and forms a significant part of the visual and performative economies of Jessica Simpson's *These Boots Were Made For Walking* (2005), Narcotic Thrust's *When the Dawn Breaks* (2005), Intenso Project's *Get It On* (2005) and the remixed version of Mariah Carey's *Heartbreaker* (1999). In fact, the use of this erotic conceit is now so well known that it is open to parody, as Pink does in *Stupid Girls* (2006).

Perhaps the logical destination of this process of pornification is the increasing production of X-rated music videos, that is to say, explicit versions of what are already highly sexualized videos, designed for late night transmission. For instance, while the censored version of N.E.R.D.'s *Lapdance* (2001) features women performing for the pleasure of their male customers, wearing just enough clothing to clean it up, in the uncensored version most of these clothes are removed, with breasts and buttocks not only flaunted and displayed, but also touched, squeezed and licked. This same strategy of exploiting images of women sex workers also describes 50 Cent's *P.I.M.P.* (2003), Nelly's *Work It* (2003) and *Tip Drill* (2004), and Ludacris's *Pussy Poppin'* (2003). Indeed, the *Hip-Hop Honeys'* series of DVDs can be seen as yet a further extension of this practice. Though not music videos in the strict sense of the term, in that they are not designed to promote a secondary product, they nevertheless feature a range of women, from both music videos and the pornography industry, acting out soft-core fantasies to a hip-hop soundtrack.

However, there are a number of other music videos proper which, though undoubtedly less explicit, are nevertheless every bit as dependent on a version of porno-chic aesthetic. And it is perhaps these videos which are by turns more interesting and more problematic precisely because their focus on a highly fetishized female body, a body that is stripped of authorial agency, is entirely unmotivated. So whereas the graphic displays of flesh in *Lapdance* or *Pussy Poppin'* are, at least partly, contextualized and justified by the lyrical performance, the same is not true for videos such as Benny Benassi's *Satisfaction* (2002), Eric Prydz's *Call on Me* (2004), Junior Jack's *Stupidisco* (2004) and Sunblock's *First Time* (2006), videos which, like the UK version of *My Neck, My Back (Lick It)* and *We Want to be Free*, attempt to filter their porno aesthetic through an ironic lens. Yet, irony simply doesn't wash here. Even if the use of irony might well have been intended as a way of putting the codes and conventions of porn in quotation marks so to speak, perhaps even as a way of capturing a kind of nostalgia for a certain moment in porn's own history, precisely the ambiguity of the irony and the incongruity of the context serve to render the enterprise inappropriate. In other words, the indirection and obliqueness of these images and the confusion over intentionality render the ironic process *too* unstable, *too* plural and, in the end, *too* dangerous. For the sexualized performances contained in these videos are merely gratuitous, that is to say unnecessary, unwarranted, unmotivated and unjustified. And it is here, of course, that the political question of pornography continues to replay itself. For whether one chooses, on the one hand, to denounce this apparent pornification of the everyday and ordinary as patriarchy passed off as postmodernism or, on the other, to write it off as part of a more general liberalization of culture, turns precisely on the question of authorship. In other words, the degree to which these images of women's bodies are politically problematic is indexed to the degree to which agency is seen to be removed from the women whose bodies are on display. In the end, regardless of how explicitly it is represented, the after-hours image of women being paid to perform sexually with/to men may be less worrisome than the all-pervasive image of voiceless women performing as fetish objects *for* men. Put simply, it is not the removal of clothes that is important but rather the removal of agency. Indeed, if the Internet is more or less the last word on the mainstreaming of porn inasmuch as it makes graphic sexual material readily available to a mass audience, then the political rub is no longer simply whether or not pornography itself is a problem, but rather what the implications might be for a culture in which the ordinary and everyday becomes pornified.

–10–

Outdoor Pornification: Advertising Heterosexuality in the Streets

Leena-Maija Rossi

Advertising imagery plays a definite role in the sexualization of urban space. Contemporary advertising and soft-core porn are connected through several representative means: exposing the body; fragmenting it by cropping and foregrounding the culturally eroticized parts of it; and using stereotypically gendering, eroticizing and racializing sets of images.[1] But how is it exactly that a pose for the camera becomes 'softly' pornographic? What kinds of poses am I, as a viewer, ready and willing to categorize and describe as soft-core in advertising? To rephrase my question using the terms launched to feminist discourse by Judith Butler (1999; 1993), what kinds of *performatives* of gender and sexuality are *reiterated* and *cited* over and over again in these poses? How are gender and sexuality *done*[2] in advertising?

And what about the issue of context? Linda Williams (2004b: 3) has coined the term 'on-scenity' to describe the 'insistent appearing' of representations once deemed obscene in the public arena. How do pornified images – for instance, the mainstream images of advertising, which cite and repeat the codes of pornography – function in the public space? And how is streetscape, the urban landscape formed by streets and city dwellers, affected by these images? In this chapter, I discuss these questions from two perspectives: first pondering how advertising imagery in general operates in the streetscape, and then looking at some specific images.

To make it clear from the start, my intention is not to oppose pornography as a monolithic, solely oppressive phenomenon (on porn's multifariousness, see, for example, Snitow 1983; Attwood 2002), but to analyse specific modes of representation and their public presentation. My aim is to bring together a queer-feminist viewpoint – criticizing the heteronormativity (Berlant and Warner 2000: 312) and heterosexism of mainstream advertising imagery – and a politically sensitive approach which que(e)ries whether people have the right not to be exposed to stiffly stereotypical representations of sexuality or eroticism in the public space. When close-reading my case study, one of the clothing company Hennes& Mauritz's ad campaigns, I also try to bring forth the possibilities and challenges of representing 'nonstandard intimacies' in public (see Berlant and Warner 2000: 322–3; also Clarke 2000).

Images do not function as a 'mere' reflection of the world. They play an essential part in the societal production of meaning, knowledge and power, thereby shaping the realities we live in.[3] As an example of this, advertising constantly produces knowledge on both sexuality and the gendered idea of beauty, fixed as a presupposition on to women and female femininity. Furthermore, the knowledge thereby produced does not concern just any kind of sexuality, but more precisely heterosexuality. The power constituting, being constituted by and entangled in that knowledge (Foucault 1990) is the normative power of the position of heterosexuality as the 'dominant fiction' (Silverman 1996: 178) of Western societies. The heterosexual regime supports, maintains and naturalizes a notion of two internally unified, 'opposite but complementary' genders that are supposed to be hierarchically and essentially different from each other. This normative, norm-producing scene – or a kind of *screen* through which we look at things (Silverman 1996: 135, 195–227) – is constantly being performed, brought in front of us by advertising in the urban environment.

'On-Scene': Pornification in the Streetscape

Media may be thought of as a key factor in the constitution of the public sphere where people 'make sense' of the world, receive information, argue about information and (ideally) participate in rational decisions concerning political and public issues (McGuigan 1996; see also Clarke 2000: 2–3). For instance Brian McNair has used the concept of the public sphere to refer to the mediation of knowledge/information on sexuality to the 'society as a whole' (1996: 23). The queer critic Eric Clarke, again, has emphasized that the public sphere may also be conceptualized as signifying a qualitative relation instead of distinct material things (such as media), or a spatial ensemble of places; thus, he writes, 'those disenfranchised from the venues that claim publicness can ask more insistently whether they actually embody this quality' (2000: 2–3). I shall, nevertheless, focus here on a particular set of spaces and images: the advertising imagery presented to the public in the street. Even from this angle, Clarke's question concerning the qualities embodied by the disenfranchised is still highly valid.

Street constitutes a space in which people move around every day, where they have their routine-bound, but also wandering and exploratory routes. Street can also be thought of as an urban landscape, the streetscape. The varying meanings of streetscape are constructed in reciprocal action, in interactive relationships for which visibility, acts of seeing and being seen, are crucial (Saarikangas 1996: 306). Mediated encounters with pornified heteronormative imagery on the street differ radically from domestic ones. At home, we do have at our disposal various filters between the images and ourselves (Poynor 2006: 44). A sticker politely telling 'No ads, please' partly blocks the flow of commercial imagery into our homes. One does not have to subscribe newspapers or magazines, own a television or even have an Internet connection. Remote control enables us to be selective in terms of incoming audiovisuality: we may switch the channels and switch off the television at will. However, home may of course also offer a space for consuming porn through television, Internet and magazines (Juffer 1998). Pornified imagery forms only a part of the knowledge that constantly obfuscates the border between the public and the private, and connects the private sphere to public networks of power. One example of the latter phenomenon would, of course, be the vast deployment, accessibility and production of amateur porn.

Home and street thus offer very different spaces for sexual encounters – even if one would take a stranger home to have sex with. One should, nevertheless, challenge the idea of a total freedom of choice prevailing in the privacy of homes in relation to watching pornified imagery. It is rather a question of relative freedom, and a different control over the space than the one we have on the street. The remote control and compulsory switching of television channels hardly remove the sexual tinge permeating the repertoire of TV programming. However, they offer the possibility of temporarily removing the unwanted visual representations from sight. On the streetscape such removal is not possible. The images are there and they stay there (even though changing into other images at a regular interval): hung along the streets, at the bus stops, inside the vehicles of public transportation, in the store windows. It is difficult for a sighted person to move around on the streetscape without looking at advertising. Jim McGuigan (1996: 26) has even argued in a Habermasian vein that the 'sophisticated communicational techniques' of advertising have 'hijacked' the public sphere.

In the public space of the streetscape, people gendered as women and men are both exposed to the multiplicity of images and at display themselves. They stand not only as looking subjects but also as objects for the looks of strangers, and potentially also objects for sexual assessment and desire. The images in the streetscape obviously do not interfere with the bodily integrity of people in the same way as the comments and suggestions presented by fellow men (possibly also women) on the street, not to mention outright physical harassment. Yet we should not underestimate the effective position of the images in the network of power formed by the streetscape. Advertising, which nowadays seems to be so central to the meaning of the streetscape (Poynor 2006: 44), does participate in the formation of sexual encounters and their conditions. Men and women are looked at in relation to the imagery of advertising and the discourses constructed by it. These repetitive images present themselves as a source of knowledge concerning beauty and desirability. On the streetscape those images, colourful, glowing sources of gendering and sexualizing knowledge-power, loci of ideals, provide an instant surface for reflection and comparison in relation to the bodily contours and surfaces of the people moving on the streets.

Jean Gagnon, who has analysed heterosexual pornography from the angle of male viewers and consumers, describes the cityscape as a 'cultural reservoir where individuals draw the representations that they more or less consciously incorporate into their lives and value-systems' (1988: 25). He categorizes pornography as a specifically urban phenomenon, part of the network of images in the cities and a quintessential part of the realm of advertising and consumerism. He also writes about the *rhetoric of the city*, which largely derives from the rhetoric of advertising images and is constituted in the interaction between the knowledges of individual consumers and the knowledges of the producers of advertising (both advertisers of the products and the people planning and realizing the ads). This rhetoric is, according to Gagnon, stereotypical and overpowered by consumer myths: a 'reservoir of stereotyped attitudes' (1988: 25–7). It is also thoroughly gendered, and continuously naturalizes and foregrounds heterosexuality. This rhetoric is in use when people move around in the streets, 'accompanied by a running commentary' (Cauquelin cited by Gagnon 1988: 220–7) consisting of the images and texts attached to them. The comments and outright imperatives presented by advertisements illustrate the idea(l) of perfection: they participate both in the production of feelings of bodily inadequacy and dissatisfaction (Grogan 1999: 94–116), and in processes through which people on the streets are urged to strive for 'picture-perfect' ideals without being able to settle for a 'good enough' (Silverman 1996: 220–7; also Poynor 2006: 37) body-image.

Gagnon also connects advertising, pornography and the cityscape to the ideology of permanent relationships – the ideology central to heteronormativity. He writes:

> In the city, solitude is never greater than when one lives in close proximity to the crowd and the possibilities of contact it offers. We should also note in passing that solitude has a pejorative connotation … If I remain solitary, I feel that I am lacking and that I have failed to obey the imperative of the urban enterprise … This pattern is maintained by some ramifications of the pornography industry. (Gagnon 1988: 32)

The urban fantasy is thus permeated by the ideology of encounter, which connects images, texts and public places to each other (Gagnon 1988: 33; see also Ahmed 2000: 32). In the urban fantasy, encounters with the gendered and sexualized characters represented by advertising become amalgamated in our reality. Nevertheless, these images and the viewers' relationship to them may also be read through the problematic of non-encountering.

Looking Back from the Image

Pornography, both soft and hardcore, has been criticized for objectifying women, or at least not subjectifying them enough – for not 'taking others seriously' (Snitow 1983). One essential guarantee for agency, claimed for by the feminist critics of visual culture, has been the right to look, and even to gaze intently, instead of just being the object or the bearer of the look (see e.g. Linker 1983; hooks 1992). Arguably it may be said that even though (hetero *and* homo)sexualizing[4] representations of the male body have become more and more common in advertising imagery, women are still more often placed in front of the camera, to be scrutinized by the gaze it represents. But what does it mean that not only do we look at the images, but they also look back at us (Gagnon 1988: 26)? Would the intense looks directed at the viewers by the models of the ads be signifiers of a potent agency, a strong subjectivity? Or could the looks, and the often soft-pornified and heterosexualized agency they represent, be rethought and made more complex through the subjectifying notion of interpellation?

The French philosopher Louis Althusser shed light on the workings of ideology by using the example of the representative of the law, a cop, hailing a man in the street (1971: 170–86). In the Althusserian interpretation the man, through this interpellation, becomes a subject in the twofold meaning of the word: not only is he *subjected to* the act of hailing, he also becomes recognized *as a subject with agency*. Judith Butler (1997: 24–5) has emphasized that the power of interpellation, or subjectification, not only resides in the law but just equally in the conventionality and the ritualistic dimension of the act. Could we, then, think that the soft-pornified public images, and their often heteronormative ideology, get to formulate, gender and sexualize our subjectivities as the images repeatedly look at us, addressing, inviting, interpelling us, over and over again? What are these images subjecting us to?

Looks or gazes directed at viewers from advertising images effectively arrest our looks. It is interesting that the authorities assessing the codes of advertising repeatedly appeal to this eye-catching ability – and this appeal also gives a twist to the problematics of arresting images. The ethical bodies of advertising may emphasize that the images of women should not be used *solely* for catching the eye of the viewers, nor should the ads represent 'sexual promises or cues which do not have any connection to the advertised product'.[5] Do the products advertised by images emphasizing the conventionally eroticized parts of female bodies always and necessarily have a direct connection to sexuality and sex? Does this apply, for instance, to women's underwear advertised in the public space? Is the main function and purpose of women's fashion, and the repetitious and citational acts of 'feminine' dressing up in general, to represent, or 'do', sexuality in public? And not just any kind of sexuality, but normative eroticism, which supposedly attracts representatives of the 'opposite sex'.

Flirt Between Women: One Soft-Core Method

Late in 2003, before Christmas, the Swedish-originating but multinationally operating clothing company Hennes&Mauritz was advertising women's underwear on outdoor billboards in the streets of Helsinki, as in many other bigger towns and cities in its vast marketing area (Fig. 10.1).[6] The advertising campaign is analysed here as an example, both typical and slightly exceptional, of the visual techniques used for selling the product *and* titillating the viewers by producing and repeating certain forms of knowledge concerning female sexuality. Close reading these images, I sketch some features in the visual grammar of the signifiers habitually used in soft-pornified advertising in public spaces, the streetscape included. The atypicality of these images, again, connects to their ways of representing inter-

Figure 10.1 H&M street advertising campaign in Helsinki, December 2004. Photograph by the author.

female relationships. Nevertheless, I suggest that even their atypicality, or non-normativity, is rather ostensible since the representations of intimacy in the campaign quite easily fall into the representational category of female friendship (see e.g. Butler 2004: 174).

The H&M campaign in question consisted of images showing three female models in several different poses and groupings: all three together, in a 'twosome' and posing alone. One of the models was black and easily recognizable as the supermodel Naomi Campbell. The other two were white and anonymous: the campaign used Campbell's status as the main attraction and she also performed alone in video clips on the company's website. The lighting and dramatic colours – the combination of 'Christmassy' red and black – used in the photos emphasized the fair skin of the white models, one of which was a blonde and the other a reddish brunette. All the models were slim (the blonde one even remarkably thin), long-haired and conventionally 'good-looking' and thus performed the dominant heteronormative idea of feminine female beauty. The deliberate choice of models representing different skin colours situated H&M as a company within the popular advertising rhetoric of tolerance, which Benetton had already launched in the 1980s (Seppänen 2001: 188–209, 222–3). This kind of rhetorical choice could be read as a self-rehabilitating move from H&M, which had been heavily criticized on ethical grounds: both for using extremely thin and young-looking models, and

Figure 10.2 The campaign used supermodel Naomi Campbell's status as the main attraction. Photograph by the author.

for benefiting from circumventing the terms of ethical trade. On the other hand, the representational use of Campbell's body – especially in the website video clips – can be seen as echoing the Western tradition of stereotypical eroticization of black female bodies (see e.g. Hall 1999: 264–9; Miller-Young in this volume) (Fig. 10.2). Neither did her status as a supermodel diminish the accent of overt sexualization. The configuration in which the black model was the famous one and the white models anonymous might of course even be read as turning the tables on racialized hierarchy – but in the end the 'equality' thus achieved merely concerned the stereotypically eroticizing display of the represented bodies.

Besides 'multi-ethnicity', the other obvious theme of the H&M campaign was intimate bodily closeness between women. This was most evident in the images presenting the 'black-and-white couple', but also in the photos showing all three women together: they had been directed to stand close to each other, bare bodies touching, arms on each others' shoulders or around each others' waists. Some of the compositions blatantly called for a reference to the traditional girl-on-girl subgenre of heteroporn in which female-to-female intimacy is frequently used for titillation of the (male) viewer: 'lesbian' scenes may serve as a metaphoric foreplay or warm-up before the 'actual' heterosexual penetration takes place, but they may also be used for arousing the viewers 'as such' (Fig. 10.3).[7] Heather Butler has aptly called these woman-to-woman porn scenes 'the lesbo-jelly in the hetero-donut' (Butler 2004: 168, 173). The poses of the female models in the H&M campaign were easy to interpret flirting with this genre of 'lesbo-jelly': horny and malleable, ready for sex. This was secured by the several signifiers conventionally referring to, and emphasizing, sex and sexuality. Sartorial codes (black, red and lacy underwear drawing attention to the breasts, the buttocks and the pubic area) formed even clichéd porn-citations. The downcast eyes or the furtive looks were used to signify seductiveness combined with submissiveness[8] while the moist-looking red lips were either invitingly parted, imitated a kiss or framed a dashing laughter. The red background of the images constituted, together with the black underwear, a colour combination which media imageries have taught us to associate with environments of sexual consumption: brothels and striptease-joints, or more mundane but 'naughty' bedroom scenes.

The women in the ads were either cuddling or looked like they had stopped in the middle of playing and frolicking with each other. One of the scenes *might have* been interpreted as representing the white woman *almost* kissing the black woman's ear. In many of the images, women not only actively foregrounded their breasts but also curved their backs in order to focus the viewers' attention to their bottom and pelvis. Was this imagery meant to be arousing while not 'revealing everything', in other words, soft-core (Williams 1989: 30)? I would say, at least close to it.

As explicitly sexualized, and not representing a male–female couple, the images might have been interpreted as representing moments of lesbian intimacy,

Figure 10.3 The poses of the female models in the H&M campaign were easy to interpret flirting with each other. Photograph by the author.

moments of 'nonstandard intimacy in public' (Berlant and Warner 2000: 322–3). This interpretation, however, requires a quite conscious reading against the grain – which has certainly historically been a standard viewing practice among the lesbian and gay identified audiences of films, television, advertising and art (see e.g. Dyer 1985). Instead of looking *at each* other in a clearly desiring way, the models either looked seductively towards the gaze of camera/the alleged viewer, or away from the image towards its edges, or they had closed their eyes. There was no eye contact between the models. This way they, at most, invited the potential viewer – not each other – into an erotic exchange. And even though one might think that this invitation was addressed to the female viewers as well (cf. Lewis and Rolley 1997), one might just as well assume that the erotically coded address was intended *mainly* towards a male audience.

The female audience may have been supposed to remain safely in the realm of identification and not to experience desire. Or it may have been thought that the 'desire' of female consumers could be channelled towards the fetishized underwear and acquiring them in order to repeat the advertised, idealized gender performance as closely as possible. This understanding of a heteronormative structure of looking, identifying and desiring corresponds to a highly conventional account of the directions of desire and identification. Even though the relationship between desire and identification tends to be much more complicated, and the border between them quite blurred (Lewis and Rolley 1997; Stacey 1994: 138–70), it is generally thought that women watch images of women as models for ideal appearance, whereas men have been thought of as getting sexual pleasure out of watching images of women, 'naturally' desiring them as objects of their 'male gaze' (cf. Mulvey 1989). Scenes of female-to-female intimacy, as represented in the H&M campaign, are conventionally read as representations of friendship, non-romantic and non-erotic intimacy – and thus as non-threatening towards the heterosexual regime. The lack of intensity between the models in the campaign can be thought of signifying exactly the non-erotic, almost platonic closeness, and thus actually forming an effective obstacle for queer reading. A poignant signifier for this lack of intimacy could be found in one of the images in which the hand of the black woman rests inertly on the shoulder of the blonde. The gesture is not caressing, but plain passive.

It may have been the intention of the designers of the campaign, and even of the advertiser, to produce a set of sexually ambivalent, multiracialized images enhancing tolerance, or even promoting diversity beyond tolerance in the public sphere (Clarke 2000: 171–2), but ultimately the codes chosen made it difficult – at least for me as a viewer – to foreground this interpretation. And, gloomily enough, almost all outdoor advertising repeats the same pattern of heterosexualizing female bodies, quite often through poses citing the codes of soft-core porn. This imagery, explicitly addressing heterosexual men and women, seems to convey generalized knowledge on women's constant wish to be desired by men, and to become partners in heterosexual exchange. The codes utilized in this knowledge production are not only heteronormative: they also normatively restrict the ways heterosexuality and hetero-eroticism may be performed (see e.g. Berlant and Warner 2000: 316, 318–20). Only certain types of bodies are represented as desirable, only certain conventions of poses as 'sexy' or erotic.

Not On-Scene, but on an Alternative Scene?

It is has been a challenge for me as a queer-feminist researcher to grasp the mundane phenomenon of outdoor pornification formed by advertising in public spaces, especially since my account is largely motivated by the conception of the urban streetscape as a highly problematic venue for exhibiting visual material influenced and inspired by soft-core porn. One may legitimately ask whether this kind of discussion even signifies a will to censor public visual culture.

As a term, censorship awakes unpleasant feelings. Jim McGuigan (1996: 156) has suggested that it is communally unrealistic to cherish the idea of abandoning moral regulation altogether. Instead of a total overthrow of the regulation, he places emphasis on discursive control, which should be open, well founded, and continuously subjected to public scrutiny. It would be desirable to connect this kind of open process of discussion to the sexualized imagery of our everyday environment, instead of banning single exemplary pieces of advertising. This would be especially critical in terms of the images of female bodies that still represent the majority of the figures used to connote sexuality. It should also be noted that there already exists a lot of tacit regulation in terms of what may or may not be shown in public. Both advertising agencies and different ethical bodies for advertising continuously negotiate this border of visibility. Nevertheless, the urban landscape, as part of the public sphere at large, seems to be saturated by spectacles of hetero-normative erotic address and intimacy (Fig. 10.4).

Rather than objects to be banned, I see representation(s) of naked bodies and different sexualities as a challenging and interesting field of visual politics. From my point of view, the dilemma Carol Vance so aptly described in the early 1990s

Figure 10.4 Outdoor advertising repeats the codes of soft-core porn. Photograph by the author.

is still valid: How could different feminisms simultaneously both decrease the sexual dangers threatening women *and* increase possibilities of sexual pleasure? (Vance 1992: xx) For me it seems obvious that it has to be possible to represent naked bodies and different sexualities in varying ways. The question remains *how* to do it in order not to reproduce trite, stereotypical and banal notions of genders (men only as voyeuristic viewers and women always as the ones solely being looked at). In academic discourse there have been numerous efforts to rethink the notion of the 'male gaze' (Mulvey 1989; Gamman and Marshment 1989; Burston and Richardson 1995). In the practices of advertising, one might dare to estimate, the efforts to bring forth alternative representations have not yet been too plentiful.

In my account on soft-pornification of advertising and the public space, I am not too concerned about the question of objectification. While this issue has been crucial in feminist critiques of porn, I suggest that every time people and things are represented in a visual form, they/we are objectified to a certain extent, and as viewers who are being looked at, we are constantly moving, sliding between subject and object positions. Put in psychoanalytical terms: when we practise looking, we are constantly posing both for the imaginary generic Gaze relentlessly 'supervising us' (often represented by the lens of a camera) and for the embodied looks of other subjects (Silverman 1996). The burning issue is, how are objects and subjects positioned and established in images representing human beings, and what kind of genders are produced through these visual set-ups? What kinds of female, male or transgendered models are chosen from the pool or repertoire of possible models? In what kind of combinations are they shown together?

And the final question is *where* to present these representations? On-scene, off-scene – or some place else? Could the pornified figures of fantasy be represented on *alternative scenes,* scenes of choice, instead of the most public of the public spaces, the streetscape? Could these images be situated in places and spaces where signification and resignification, the corporeal feelings and affects the images arouse might be faced as a result of at least relative choice? Even though I whole-heartedly embrace the politics of the radical proliferation of genders and sexualities, and especially since I understand how important, how productive a role representations have in this process of proliferation, I still cannot see how the soft-pornified representations of women in the streetscape – also the ones only ostensibly queering the female intimacy – might contribute to the politics of cultural diversity.

–11–

Insatiable Sluts and Almost Gay Guys: Bisexuality in Porn Magazines

Jenny Kangasvuo

Are bisexuals weird horny freaks who have sex with anything that moves? Are they products of a twisted upbringing or an unhappy childhood? Where do they come from and who are they? *Exit* studied the issue and now our writer reveals everything that is really known about bisexuals. Maybe even you are bisexual? (*Exit* 3–4/1999: 41)[1]

This list of questions is presented in an article entitled 'The X-files of Bi-sexualism' in *Exit*, a Finnish porn magazine for women. Bisexuality is depicted as a titillating and fascinating mystery. Since solving this mystery would erase its possible pleasures, the article sways away from closer description of bisexuality. This chapter poses a different set of questions on bisexuality: Namely, how is bisexuality described in mainstream pornography? What kinds of situations or people are labelled 'bisexual'? How is bisexuality gendered? And what kind of dynamics are there between the eroticized depiction of bisexuality and heteronormativity? In order to explore these questions, I analyse porn magazines. However, unlike *Exit*, I will not claim to 'reveal everything that is really known about representations of bisexuality in porn'.

My research material consists of hardcore porn magazines published in Finland between 1995 and 2005.[2] The magazines of my sample have slightly different foci and profiles. According to its advertising, *Exit* seeks its audience among 'bold women and erotic men' and *Haloo!* presents itself similarly as a woman-friendly porn magazine serving 'sex-positive couples' supposedly consisting of a woman and a man.[3] *Tabu* concentrates on fetish and BDSM porn while *Hustler* is the Finnish edition of the well-known American magazine. *Kalle*, the oldest and most classic porn magazine of my sample, is the only magazine publishing gay porn in Finland (Fig. 11.1).

I have analysed all explicit mentions of bisexuality in the magazines while excluding depictions not making use of the term. I am interested in the contexts in which the concept of bisexuality is used. For instance, a 'threesome' of two women and a man having sex is one of the most conventional scenarios of mainstream

Figure 11.1 Photo collage by the author.

heteroporn. In these scenes it is self-evident, even compulsory, that women fondle each other as well as the man (Williams 1999: 127). However, the scene or the women attending it are not usually named as bisexual, although they would seem so from a commonsensical point of view.

In general, bisexuality denotes a person's ability to feel sexual, romantic and emotional feelings towards people of different genders[4] or regardless of their gender. A bisexual person has this ability and, more to the point, defines him- or herself as bisexual (e.g. Firestein 1996: xix–xx; Geller 1990: 106; Kangasvuo 2006). The concept of bisexuality is firmly anchored into Western sexuality and the gender system, in which homo- and heterosexuality are separated as totally different and mutually opposing categories. As a concept, bisexuality could not be comprehensible without the concepts of homo- and heterosexuality.

'I'm bisexual, I like both girls and boys', says the Finnish porn star Rakel Liekki (*Kalle* 7/2002: 76). Her statement is the simplest possible definition of bisexuality (especially in comparison to formulations posed by bi-theorists): liking both girls and boys marks bisexuals apart from straight and gay people. In porn magazines, the term 'bisexuality' serves multiple purposes and it is not pinned down. Its central aim is to knowingly titillate and excite the reader: people, positions or relations labelled bisexual become objects of desire and arousal. 'Bisexual' is comparable to terms such as 'whore', 'slut', 'teen', 'lesbian' or 'nympho' widely used in porn in such a way that their actual meaning or accuracy is secondary to their libidinal affect. In a feature article listing sixteen different sexual fantasies and fetishisms ranging from golden showers to mud wrestling, bisexuality ranks ninth: 'Steamy flesh is steamy flesh, whether it has balls attached or not, and tight orifices feel good across gender boundaries' (*Haloo!* 4/2002: 19). Here bisexuality is just another sexual habit to be used as a fantasy, in parallel with anal sex or spanking. The frequent use of the word bisexual does not shake the stable polarities of gender and sexuality: bisexuality is depicted as a sexual quirk or a means to spice up one's sex life rather than an identity category or identification similar to hetero- or homosexuality. While Rakel Liekki might define bisexuality in simple terms, the meanings of bisexuality are actually slippery in porn.

We bi-girls are wilder than lesbians and straight women'

'It has been proven that women are more inclined to bisexuality than men. More ready to surrender to girlie sex than men to each other', states a caption to images of two women and a man having sex (*Haloo!* 2/2004: 50–1). The practice of labelling women bisexual is not limited to a certain type of pictures or text but is present everywhere in porn magazines. Captions in particular often name women bisexual, as if to remind the (male) reader that despite the absence of men the women are still available.

However, sex between women is also such a well-established porn convention that there is no need to specifically name it – unless the naming is intended to titillate the reader. Sexual acts or erotic intimacy among women do not alone suffice to classify them as lesbian or bisexual, since such activity is framed as a natural and inherent part of female sexuality in porn (Williams 1999; Williams 1992: 252–3; Butler 2004: 173; Kalha 2005: 48–51). Women engaged in sexual acts with each other can be named lesbian, bisexual or be left without specific labels, depending on the context. The difference between bisexual and non-bisexual women does not lie in their desire to have sex with other women, but in their openness about the desire. According to porn magazines, any woman can be seduced to have sex with other women, whereas a woman who names herself bisexual is more open, modern and sex positive than other women. She is also more lustful and more ready to have sex with anyone. Being named bisexual, a woman is also labelled insatiable and hypersexual. As a speech bubble beside a close-up of a vulva reads:

> It might be truth or myth, but sexually active and bold women are often bisexual. I like to make out with women too. It's so different with girls, although I have to admit that making love with a man is even better. Variety is the spice of life, and 'cause men have that invincible tool, lesbian love is mostly just an extra spice. (*Kalle* 1/2001: 48)

The bisexual woman is defined as sexually open and enjoying sex with anyone, yet it is the penis that gives her the most delicious pleasure.

The arousing nature of the term bisexuality is apparent in how women are categorized in porn stories featuring male protagonists. A short story called 'Once in a lifetime' starts with the following sentence: 'I'm mortally in love with my bisexual wife' (*Haloo!* 2/1995: 36). The story meanders through the male protagonist's first date with his future wife and reaches its climax in their first sex act. The story concludes: 'I will penetrate her again while she is still asleep and wet from my semen. I will be in love with my lovely bisexual wife until the end of my life.' (*Haloo!* 2/1995: 37) References to bisexuality help to render a rather ordinary description of heterosexual dating and intercourse more interesting. Bisexuality promises continuous sexual pleasure – a bisexual wife will never have a headache or say no to a man who fulfils her needs completely. Here female bisexuality is something that excites, but also something that needs to be tamed.

Bisexuality has a peculiar position in porn stories depicting sex between women. On a surface level, bisexuality is present in the stories – and explicitly mentioned – since female characters have sexual feelings towards both women and men. On a deeper level, the stories nevertheless keep the heterosexual hegemony intact by depicting sexuality between women either as foreplay to heterosexual intercourse or as a one-time experience. The characters may call themselves bisexual but they will eventually return to their boyfriends' waiting arms. Even women presented as each other's girlfriends and lovers are said to yearn for sex with men.

Porn stories recurrently allude to an alleged heterosexual male fantasy of watching two women having sex together. Male characters can experience this dream once they meet a bisexual woman horny enough to convince her lesbian girlfriend to have sex with the man, or even to deflower her own sister. In this equation, bisexuality signifies insatiability: bisexual women will have sex with each other, with a man, back and forth, again and again. Even when the protagonist is female, bisexuality can be used to explain her readiness to experiment. The female protagonist of 'Fantasy fulfilled' calls herself and her girlfriend bisexual: 'We are both bisexual women, sex has a central place in our lives and we are ready to try most extraordinary things' (*Haloo!* 3/2003, 43). The 'extraordinary thing' presented in the story is a lesbian show for three men, followed by a gangbang.

Women in porn – straight, lesbian or bisexual – are constantly available and willing to have sex. This utopian stereotype of female insatiability and lecherous women precedes the era of (audio)visual pornography, dating back to literary pornography (Williams 1999: 174–83). However, before the 1980s, female insatiability was mainly depicted as comical or threatening, whereas contemporary porn frames it in decidedly positive terms. Given this, bisexuality does not present a departure from more general representational conventions of hypersexualized femininity. It is nevertheless noteworthy that since the 1990s, 'whores' and 'nymphos' have been, if not replaced, at least paralleled by bi-women. The bisexual woman is an updated version of the ideal woman of porn: active, open and ready to fulfil all possible fantasies.

The Ideal Woman of Porn: 'I'm very grateful to porn'

Bisexual identification appears almost compulsory for female porn stars interviewed in porn magazines. Porn star Bobbi Eden criticizes performers who do not seem to enjoy lesbian scenes and do them just for the money. 'Did I mention that I was completely bi even before my porn career?' she snaps (*Haloo!* 3/2005: 60–2). Bisexuality becomes a guarantee of Eden's true porn stardom and, paradoxically, of her professionalism in comparison to her straight counterparts who merely pretend enjoying scenes with other women.

Stripping and acting in porn films are often represented as a means of self-realization for bisexual women who are apparently just too sexual to lead a life outside the porn business, in a monogamous relationship and a dull job. 'I love my job, it has made it possible to fulfil even my most secret fantasies', tells Janine Lindemulder, 'lesbian porn queen' and says: 'I'm bisexual, each and every cell, but I would never have dared to approach all those wonderful women had I not worked in the porn industry. I'm very grateful to porn for that.' (*Haloo!* 3/2002: 27) In her analysis of media representations of the Finnish professional dominatrix Veronica, Kaarina Nikunen (2005) notes how the porn industry is presented as the saviour of an unhappy hooker. Porn magazines similarly present the industry as providing women independence and the possibility to gain personal satisfaction.

Bisexuality is not a similar requirement for male porn stars. The only male porn star labelled as bisexual is Jeff Stryker who makes films for both gay and heterosexual markets. When asked about his sexual preference, Stryker replies: 'A hole is a hole, both suit me. The most important thing is that I can work with people that have some class.' (*Tabu* 3/2000: 60) While female stars discuss their self-realization through porn, Stryker's interview focuses on his potency and business: how many films he has made, how he entered the porn business and the kind of shows he does. In contrast, even the female producers, directors and photographers working in the porn industry often label themselves, or are otherwise labelled, bisexual. An article on the Danish hardcore photographer Bettina Bergemann claims that her photographs have better quality than ones by straight men: 'Bettina, a.k.a. Big B, is an active bisexual and she knows very well what belongs to love between girls. The models feel comfortable posing for her.' (*Haloo!* 4/1999: 18–19) The recurring requirement of female bisexuality blurs the meaning of the very concept: if every female porn star is bisexual, bisexuality hardly poses a challenge to heteronormativity (cf. Nikunen 2005: 220).

In porn magazines bisexuality is set as an ideal for all women. In addition to international porn stars, magazines such as *Haloo!* and *Tabu* introduce and interview 'ordinary bisexual women' with (self-evident) boyfriends or husbands. These women usually have a special trait – they might be members of an SM-club, enjoy wife swapping or posing for the camera. An interview with 'experimenting bi-girl Sanna' is illustrated with two amateurish photos where Sanna fondles her breasts and spreads her legs (*Haloo!* 1/2002: 23). The pictures parallel her with professional performers who are set as ideal for all women wishing to manifest their lack of inhibitions. *Tabu* publishes a regular series of pin-up photos and interviews with amateur fetish and SM models. One of the regular questions posed concerns bisexuality: 'Are you bi-inclined? Do you enjoy love between women?' All models interviewed in my sample gave an affirmative answer varying from a simple 'yes' to the more enthusiastic 'Absolutely!' (*Tabu* 2/2005: 93) and 'One hundred percent!' (*Tabu* 2/2004: 103).

Both amateur models and porn stars seem eager to confirm their lack of inhibitions with the label of bisexuality. In all interviews, bisexuality is depicted as a positive trait, something that makes a porn career or activity in fetish circles appear natural. While all women in porn are presented as inherently interested in each other, naming oneself bisexual is a way to prove one's up-to-date attitude. Smart women know that it is useful to be bisexual.

Bisexuality as a Threat: 'We are not lesbians or even bisexuals'

Despite the depiction of bisexual women as ideals, they can also be seen as threatening in their alleged insatiability. In some cases bisexuality – and lesbianism – are disavowed even when featuring sexual acts among women. In one example, photographs of two women having sex are used to illustrate a story in which a photographer picks the women up and asks them to pose. 'We are not lesbians or even bisexuals, said Kelli as she tasted Brandy's tumescent cunt. This is just play, just to tease men. Sometimes we do pet each other until we reach an orgasm, but for real lovemaking we need a man and a real cock.' (*Kalle* 7/2003: 46) Sex between women is detached from any notions of lesbianism and tamed into a spectacle tailored to male needs.

Although most 'lesbian' scenes in mainstream porn are not *named* lesbian, the word lesbian is frequently used in porn magazines, albeit with one exception. Targeted at female readers, *Exit* has few references to lesbians whereas gay men are regularly featured on its pages. Gay photographers and make-up artists are interviewed and gay rights discussed, yet 'love between women' is addressed in terms of sexual exploration of predominantly straight women. Avoiding references to lesbianism, whether actual or fantastic, is – somewhat paradoxically – a means of marking the magazine as 'woman friendly'. Leaving lesbian themes out, *Exit* may emphasize its role as an erotic magazine for straight women while still maintaining the pornified view of female sexuality as fluid and sexuality between women as inherently natural to all women. *Exit* shuns lesbianism as a separate identity but embraces sexuality between women as something exquisitely erotic that any woman may enjoy.

Lesbianism has an interesting position in porn. On the one hand, the term 'lesbian' is used in labelling acts, desires and people without describing any fixed state of sexuality. Like the word 'bisexual', the word 'lesbian' may be arousing in itself: 'hot lesbian pussy' promises something quite different than 'women licking each other'. The term lesbian creates a special framing: a woman labelled lesbian seems unattainable and can only be won over by a special man. In addition to enjoying the visual spectacle, male readers are invited to fantasize being the one to achieve this (Kalha 2005: 48–51; Williams 1999: 173–4, 256). On the other hand, the word lesbian can also be a deterrent. A short story about a girl's first sexual experience with a woman depicts lesbians as sexual predators: 'I had met the first lesbian of my life and fallen into the trap like a little girl … That night taught me a lot. Actually, as much as it is possible for a girl in her twenties to learn about love between girls and survive it without turning into the goddess of Lesbos.' (*Haloo!* 5/1995: 33–8) Lesbians may give pleasure but they also threaten to turn women into lesbians – a transformation deemed ultimately undesirable. In mainstream porn, bisexual woman, as hypersexualized and enticing as she may be, can slip dangerously close to being lesbian.

The danger is frequently played with. 'Harmless play made girls bisexuals', exclaims a caption from a photo series juxtaposed with a story in which women tease a man by caressing each other, only to realize that they are actually enjoying it (*Kalle* 5/2003: 112). The male protagonist fears that the women are too excited about lesbian love – they have already turned bisexual and what if they turn lesbians too? There is, however, no need to worry:

> Lesbian game was just a show', reads the caption positioned on a close-up photo of a vulva. The story ends by averting the possibility of lesbianism and ensuring the availability of bisexual women: 'Fortunately, we can be sure that lesbian play was just

fooling around and that, despite their bisexuality, the girls still prefer a masculine, erect cock. That gives all of us hope for a better future. We'll never know when we'll meet one of the girls – or both at the same time. (*Kalle* 5/2003: 114)

Bisexuality and lesbianism pose a threat not because of women having sex with each other but because they might prefer doing this on a permanent basis. The idea of stability threatens the pornographic ideal of female sexuality as open, fluid and oscillating (Williams 1992: 253). The concept of bisexuality can be used in depicting fluid, hypersexualized and insatiable female sexuality, as well as closed, stable and identity-based sexuality. By denying the possibility of bisexuality or lesbianism, the ideal of female sexual fluidity is safely distanced from associations of stability linked to the concepts of bisexuality and lesbianism as markers of identity. In pornography, bisexuality is not allowed to be interpreted as an identity and must correlate with fluidity in order to be acceptable. Porn recycles fantasies of insatiable bisexual women and slightly more easily satisfied straight women also willing to have some lesbian fun. Since all women in porn are ready to have sex with other women, bisexuality loses its commonsensical meaning. The concepts used to discuss female desire and sexuality are emptied in the process.

Bisexual Men: 'Could it be that the man is gay!'

Unlike women, the men of porn cannot be generally labelled bisexual. Porn magazines keep male homo- and heterosexuality strictly isolated from each other. Male heterosexuality also requires the constant rejection of homosexuality. Sex between men seems to be one of the strongest of taboos in mainstream porn (Williams 1992: 252.) Sex between men is very seldom referred to in porn magazines, and the few men who appear to desire men are usually not called bisexual. *Kalle*, the only magazine in my sample publishing gay porn, limits it to special 'gay pages'. In other parts of the magazine, homosexuality is occasionally referred to but usually in a ridiculing and homophobic manner. The separation of homosexuality and heterosexuality is blatant: gay pages are an airtight all-male space in which women do not exist, whilst other parts of the magazine almost completely ignore sexuality between men.

Mainstream porn stories are quick to deny the possibility of homosexuality in men having sex together: 'I consider myself a pure-breed hetero who just seeks pleasures that my girlfriend doesn't want to give. If Mira would suck my cock and give ass, I wouldn't go to Tomi', complains the protagonist of a story centring on anal pleasures (*Kalle* 5/2004: 35). Sex with other men is presented as either a substitute for straight sex or as an exciting one-time experience insufficient to turn the protagonist gay. Porn stories also feature compulsory female characters that ensure the non-homosexuality of the men, even if their role is minor.

Since the gay pages of *Kalle* never show women, the possibility of male bisexuality is ruled out on the visual level. Bisexual men are nevertheless presented as objects of gay male desire: 'It's especially exciting to fuck an inexperienced, married semi-straight man ... I'm used to fucking with gay men but I have a soft spot for these bi-men. My arousal is stronger if the man is inexperienced', confesses a pin-up boy 'Andy' in an interview most likely written by the editor (*Kalle* special issue/2005, 40–1). While bisexual women are presented as sexually uninhibited, experienced and open, bisexual men are presented as married and closeted gays who need a gay man to give them some cock. The male homosexuality of *Kalle*'s gay pages is just as monolithic as the heterosexuality elsewhere in the magazine – and elsewhere in my research material.

This monolithic nature of gayness owes partly to the function of porn in supporting gay identity, desire and community (Dyer 1992; Cante and Restivo 2004: 142–53; Mowlabocus in this volume). Heteroporn is similarly used in building straight male identity and homosociality (Kalha 2005: 32). Given all this, it may be understandable that references to male bisexuality are avoided in porn magazines and that bisexuality is presented as a phase preceding the discovery of one's homosexuality. The rigidity of homosexuality also protects the uniformity of heterosexuality.

The only photo feature in my sample depicting men having sex together *and* with a woman is published in *Kalle* (1/2001). The title 'Bisexual fuck-mix' makes explicit reference to bisexuality whereas features showing two women and a man having sex tend to be named after the characters or the setting. This photo feature is accompanied by a fictional story written by the editor. The first caption states: 'For Ben and Peter, masculine men, it seems to be extremely important not to be called gay. Despite the fact that they have steamy sex together, these knights claim that they like women as well, in other words they are bisexual. "It's completely different from being gay", the boys say.' The tone of the story is humorously sceptical. '"We are not gay, we really aren't!" shouted the dark haired Ben, whose voice made windows tremble. "Says a man who has been caught in the act of fucking his boyfriend in the ass," I argued. "Gays, no way," blonde Peter tried to repeat ... Don't try, your names are so Swedish that there is no need to dispute it.' (*Kalle* 1/2001: 4–5)

The story ridicules men trying to prove their non-homosexuality: if a man has sex with other men, he is definitely gay, independent of his objections. A Swedish name works to confirm gay identity, at least according to the Finnish vernacular comic tradition of Swedish men being particularly prone to homosexuality. In spite of this evidence, Ben and Peter assert their bisexuality: '"As a journalist you must know the word bisexual," continued Ben and picked a dictionary from a bookshelf ... "it means 'a deviant person whose sexual attraction is oriented towards both genders' ... We really like women just as much as each other ... or some other guys."' To prove their bisexuality, the men agree to a photo-shoot with a woman:

'let's show what bisexuality means in practice, in other words we fuck the woman but also each other.' (*Kalle* 1/2001: 5–7) Verification of male bisexuality is a difficult challenge: 'Our guys try to prove their bisexuality with the help of a girl' (*Kalle* 1/2001: 10).

At first the story seems to have a happy end: 'The classic queue in which the first man fucks a cunt and the other guy fucks his ass is preserved on film. Everything seems to be fine and the evidence is clear. Ben and Peter really are bisexual.' The queue is presented as the ultimate proof of bisexuality. A caption verifies the suitably straight climax: 'Semen is thrown on the breasts and mouth of the girl'. The editor sums up: 'the whole operation was put up just to give Ben and Peter a chance to prove that they are not gay'. (*Kalle* 1/2001: 16–7) Nevertheless, a surprise is in store. As the editor checks the photos, he notices that: 'I couldn't find one in which Peter's member was inside Tarja's cunt in any of the forty pictures I got, although it was several times in her mouth. What kind of conclusions can we draw from this? Maybe we can't draw any, but I still have a small suspicion; could it be that the man is GAY!' (*Kalle* 1/2001: 17) The word 'gay', written in capital letters is the last word of the story. The story restores the binary sexual division, assuring readers that a man desiring other men is ultimately gay, independent of his self-identification or any other sexual acts that he may perform. Male bisexuality is ridiculously impossible since attraction towards other men, let alone sex with them, marks the man as gay.

While male bisexuality is virtually absent in images and texts intended to arouse the reader, it remains a recurring theme in counselling columns. A letter entitled 'Real me?' (*Kalle* 4/2005) is a typical example of the threat of gayness. In the letter, 'Juha' tells of his dream in which he had sex with a man. He woke up beside his wife with his pyjama pants wet and his mind deeply troubled: 'Does my dream reflect my real orientation, in other words is it possible that I have turned or am turning gay, or do we all have a small gay in us. And should I be worried about my situation?' The counsellors generally neutralize the threat of gayness with the term bisexuality, considered a safe label in comparison to the threat of 'turning really gay'. The letters published in counselling columns reiterate stigmatic links between male homosexuality, sickness, shame and dirt (cf. Warner 2000). They also reflect insecurity concerning male sexuality. While sex and desire between women is constantly present in heteroporn, sex and desire between men is depicted as either ridiculous or problematic. The term bisexuality can refer to all women but bisexual men are presented as either the troubled souls of counselling columns or pathetic clowns who fail in their attempts to prove that they are not gay. The imbalance between the nervous questions published in the columns and the ridiculing treatment of male bisexuality elsewhere in the magazines is close to tragic.

The Most Exciting of Fantasies?

'They decided to fulfil the most exciting of fantasies – lovemaking with a bi-sexual [*sic*] woman', describes a feature article tackling sexual fantasies (*Haloo!* 4/1995). In porn magazines, bisexuality is used in labelling people, sexual acts or relationships, but is also a source of pleasures and fantasies. Naming an act, a person or a situation bisexual has added value: in pornography, bisexuality is never used as a neutral term. Bisexuality can function as a sexual fantasy, a fetish to be experimented with – maybe just once – or a source of humour. The bisexuality of men, in particular, crossing as it does the sacred border of hetero- and homosexuality, is depicted as embarrassing, revolting or humorous. The possibility of bisexuality can be disturbing and the anxiety it evokes is neutralized through ridicule.

Depictions of bisexuality in porn are oddly twisted. While the concept of bisexuality has many interpretations and uses, it is still most frequently used in reference to women who do not drastically differ from other women in porn. Female lust can be oriented anywhere: its object can be male, female, she-male or a phallus-like object. Such lust can be labelled bisexual, but lesbian and straight are equally possible terms since female sexuality is open to renaming – the object of female desire is not definite but contingent. The object of male desire, however, must be defined. Even a dildo in a man's anus, handled by a woman, creates suspicions of homosexuality. Male bisexuality and homosexuality lie frighteningly close to each other.

Magazines

I refer to my material only by the issue of the magazine. The names of the writers are not usually given, and if they are, they are often nicknames, like 'Onnellinen alainen' ('Happy subordinate') or humorous pen names of the editor, like 'Usko-Voitto Etuseisiö' ('Faith-Victor Frontboner'). Therefore these names do not have relevance in identifying the writer.

Exit. Helsinki: Exit Publishing. Volumes 1996–2005.
Haloo! Helsinki: Monimediatalo oy National Tele. Volumes 1995–2005.
Hustler. Järvenpää: HF Publications. Volumes 2000–5.
Kalle. Tampere: Pop-lehdet. Volumes 2000–5.
Tabu. Helsinki: TV-kustannus. Volumes 2000–5.

–12–

Bend over Boyfriend: Anal Sex Instructional Videos for Women

Michelle Carnes

Although porn films regularly feature anal sex (and female performers apparently begging for it), three women decided to make 'guide' films to help viewers have anal sex. What does it mean that these films frame their viewers as women or as adventurous couples (rather than addressing heterosexual men singularly) and how does this impact women's and couple's access to these how-to films? Finally, is it the goal of these three film series to change the anal sex taboo, to 'normalize' anal sex?

This chapter explores five how-to films for women and couples demonstrating and demystifying anal sex – a sex act with a stigmatized past and (as evidenced by these films) a changing future. Tristan Taormino's films, *The Ultimate Guide to Anal Sex for Women* (1999) and *The Ultimate Guide to Anal Sex for Women 2* (2000) followed her trailblazing book of the same title (1998). Co-directed with porn director, Ernest Greene (a.k.a. 'ButtMan'), Taormino's films are the most recent and best known but were preceded by series by Nina Hartley and Carol Queen. *Nina Hartley's Guide to Anal Sex* (1998) is one of a series spanning nearly thirty Hartley's 'Guide To' videos. Carol Queen's *Bend Over Boyfriend* (1998), featuring women strapping on dildos to penetrate a male partner, went on to enjoy something of a cult status, giving rise to *Bend Over Boyfriend 2: More Rockin', Less Talkin'* (1999).

Despite the prevalence of anal sex in mainstream porn, the three sets of films represent a specific moment when women were increasingly creating their own visions within the porn genre. Creating how-to films to educate but also to inspire viewers is a statement about the potential for pornography, for sex education and for the continued attention to women and couples as porn spectators.

Because of the nature of these three women's video series, the techniques used to demonstrate the mechanics of anal pleasure and to explore new ways of filming sex (particularly to reflect the films' access to women) do differ among the films. As women got behind the camera, they responded to the commonly held idea that porn did not 'speak' to women and different approaches were needed to reach them. All three of the video series begin with an anatomy lesson, a communication lesson and then move on to hardcore action sequences, indicating a shift from *thinking* about it to *doing* it. The beginning of each anal sex guide film (or two-part series on anal sex, in the cases of Queen and Taormino) serves to *demystify* through information and diagrams. The remaining, longer part of the videos, the sequences of sexual play often culminating in anal penetration, functions as a way to *re-mystify* the act all over again. While it seems paradoxical, the demystification/re-mystification dynamic is present in each of the anal sex guide films discussed here.

While Hartley, Queen and Taormino pioneered anal sex guide films in their assertions that anal sex can be 'for women', not all female porn directors agree on this point. Candida Royalle's well-known project of creating female-centred pornography from 'a woman's perspective' places her work as an oft-cited representation of 'what women want to see'. Her explicit films for women seem to dispel a common, gendered assertion that women's sexual lives exist primarily in our heads, that we need soft-core sex with character development and plot, or at least a narrative-based context for hardcore imagery. For all of her transgression in targeting hardcore imagery to female viewers, much of Candida Royalle's work still indicates a strong adherence to gendered notions of 'what women want', which also inevitably defines what women *do not* want, at the top of that list being anal sex. In Royalle's films, anal sex is still a frontier yet unexplored:

> When I was negotiating with the distributor, the guy says ' … what you need is more anal sex in your movies.' More anal sex? I didn't have any anal sex. 'I know who watches these films,' he says. 'It's the husbands who buy these movies, to show their wives what they want them to do.' I was horrified … Here I am, a woman wanting to make movies from a woman's point of view, and you're telling me to make something that the husband can bring home and talk their wives into doing. I was really appalled, and after that I started my own distribution. (Royalle 2000: 547–8)

Although Royalle is clearly objecting to the idea that her videos are actually for a male audience, she is also hinting at an anal sex myth: that men coerce their partners into anal sex with the assistance of pornography. Ironically, Royalle's words invoke antipornography feminist notions of the coercion of women into sexual activity and into the role of porn performers while defining the women in question as heterosexual (and married). Her quote implies that women are coerced into anal sex, that no woman would choose that act freely.

Films with titles such as 'Guide to Anal Sex' and the bending over of one's boyfriend send a different message from Royalle. Not only can women enjoy porn that reflects their experience (hardcore action included), the films' titles and descriptions insist that being penetrated anally can be a powerfully pleasurable experience, that penetrating a male partner can be fun – and women can be teachers of anal sex to other women and men. These films directly counter Royalle's demarcation of anal sex outside the boundaries of female pleasure while incorporating anal sex in the 'porn for women' discourse.

More Than Sex Ed

The cultural connection between anal sex and HIV has fed into the taboo qualities of anal sex, directly conflating 'abnormal' pleasures with a degenerative infection and heightening the relationship between sex and death: a delight so transgressive it can kill. As though 'gay men's "guilt" were the real agent of infection' (Bersani 1987: 210), HIV and AIDS came to be associated with gay male promiscuity and 'insatiable desire ... unstoppable sex' in the 1980s, leading to a public discourse conclusion that 'homosexuals are killers' (1987: 210–11). Georges Bataille articulates the relationship between taboos as, 'diametrically opposed' since 'death is really the opposite process to the process ending in birth' (1986: 55). Like the culturally inscribed horror at seeing something that is dead or decaying, we react similarly to 'aspects of sensuality we call obscene. The sexual channels are also the body's sewers; we think of them as shameful and connect the anal orifice with them' (Bataille 1986: 57). The perceived link between HIV and anal sex has persisted to the degree that anal sex is mythologized as having caused HIV infection spontaneously.

One unifying similarity surrounding anal sex myths, as presented in the videos' demystification sections, has to do with a sense that anal sex fundamentally changes you, irreparably, at the moment you do it, whether by penetrating or being penetrated. Anal sex fears range from permanent wreckage to your bowels, turning a straight man gay and even spontaneously manufacturing disease. The myth is that, once a person engages in anal sex, s/he will never be able to recover physically or psychologically. Either your body will fall apart from disease and 'misuse' or you will succumb to homosexuality or uncontrollable lust, not unlike the 'domino theory' (or 'slippery slope') of sexuality: that there is a cultural line 'between sexual order and chaos' (Rubin 1984: 282) and taking just one step over the edge is a one-way ticket to sexual heresy (1984: 287).

Addressing anal sex mythology begins the process of demystifying anal sex and replacing its reputation as dangerous, painful and unhealthy with a message of safe methods, pleasurable techniques and prevention of infection and irritation. Part of each film's function in addressing the taboo is simultaneously to open the door to the viewer's own willingness to explore anal sex and also to help maintain the viewer's sense of normalcy, of the acceptance of anal sex as a positive experience.

All three anal sex guide series begin in the same manner: Hartley and Queen each start by speaking to the camera, fully clothed, directly addressing the audience – and dealing with anal sex myths. Both spend a significant portion of screen time dedicated to educating viewers about anal sex, replacing myths with information (usually presented as medical discourse) to help provide a positive context for the sex scenes seen later on in all the films. In Hartley's film, anatomy charts roll out, complete with pointers. Carol Queen's partner, Mike, joins her as co-presenter of anal sex information at the start of *Bend Over Boyfriend* (BOB) and her credential as Dr Queen is emphasized (whereas her books do not typically make mention of this status). BOB also features occasional commentary from a 'naughty nurse' sex educator adding medical guidelines, complete with cleavage-revealing nurse outfit and a gleam in her eye.

Carol Queen's extensive lecture at the start of BOB, nearly epic in its length and concentration of information, makes clear why the second film is titled *Bend Over Boyfriend 2: More Rockin' Less Talkin'*. As promised, BOB2 moves directly into anal sex scenes. Instead of sex education, we meet BOB fans who are waiting in line at a progressive (queer?) bookstore to purchase the first film, just released on DVD, and express their excitement over the release of the film we are watching. As the faux journalist interviews the fans, we learn how BOB has helped them in their sex lives alone and with partners. Fans are often standing in line with someone appearing to be their partner and they muse together about the film's impact on their sexual practices – same-sex and different-sex couples are united in their enthusiasm for the first film and their anticipation of BOB2.

One couple – notably, white, gay and male – comments on how helpful BOB has been to the inclusion of anal sensuality in their relationship. This interview serves as a reminder that anal sex practices do not come 'naturally' but are '*learned* – learned by participating, in scenes of talk as well as in fucking' (Warner 2000: 177). Stereotyping of gay male identity has virtually revolved around anal sex, which has then become a defining feature of being gay (what gay men do and, therefore, who gay men are). For BOB2 to suggest that gay men do not, by definition, practise anal sex, redefines these understandings. Rather than being a particular sexual identity, an activity like anal sex becomes simply a matter of information and practice: armed with the facts and tips offered, anyone can engage in and enjoy anal sex.

Taormino's *Ultimate Guide* films depart from this dynamic. She laments the dearth of available information about anal sex, particularly representations of women enjoying anal sex. In contrast to all the sex books on SM, sex after fifty and phone sex, Taormino found just one volume dedicated to 'fun with the ass': Jack Morin's 1986 book, *Anal Pleasure and Health*. Consequently, she recognizes accessibility as a factor for women's consumption of sexually explicit material, whether called 'porn' or 'sex ed'.

Perhaps as a result of the extensive anatomy lessons and guidelines contained in her book, Taormino spends considerably less time providing a sex ed lesson at the start of her films. *Ultimate Guide* begins with a trip to Ernest Greene's studio. As Taormino walks through the parking lot, she talks about her long-standing wish to create an anal sex film for women. Well known for his successful, commercial anal sex focused porn, Greene ('ButtMan') is a clear choice for partnering to create the *Ultimate Guide* films. He indeed agrees as long as Taormino can get porn star Ruby to accept something in her anus (which she had not to done prior to the scene). Taormino – thoroughly prepared with lube, gloves and toys – walks Ruby through each step, successfully initiates her into anal sex and earns ButtMan's respect. This is the first scene of the film and although Taormino demonstrates her techniques, there is little separation between porn action scenes and anal sex instruction.

Money Shots Reinterpreted: Nina Hartley and Tristan Taormino

Nina Hartley, being the first in the genre of anal sex instructional videos for women, introduces a new form of the money shot, marking her film as porn and yet as different from traditional porn by reworking this cornerstone of porn imagery. Hartley's first action scene is a demonstration of anal relaxation techniques, the importance of lube and communication with her partner in the scene, porn star Anna Malle. As the action builds, Malle tells Hartley to go ahead and 'fuck it' since she's going to have an orgasm. The camera angle that has focused on Hartley's fingers and between Malle's legs suddenly cuts away to focus on Malle's face. We watch her eyes flutter and her smile widening but do not actually see what Hartley, the vibrator or Malle's lower body are doing. If this were still a lesson in technique and anatomy, would not the camera still focus on Malle's anus and crotch during the moment of climax?

First, if the video's intent is to reduce female viewers' anxiety about anal play, the aim might be to reassert that feeling good is the ultimate goal, rather than making sure fingers are properly in or vibrators angled just so. While the video makes it possible for the viewer to mimic the actions of Malle and Hartley, the concern here might be that if a female viewer replicated the scene without reaching orgasm, she might conclude that she is 'doing it wrong'. The message is emphasized by Hartley and Malle's repeated suggestions to take it slow: they point out their professional status and that the same result may not occur at home.

Rather than focusing on a squirting penis, the classic 'money shot', the orgasm's origination is redirected to the face – giving the phrase, 'it's all in your head' new significance in the context of anal sex.[1] Hartley asserts that one's body and mind must be relaxed and 'one's heart must be in it'. Hence the focus on the face during orgasm further reinforces the stated necessity of the heart, the brain and anus working together in concert – each contributing to a full-body pleasure experience. Although the film isolates the anus as a body part with its own personality, attitudes, likes and dislikes, Hartley's how-to opening scene reflects a holistic approach to orgasm, one that goes well beyond the penis and clitoris.

In *Ultimate Guide 2*, Taormino confesses to fantasizing about Ava, a porn performer. Taormino comments to other people on Ava's innocent looks and how enjoyable performing anal sex on her would be. The scene dissolves into Taormino arriving in a private room with Ava already dressed in a skimpy outfit. A fade-in reintroduces Taormino wearing a 'dominant' outfit: a black, shiny zippered dress with military-themed striping on the sleeves. The 'warm up' scene consists of oral sex and the use of sex toys, first on Ava by Taormino. Ava communicates with Taormino about what feels good, when to progress to anal activities (such as the introduction of toys, vibrators and a strap-on dildo), and her orgasm is evident through a series of quick, convulsive movements throughout her body. This appears to be a version of a female 'money shot'. Nowhere in Taormino's videos are there pretty, polite orgasms with women's heads thrashing about and wild screams emitted for the illusion of pleasure. Female orgasm seems to occur nearly without warning but the action does not stop once a woman has an orgasm. Women are seen experiencing multiple orgasms as the sexual act continues.

The amateur filming style of the *Ultimate Guide* series adds to an air of realness and spontaneity. Lighting comes from the natural light sources in the room, the sun when outdoors. The camera shots are bouncy and sometimes unsteady. The first *Ultimate Guide*, in particular, features glitches where the camera does not focus correctly or the light is not exactly right. The camera lens actually steams up during a close-up shot in the first video. All this results in a film with a realistic and personal feel looking more like a home video than a professional production with famous porn stars. The amateur look of the scenes, following Greene's spontaneous film style, works to bring the viewer closer to the experience because it is presented as unstaged and real. This look contributes to the message that the viewer is not so different from the porn star and can experience events depicted in the film. Performers select the toys they want to use and express a preference for performing with a particular colleague: the performers are presented as having a choice and expressing their likes and preferences as people rather than as porn stars.

Taormino further reinforces the individual personalities and preferences of the porn stars by including the performers' own words and shows them talking about what they like to do sexually in their personal lives, separate from their employment. Taormino as the director and 'teacher' talks during the anatomy lessons and technique advice, but so do the porn performers. They contribute their ideas and suggestions and express what they like to do and what feels right for them. This brings the viewer (presumably not a porn performer) and the porn performer closer together, possibly making them seem more alike than the viewer may have previously thought.

One of the key points of Taormino's films is a sense that anal sex takes time and that the receiver of the anal pleasure must be completely engaged in the act and ready for it to happen: 'There's no zero to sixty … not for anyone' (*Ultimate*

Guide). When porn performer Inari Vachs needs more time to warm up to anal sex with porn performer Tony Tedeschi in the threesome scene in the first *Ultimate Guide*, she stops and asks for more warm up and lubricant. When her body does not cooperate, she requests more time and her requests are honoured on screen. This reinforces the ability of women to control what happens to their bodies and to express their needs both during anal sex and within a pornographic film.

It is not easy for all performers to perform anal sex in front of the camera. Some have trouble with the toys, some experience difficulty or pain and some others cannot graduate to larger objects, but there is no pressure to continue the scenes. Performers communicate, adjust and accommodate. The viewer is left with the impression that this was made not just with the viewer's pleasure in mind but also that of the performer. Usually edited out of other pornographic films, the 'oops' scenes remind the viewer that performers have difficulties, even if the editing process removes the evidence of their fallible bodies in other films. Through the intentional inclusion of performers' occasional difficulties, the film further disputes assumptions that anal sex, indeed any sort of sexual act, 'comes naturally' to anyone.

By asking performers what is right for them sexually, Taormino also continues the educational or guiding theme alongside hardcore action throughout her films. This can be seen as implicitly assigned 'get to know your body' homework in preparation for the viewer's own anal sex experiments. In addition to information about anal sex, the videos guide viewers in how to begin exploring her own body and communicate their wants and needs with a sexual partner.

Anal Sex As Gender Equalizer: Bend Over Boyfriend

In *Bend Over Boyfriend*, Queen includes heterosexual couples watching her film as representative of the 'normal, everyday' people who may be strapping on dildos and penetrating butts. They seem to be there to reassure any straight couples holding the remote control that they are 'just like us', thereby making strap-on sex more accessible to straight audiences. At first glance, these films may seem like 'couples videos' that attempt to set themselves apart from hardcore pornography. However, one of the key markers of the couples' how-to videos is a reinforcement of morality. Couples videos often distinguish themselves from pornography and imply that sex in a committed relationship is the best kind of sex:

> Sex education videos for couples also illustrate the complicated position that domesticated porn occupies: they sometimes use excerpts from hardcore porn in order to emphasize the importance of female orgasm through clitoral stimulation, yet they usually legitimize the images through their emphasis on a better partnership, often referring to marriage and monogamy. (Juffer 1998: 7)

Could a video dedicated to different-sex couples engaging in such gender-bending acts as penetrating a man's anus with a strap-on dildo be a reinforcement of 'marriage and monogamy'? According to Heather Butler, 'although Carol Queen explicitly states at the beginning of the film [BOB] that this video lends itself to people of any sexual preference, it is indeed a video addressed to heterosexual couples' (Butler 2004: 189). Butler also notes that the film, made by lesbians, displaces the male phallus with sex toys and serves as an example of 'lesbians instructing heterosexuals on new ways of sexual expression' (Butler 2004: 191).

Despite addressing heterosexual couples, there is no message here about improving a relationship (except, like Taormino's films, the emphasis on the need for trust and communication, which is instructive about talk during sex rather than relationship-building) or use of terms such as 'husband' or 'wife' during anal play. This film (and BOB2 as well) is a how-to guide about women penetrating men, about the anus as the equalizer. Because the anus is neither unique to men nor unique to women (but shared by all), the eroticization of the anus creates a new playground for women partnered with men. The penetrated male anus – a pleasure associated with gay male sexuality – becomes incorporated in a 'straight' sexual diet. While I agree with Butler that the film does focus on heterosexual couples and is seemingly intended as such, I see the films as transgressive in terms of gender and normative understandings of 'normal' heterosexuality.

Demystify/Re-mystify

After the information session at the beginning of each of the film series discussed in this chapter, the subsequent *re*-mystification serves to entice the viewer to try anal sex. Nina Hartley states at the start of her film that the goal is 'anal eroticism', rather than anal penetration. The attempt to take the focus off anal penetration, however, also allows it to remain the ultimate taboo act and threshold reached during the course of all five of the films. Information serves to demystify anal penetration and to redefine it as pleasurable, safe and fun, counter to myths of dirtiness, remoteness and unpleasantness. The double movement of demystification and re-mystification helps to make anal sex acts accessible while still retaining some of their transgressive quality.

The implication is that one can experiment with anal sensuality, or 'go all the way' with anal penetration. In fact, the timeline of the films' release reflects this: after one has learned some basics from Hartley, s/he can try out male receptive anal sex (BOB) and if s/he has already done that, s/he can try enemas or group sex with dildos (Taormino). With each film come new sexual frontiers, allowing the female viewer to determine her level of adventurousness. Whatever form of anal sex the video may show, there is always the implied next level: trying anal play allows one to 'graduate' to full anal penetration and go further by switching positions and roles, using toys or introducing new partners. In a way, all three of the series signify that ultimate sign of anal sex mastery: making an anal sex how-to video.

It is worth noting that while the films include anal penetration of some variety, none of the series features male–male penetration. Consequently, male-on-male penetration is relegated to the realm of gay male pornography and it remains the invisible 'ultimate' form of anal sex – but also the one most rife with myths (anal sex 'makes you gay'; anal sex 'causes' HIV; anal sex is 'unnatural'). In fact, the only identifiable men who have sex with men are the two we see in BOB2, standing in line to buy BOB on DVD. Male-on-male sex is not included as something that women of any sexual identity would enjoy, nor as something a man partnered with a woman would be interested in seeing as part of their anal sex education. This distance, while it helps to destigmatize anal sex among women as penetrators and penetratees (as well as their male partners' interest in the same), privileges heterosexual couplings (particularly in Hartley's and Queen's films) and reduces women's same-sex anal play to fun frolicking. Anal sex remains a fun add-on to sex life that does not necessitate a re-evaluation of one's sexual identity.

Another notable omission is that of excrement. Although 'blooper' scenes seem to be all part of the fun as performers adjust and reinsert, the anuses are tidy and free from crap. The first *Ultimate Guide* film includes an enema scene in a bathtub, where the virtues of enemas are described and the intense feelings of being 'full' are articulated, with a doctor-like male figure there to supervise the woman receiving the enema. When asked what happens when the enema bottle is removed, the forceful exit of water and excrement is explained – but absolutely not shown. When the woman is ready for the enema bag to be removed, the shot fades to black and this viewer wonders if the expulsion was filmed and then edited out later. Although the pleasures of receiving the enema are included, the entire process is not included as visually pleasurable, keeping excrement completely out of view for all five films. Despite the myth-busting rhetoric (and qualities) of the films, there are some taboos left intact: indeed, left alone.

Pornography and Transgression As Cultural Mirror

Exploring the three film series and investigating their dynamics and the blurring of sex ed with pornography, where does this leave us? First, having control over one's own sexual imagery is a powerful way to claim one's own body and sexuality. If women create their own pornography, facilitate access to that pornography as well as expand the sexual landscape for other women (by making porn into a teaching tool), the potential for greater sexual power and expression is increased.

These films do not seem to normalize anal sex but simultaneously to make anal sex and porn more accessible and to keep it hot. Sex ed material has, historically, sought to educate about the birds and the bees but is usually heavily invested in the 'right kind of sex' and presented in a sanitized way, relying on biological information rather than successful and pleasurable technique. These films straddle the boundaries of sex ed and porn, blurring their distinctions. Marketing the films as 'how-to' can make them more accessible to women, a non-traditional porn audience. Rather than a statement about their content, the how-to label serves to reduce potential stigma by presenting images in an educational context, even if the content is as hardcore as any porn film with no specified educational goals. Although they knowingly make use the stigma of anal sex they seek to reduce, these films by Nina Harley, Carol Queen and Tristan Taormino transform learning into yearning.

Videos

Bend Over Boyfriend: A Couple's Guide to Male Anal Pleasure (1998), dir. Shar Rednour. With Carol Queen and Robert Morgan. Fatale Video.

Bend Over Boyfriend 2: More Rockin' Less Talkin' (1999), dirs Shar Rednour and Jackie Strano. With Carol Queen and Chloe. S.I.R. Productions.

Nina Hartley's Guide to Anal Sex (1998), dir. Adam and Eve Productions. With Nina Hartley, Anna Malle, John Decker, Hank Armstrong. Adam and Eve Productions.

The Ultimate Guide to Anal Sex for Women (2000), dirs Tristan Taormino and Ernest Greene. With Tony Tedeschi, Kyle Stone, Nacho Vidal, Chloe, Ruby, Inari Vachs, Nina Hartley, Sydnee Steele, Jewel Valmont, Chandler, Jazmine. Evil Angel.

The Ultimate Guide to Anal Sex for Women 2 (2001), dirs Tristan Taormino and Ernest Greene. With Jewell Marceau, Kate Frost, Ava Vincent, Lola, Bridgette Kerkove, Jewel De'Nyle, Joel Lawrence, Mr. Marcus, Mickey G. Evil Angel.

–13–

Epilogue: Porn Futures

Susanna Paasonen

The proliferation of alternative, independent, queer, artistic and amateur pornographies on the Internet has given subcultural products and tastes unprecedented visibility. From the activists collecting funds for the preservation of tropical forests with the 'Fuck for Forest' project (Fig. 13.1) to the naturally hairy graces of 'Hippie Goddesses', the tattooed and pierced post-punk models of alt porn sites, hot grannies and image galleries on (virtually all kinds of) shoe fetishism, online pornography has captivated the attention of Internet users, journalists and researchers alike. Such sites do indeed support Michael Warner's (2000: 185) view of porn as possibly enabling 'unpredicted forms of experience', surprises and discoveries that work to broaden one's understanding of sexuality and desire beyond preconceived identities, labels and categories (also Chun 2006: 104–6; McLelland 2006; Mowlabocus in this volume).

Alt porn (also referred to as 'alternative', 'indie' and 'alt.porn'), a term coined as a means of differentiation from mainstream commercial porn, has become a well-recognized category for pornography featuring subcultural styles – most notably tattoos, piercings, punk and Goth coiffures on sites produced in the USA. Compared to so-called mainstream porn, alt porn models are mostly non- or semi-professionals (in the sense of coming from outside the industry) lacking in silicone implants and other standard porn star enhancements. The sites insist on the authenticity of their model biographies and interviews as well as the centrality of community building – in terms of music, lifestyle and attitude – for their principles of operation (Mies 2006). In addition to post-punk influenced styles, a variety of non-mainstream pornographies are distributed online from fat porn to BDSM. Independent porn producers (not necessarily but possibly producing alternative porn) are making use of the Web as a publishing platform and hence questioning the forms and limits of porn as an industry (Tola 2005). All in all, the increasing specialization of porn sites catering to particular sexual preferences, fetishes and niches is a trend recognizable even on the level of governmental reports (Thornburgh and Lin 2002: 82–3; also Lane 2001: 223–7). Independent, artistic and amateur productions have been invested with possibilities of redefining the conventions of sexually explicit representation outside the confines of mainstream

Figure 13.1 Porn as activism: Fuck for Forest. Image courtesy of FFF.

porn marketed in print and on video, and diversifying the available economies of desire. To the degree that new media in general is seen as indicative of things to come, future pornographies have been seen as diverse, alternative and distributed on the Internet (e.g. Jacobs 2004b; Patterson 2004; Villarejo 2004; Halavais 2005; Dery 2006).

In his studies of Usenet amateur alt.fetish groups, Sergio Messina (2005) has coined the term *realcore* to describe their displays of sexual acts and desires. Separating digital amateur photography (as featured and distributed on Usenet) from the familiar concepts of hardcore and soft-core, Messina argues for the real-ness of the performers, settings and events depicted. Distributed mostly for free, realcore is a gift economy for various highly specialized interest groups, published without the aim of financial gain (cf. Jacobs 2004b). Unlike websites identified as personal projects of individual amateur women but actually run by far less amateur companies, Usenet porn seems to offer more than a fantasy of amateur sexual self-expression (Lane 2001: 209–12). Porn exchange economies have been equally active in peer-to-peer (P2P) networks, although these practices have also been heavily regulated. Katrien Jacobs identifies P2P practices in general as ones having the potential to challenge the normative codes of porn as well as the divisions separating porn performers from their audiences (Tola 2005). Furthermore, sexual experimentation and more or less playful interaction online – via chat, instant messaging, web cameras, etc. – similarly enable novel kinds of sexual experiences and relationships in which one is simultaneously performer and audience, and which stretch the notions of sex and sexual acts (Attwood 2006: 79–81). Doing this, they also stretch the notion of the pornographic. Porn may provide templates for expressing arousal, desire and pleasure in cybersexual exchanges, and the ensuing messages and chat logs can be identified as pornographic: in this sense they are exemplary of the blurred boundaries between porn and sexual self-expression. However, to the degree that porn is not only an aesthetic category but also one denoting a certain logic of capitalism and commodification, non-material exchanges seem to slip from its confines.

All in all, the categories of amateur and professional, alternative and mainstream, non-commercial and commercial are hardly self-explanatory when discussing online pornographies. Alternative pornographies have – from kink sites to subcultural pornographies – fed back to the imageries of commercial pornography that they seem to subvert. If independent porn productions appropriate poses and elements from mainstream porn while abandoning or disregarding others, this is also the case vice versa. The notion of the mainstream is porous and contingent. New categories and sub-genres are introduced and mainstreamed and they undergo transformations in the process. Transgender porn – known as 'she-male' or 'chicks with dicks' – is one example of a sub-genre shifting from the margins of porn towards its mainstream. Produced in South America (Brazil) and South East Asia (Thailand), she-male pornography used to be consumed by highly specialized niche audiences whereas in the 2000s it has become mainstreamed to the degree of being a key category (along with straight, gay and SM) in the online video service of the largest Finnish adult portal, Seksi.net. She-male porn, as featured on sites such as 'Tranny Ranch' or 'Tranny Surprise', remains a specialized genre and in this sense also an 'alternative' one. The degree of commodification at play, however, suggests it having a far less alternative position. The increased popularity of *hentai*, pornographic Japanese anime, is another example of such oscillation. Considered too extreme for video distribution in the 1990s, hentai – featuring BDSM and non-consensual sex involving alien/demon tentacle-penises – has become part of the diet of mainstream porn websites as a 'taste, genre, or preference' presented to wide audiences (Dahlquist and Vigilant 2004: 93). In sum, it seems that the body of 'mainstream porn' leaks towards niches and paraphilias, incorporates them and becomes transformed in the process – no matter how gradual or slow such transformations may be.

There is little doubt as to the Internet contributing to the politics of visibility of various sexual tastes, the diversification of porn imageries and understandings of the very concept of pornography. As Ginny Mies (2006) points out, alt porn sites are 'known for countering the porn industry's images, ethics, and business practices', yet the category of alternative has also become to signify the aesthetic rather than the economical or the ethical. As alt porn became business, 'SuicideGirls', one of the most successful alt porn sites launched in 2001, was repositioned as a point of reference that radical and queer porn sites use for marking themselves apart (Mies 2006; also Cramer 2006).

Porn in Media New and Old

Novel distribution possibilities have facilitated the creation of a conceptual chasm separating online porn from other kinds of pornographies, following the familiar divisions of new and old media. In such formulations, the digital format of pornographic images, texts and videos, as well as the distribution and interaction possibilities of information networks, mark a clear departure from older pornographies, their aesthetics and consumption practices. Anna Reading (2005: 125–6), for example, sees the increased accessibility of porn, along with the anonymity of its online use, as reconfiguring articulations of sexuality within and between private and public spaces. The success of online porn has increased the range of available pornographies while also enabling exchanges between performers and users (even to the degree that these are blurred, as suggested above). In addition to image galleries and videos, alt porn sites such as 'DeviantNation' or 'SuicideGirls' include journals and blogs by the models introducing users to their thoughts and ideas, rather than just sights of their bodies (Epley in this volume). Amateur erotica writers can publish their stories on sites with massive story archives and receive feedback from readers and other authors and, if they so desire, provide self-made illustrations for their texts. Before registering as a member of a pay site, users can familiarize themselves with free introductory materials, or search for content evaluations published by those who are already members.

The general division of new and old media has been specified with a conceptual division separating 'netporn' (or net.porn) from 'porn on the Net': netporn refers to pornographic specific to the Internet – including peer-to-peer porn, realcore and alt porn – and the latter to the recycling of pornographic images and texts from print media, video and film, on the Internet (Shah 2005).[1] Defined in this vein, netporn refers to media specificity, the ways in which online technologies restructure the pornographic impossible in other media. However, it also risks creating a hierarchy between netporn (as networked, interactive, novel, intellectually and aesthetically challenging) and porn on the Net (as representative of the logic of the same, commercial, predictable and dull) that renders the latter as a secondary concern in studies of the Internet. Such a media-specific framework accommodates only certain examples of online porn, foreclosing many and leaving yet others in a liminal category of the in-between.

Importantly, the division of netporn and other kinds of porn disables analyses of pornography's fundamentally intermedial nature. Print magazines have been marketed with free bonus VHS tapes and DVDs since the 1980s; video and print publishing companies have branched out to online markets; online distribution has led to DVD production; the same companies are involved in the production of websites, mobile entertainment and digital television channels; the same images are recycled in print and electronic formats while old porn films make their comeback as collector DVD editions. Pornographic texts and products transgress the boundaries of individual media, and content is recycled from one platform to another.[2] In other words, a clear-cut division of 'old' and 'new', 'offline' and 'online' pornography is ultimately simplifying in terms of porn economy and representational conventions alike. In a media historical perspective, the question could be phrased as one of both continuity and change.

In Alan McKee's (2005: 277) empirical study on the use of pornography in Australia, over 63 per cent of respondents used DVDs to view pornography, in comparison to 42 per cent accessing porn online. Less than 6 per cent of McKee's respondents were members of pay sites that tend to feature 'non-mainstream' or high production value materials. The question of membership fees and quality in online porn is, however, more complex than this reference implies: niche pornographies are widely published for free on both Usenet and the Web while much visited free sites may also be representative of anti-normative, premium content (McLelland 2006). Nevertheless, McKee points out two important things: that the Internet is not automatically the most popular of contemporary distribution forms, and that addressing and defining online porn through the more artistic and experimental examples may lead to myopia towards the continuing dominance of mainstream, commercial heteroporn. As conceptually and aesthetically interesting as alt pornographies are, they should not be conceptualized as the norm when considering online or future pornography. A visit to the site 'PornFuture.com' would suggest that the porn of tomorrow looks fairly much like that of yesterday: with blonde feminine female performers, promises of hardcore videos, amateurs, teens, blow-jobs, 'pussy shots', XXX action and the requirement of a membership fee.

Internet: The Empire of Smut?

Media technologies function as a horizon of possibilities that condition available forms of expression, interaction and circulation. Yet pornography is also extremely slow to change in terms of its generic conventions that travel from one medium to another. Porn futures are not altogether novel but echo past decades, familiar poses, styles and looks. The Internet has been heralded as a realm of possibilities in terms of small-scale productions that can gain as much attention and popularity as ones backed up by heavy corporate machinery (Lane 2001: 140–3). While the publication of numerous 'how-to' books on adult site publishing and quick financial gain might suggest otherwise, the position of small companies and independent producers is not necessarily easy. Well-established adult entertainment companies have bought alt porn sites and small companies continue to struggle with their distribution and finance. My conversation with a Finnish adult site producer points to a centralization, rather than diversification, of the porn industry in terms of companies in operation (see also Thornburgh and Lin 2002: 79).[3] Within the European Union, legislative differences between the different countries have obvious benefits for porn distribution as contents unacceptable in one country can be uploaded to a server located in another one. International networking and centralization of ownership has increased with both digitization and the expansion of the EU. Venture capital pays an active role in the porn economy and large international companies own shares of smaller ones. European porn distribution is both internationally networked and somewhat centralized – and the dominance of large companies is equally evident in the United States (Esch and Mayer in this volume).

There has been convergence for decades in the production and distribution of print and video porn. Portals, mobile services, image galleries, chat services and DVDs merely represent newer stages of the development. Nevertheless, it is the Internet (even more so than video) that has been associated with pornography in both public debates and journalism. Porn has been seen as integral to the development of the Internet as a commercial medium and even as its driving force (O'Toole 1998: 285). The Internet has been envisioned as saturated with smut and populated by porn addicts at least since the notorious 1995 *Times* article that liberally categorized 83.5 per cent of all photographs online as pornographic (see Chun 2006: 77–80). The availability – real or imagined – of pornographic content has given rise to various moral panics, most of which concern children's access to porn and possibilities of paedophile networking. Filtering software and age verification systems have developed in synch with local regulation practices in Europe, North America, Asia and Australia (White 2006: 20–2) and efforts such as the Bush administration's 'war against pornography' in the United States. Filtering software makes little differentiation between hardcore porn, sex education and information resources for sexual minorities (equally filtering all) while Internet regulation in countries such as China, Singapore or Iran concerns political discussions as much as displays of sexuality.

The vocal, insistent linking of porn and the Internet has also worked to feed user interest towards online pornographies: if the Web is assumed to be awash with pornography, it makes sense to make use of it for accessing porn. Pornography takes take up a considerable amount of bandwidth in web traffic due to the use of images and video (Thornburgh and Lin 2002: 72–3; Perdue 2002: 33–5). Nevertheless, the volume of so-called adult material in terms of active websites as a whole has been decreasing since the mid-1990s – in spite of impressions created by public exclamations and ungrounded arguments on the mass of pornographic material on the Internet. While new porn sites are launched with vigour, existing ones are closed down and bought up. Web searches for sex and pornography have, according to a recent study by Amanda Spinks, Helen Partridge and Bernard J. Hansen (2006), decreased from 16.8 per cent of all searches in 1997 to 3.8 per cent in 2005. Out of the approximately 100 million sites currently available, an estimated 1.5 to 5 per cent are pornographic – although some sources, including ones associated with filtering software and conservative Christian groups in the US, offer numbers as high as 12 per cent or 260 million pages. Since such inflated figures are enthusiastically circulated and presented as statistical facts, they are also referenced as objective findings in overviews on online pornography.[4] Internet porn is financially profitable and plentiful, yet hardly as ubiquitous as public discourses and moral panics would suggest.

As the lack of reliable statistical information on the uses of porn, the amount of pornographic sites or the total volume of the porn industry on a global scale makes evident, discussions on pornography and its role in media culture continue to be marked by assumptions, ideological and political interests rather than empirical knowledge. Pornography has been politicized for the past three decades in various ways by religious groups (be these Christian, Muslim or other), queer, anti- and anti-antipornography feminist activists, freedom of speech lobbyists, moral conservatives and various parties speaking in the name of children: for some, porn represents a moral dilemma and a symbol of unacceptability while others identify porn with individual and collective self-expression and radical transformative potential. In both instances, porn comes to stand for certain values and is tied to certain political aims and goals. Search engines routinely exclude pornography from their published listings of the most popular search terms while scholarly overviews on media economy or media history pay equally little attention to porn. This aversion towards porn owes perhaps to the history of its politicization – the implication being that this is a topic best avoided. Consequently, online pornography seems to be simultaneously everywhere and nowhere to be seen, ubiquitous and a public secret.

Forms and volumes of available pornography have increased with the Internet while soft-core aesthetics are enthusiastically recycled in the imageries of popular culture across a wide range of media. The diversity of specialized images, videos and texts categorizable as pornographic calls for analytical reconsiderations of the category in question – as in the case of 'balloon people' (enjoying confinement in large rubber/plastic balloons), velvet or sneaker enthusiasts addressed by Messina. It is increasingly difficult and problematic to pin down the meanings of 'pornography' as a point of reference, be this in terms of aesthetics or gender politics.

Meanwhile, porn debates remain dangerously simplified in their accounts of the meanings of pornography.

Problems with Generalization

Diagnostic texts on the role of pornography in contemporary culture, such as Pamela Paul's *Pornified* (2005), hint at ever-pornified futures in which hardcore porn is increasingly accessible and porno chic a naturalized component of popular media culture. As important as such diagnoses are in stirring public debate on contemporary culture and politics, they tend to be marked by a level of simplification that renders them ineffective in tackling the nuances involved. Paul references a 'major study' according to which 'with each iteration in technological advancement, pornography has become increasingly violent and nonconsensual' (2005: 58). This reference would seem to imply that, according to authoritative research, technological development feeds violent pornography and that the more advanced the technology, the more violent and non-consensual the pornography is bound to be. Doing so, it frames developments in both technology and pornography in definitive and deterministic terms.

The study in question is Martin Barron and Michael Kimmel's 2000 article comparing violent pornography in porn magazines, videos and Usenet (with fifty examples from all three platforms). According to Paul, Barron and Kimmel concluded that 'as new pornographies technologies emerged, pornography would become increasingly violent' (2005: 59). The authors, however, rebuke such explanation as partial while arguing for more contextual and content-based analyses (Barron and Kimmel 2000: 165–6). Barron and Kimmel did indeed find out that violent and non-consensual content had increased from print to Usenet (the increase between magazines and videos not being considerable). Magazines and videos depicted women more often than men as the victimizers and violence as consensual, while the case was the contrary in Usenet stories. Barron and Kimmel (2000: 166–7) explain the rise in violent content with the specific features of Usenet as a non-commercial homosocial forum where competition over the raunchiest of stories results in the reproduction of hegemonic masculinity. In this context, the non-consensual nature of the stories is a product of specific social practices and technical platforms. Usenet is historically and economically a different kind of publishing forum than the Web. Hence analysis of one Usenet group says little of online pornography as a whole.

Such considerations are effaced in Paul's reading through intentionally partial referencing. *Pornified* isolates violent oral sex and bukkake (a Japanese genre in which men ejaculate on a person, usually female, *en masse*, often in scenarios depicted as non-consensual and humiliating) as forms of online porn consumed by her (straight male) informant – and as examples of online porn in general. Scenes of women drinking semen ejaculated into their anuses by groups of men, as well as simulations of 'vivid rape and murder scenes of women' are again argued not to differ 'substantially' from more mainstream porn on the Web (Paul 2005: 61, 239–40). Porn sites may be rife with the terminology of 'cum-drinking sluts' used to spice up standard videos and images (Kangasvuo in this volume) but this hardly makes extreme scenarios the norm. Paul detaches her perspective from antiporn stances yet seems to draw on their legacy in choosing random, de-contextualized and extreme examples of violent pornography as representative of porn, as has been done by antiporn authors since the 1970s (Paasonen 2007b: 48–9). Such logic invests virtually any isolated example of pornographic material with metonymic abilities that again enable knowledge over pornography as an assumedly singular entity. The creation of this kind of knowledge seems difficult to resist.

As this example illustrates, the polarized legacy of the sex wars continues to obstruct analysis of the forms and meanings of pornography while the lack of reliable data helps to render the discussion into one based on assumptions and preconceived attitudes. Also, 'Ongoing debates about pornography and its place in society tend to hear mostly from those commentators whose expertise is based on not being familiar with the genre' (McKee 2006: 534). All this contributes to an inability to grasp transformations in displays of sex and sexuality, or their meanings in terms of contemporary culture. The US-centrism of porn debates creates a problem of its own: not only have the lines of battle for and against pornography been largely drawn and contemporary analyses of pornification written in the United States, but studies and theorizations of porn carried out elsewhere also tend to be read in their terms. Independent of the local debates and historics through which authors enter porn discussions, their contributions are easily rendered into ones of either for or against, and understood in relation to the political investments of North American debates. What is needed is both a step away from the polarized logic of debate and increased attention towards differences in local contexts, debates and regulatory practices – and, consequently, the variety of issues that have become discussed under such umbrella terms as pornography and pornification.

Future Pornographies, Porn Futures

The title of this concluding chapter can be interpreted in various ways, as pointing to the future of pornography, future forms of porn or futures marked by porn (in the sense of 'pornified tomorrows'). Independent of which approach or meaning one chooses, porn futures need to be through of as plural. Pornography should not be approached as a singular entity, nor should pornification be seen as a definite process with obvious symptoms and outcomes. It is easy to agree with Rick Poynor's (2006: 136) diagnosis that future displays of sexuality are likely to draw on pornography as a kind of cultural reservoir for sexual imageries (to the degree that they have become *the* reservoir to draw on) and that such displays are not likely to decrease. The likeliness of continuous proliferation of not only pornographic imageries but also ones blurring the boundaries of porn and mainstream media does not, however, mean that the process will result in an avoidable logic of the same involving only the most generic and heterosexist of texts.

As the individual contributions in this book point out, we need to remain dedicated to contextualization, sensitive to histories, aesthetics, discourses, contexts of production, distribution and consumption when conceptualizing a text or a phenomenon in terms of pornification. This does not translate as relativism but as situated knowledge, answerability of the claims one makes over contemporary culture as well as awareness of their inevitable partiality (cf. Haraway 1991: 188–90). The concept of pornification does not explain anything as such. It should be understood as an analytical tool for figuring out transformations in the cultural status and visibility of different pornographies and aesthetics in a social and historical context, not for conflating the increased accessibility of hardcore pornography and the ubiquity of various kinds of soft-core aesthetics into a single, undifferentiated master narrative. Such a narrative will be effective in blocking views of alternative futures – pornographic and other – that one might actually want to advance.

Notes

1 Introduction: Pornification and the Education of Desire

1. The role of pornography in the schooling of desire tends to be discussed mainly in the context of minors – a theme not addressed in this volume but abundantly discussed elsewhere (for an overview, see Heins 2001). Due to its increased availability, porn has become the most influential form of sex education (Mason-Grant 2004: 148). Public debates and moral panics have largely revolved around children being (involuntarily) exposed to porn online whereas less attention has been paid on the obvious fact that children and teenagers actively search for porn as they did porn magazines and videos during the earlier decades. Porn is a tool of 'sex ed' – and peer sex ed in the sense that it is circulated among minors. To the degree that it is effaced from official forms of sex education, porn retains its pedagogic function in demonstrating sexual acts and positions in vivid detail. Hence the generic specificity of porn is effaced and porn comes to stand for sex.

2 The Golden Age of Porn: Nostalgia and History in Cinema

1. E.g. *Wadd: The Life and Times of John C. Holmes* (USA 1998), *Desperately Seeking Seka* (Sweden 2002); *Debbie Does Dallas Uncovered* (UK 2005); McNeil and Osborne 2005.
2. The story of John Holmes, again, has been recounted in the documentary film *Wadd* (1998), as well as the feature film *Wonderland* (2002) focusing on his extra-pornographic adventures.
3. The films almost seem to follow a certain 'Aristotelian' logic. According to Aristotle, the tragic hero facilitates reader experiences of pity, joy, fear and finally the relief of catharsis. In tragedy, a hero with a modest background faces success followed by difficulties and destruction hastened by *hamartia,* his mistakes, bad choices and excesses. After the enemy has made the final attack and the hero has fallen, the audience forgives and awards the hero.
4. In *Boogie Nights*, the New Year's Eve party of 1980 ends in a murder-suicide and marks a change in the overall tone of the film. 'The Party's Over' is the

title of a section discussing the years 1984–87 in the oral porn history of McNeil and Osborne (2005). The party also ends in the films *54* and *The Last Days of Disco.*

5. The 1970s is hardly the only decade idealized in American popular culture, and nostalgic turns have been identified in Western societies since the industrial revolution (Grainge 2000, 28; Lowenthal 1986; Turner 1987). Each epoch seems to have exhibited – and bemoaned – their own variations of nostalgia, and these have in their part been objects of constant critique. Nostalgia has been dismissed on the grounds of commercialization, superficiality, vulgarity and the promotion of conservative values and, as David Lowenthal (1986: 27–30) argues, critiques of nostalgia are as recurrent a discourse as nostalgia itself. In this sense, the notion (or accusation) of nostalgia does not have much analytical power as such.

6. Veteran director Jim Holliday states in his review of the DVD release of *Opening of Misty Beethoven* that the film's uniqueness is partially due to the gay sex scene nowadays completely missing from heteroporn.

7. The reviews were published in the Finnish 'populist-elitist' film magazine *Elitisti* (http://www.elitisti.net) and film enthusiast magazine *Film-O-Holic* (http://www.film-o-holic-com).

8. In Lukas Moodysson's film *A Hole in my Heart* (Sweden 2004), shooting porn in a suburban apartment is used as an allegory for contemporary estrangement. Similar theme occurs in Michael Turner's novel *The Pornographer's Poem* (2004) remembering the 1970s.

3 Let Me Tell Ya 'Bout Black Chicks: Interracial Desire and Black Women in 1980s Video Pornography

1. I use the terms 'pornography' and 'hardcore' together and interchangeably in this text to denote the production of sexually explicit media by the 'adult entertainment industry' (professional or corporate and professional-amateur or 'pro-am' producers, distributors, and retailers). The distinction between 'erotica' and 'pornography' is highly subjective and contested. Many pornography producers and performers prefer the term 'adult entertainment' to pornography, as it is less stigmatized by a tradition of state and social regulation. 'Hardcore' refers to pornography that graphically highlights penetrative sex acts, aroused genitalia and often external ejaculation, while 'soft-core' is viewed as sexually suggestive media that presents nudity and/or simulated sex. In this essay, I focus specifically on hardcore videos produced during the 1980s; however, I discuss black women performers in soft-core pornography in my larger project. Estimates of the adult industry's value in the United States have been widely contested, assumed number of between 9–14 billion

dollars a year. The most common figure used is 10 billion dollars a year. See O'Toole (1999: 104) and Rich (2001).

2. On the transgressive politics of pornography see Kipnis (1999).

3. On black women's sexuality, see Davis (1971); Giddings (1984); Jones (1985); Collins (2004).

4. VCRs were invented in the 1950s, but VHS really came on the market in 1971, remaining a specialized technology until the early 1980s.

5. On stereotypes of African Americans such as the 'coon' or 'stud' see: Smith (2003) and Bogle (1992).

6. See Gray (2004) and Acham (2004).

7. Bill Margold. (2002), Personal interview. Los Angeles. December.

8. On stag films. see Williams (1999); Thomas Waugh, (2001), 'Homosociality in Classic American Stag Films: Off-Screen, On-Screen,' *Sexualities* 4(3): 275–291.

9. According to Mark Kernes (2004), editor at *AVN*, manufacturers lacked the technical skill and experience in making adult videos, resulting in thousands of poor quality videos flooding the market.

10. I would like to thank private collector 'VideoSan' for obtaining a rare copy *Black Chicks* for me.

11. Sapphire is a trope for aggressive, stubborn and bitchified black women, a stereotype developed during the Depression era and made popular in the *Amos 'n Andy* radio show, television show, cartoon and films.

4 Pin-ups, Retro Chic and the Consumption of Irony

1. In contrast to the long-time disappearance of pin-ups in the States, the British Page-Three girl achieved, during the same period, the status of a proud national tradition. Outside the US, the classic pin-up has also been perceived as part of, or even symbolic of, American cultural hegemony. In his 1946 essay, Andre Bazin characterized the pin-up as 'Rapidly perfected, like the jeep, among those things specifically stipulated for modern American military sociology, she is a perfectly harmonized product of given racial, geographical, social, and religious influences... . Manufactured on the assembly line, standardized by Varga, sterilized by censorship' (Bazin 1971: 158, 161).

2. At one point an artist was hired to paint new backgrounds onto some of Elvgren's pin-ups so they could be republished as new (Martignette and Meisel 1996: 162).

3. Notably, Taschen's list includes popular books on Betty Page and the photography of James LaChapelle, who shot many of the Skyy Vodka ads.

4. So-called 'alternative' subcultures are today more than just 'related', they are better described as 'allied'. Celebrations of 'fetish' culture, for instance,

unites a wide range of subcultural practices, including goth, paganism, BDSM, leatherfolk, fashion, and a lot of work self-identified as 'pin-ups'. Interesting articulations between fetish and pin-ups include Zombiepin-ups.com and the very popular work of Dita Von Teese (Dita.net), not to mention Bettie Page's bondage modelling for Irving and Paula Klaw. Membership of these multiple subcultures overlaps, of course, but the different fetish subcultures also actively support the practices of other groups even as members are anxious to distinguish their own particular subcultural practices. Retro culture is similarly organized as a set of allied and overlapping subcultures whose members may self-identify quite differently. Consider, for instance, RetroKitten.com, which promotes itself as 'a networking tool for models, photographers, artists and performers working in alternative genres (pin-up, gothic. rockabilly, punk and retro)'.

5. As Buszek chronicles, feminist visual artists have, since the seventies, riffed off pin-up iconography in order to destabilize its common-sense sexism.

6. This ideal of empowerment, according to some reports, is more mythos than ethos. Suicide Girls contracts with models give them little control and no ownership of their images and some blog posts have been censored. A number of models have angrily left the site over these and other labour issues, and several have bitterly attacked the site's pro-women marketing as hypocritical (Koht 2005).

7. Despite its having been taken up by a few niche-marketed features – such as the high-end 'shot on film' videos directed by Andrew Blake (See Andrewblake.com) and the Vivid Alt line (see vividalt.com), classic pin-up iconography does not seem to be a trend in American pornography more generally.

8. The links page of HotPunkGirl.com lists almost 100 sites devoted to 'atypically gorgeous and attitude-driven divas of the underground'. The page does not link to Suicidegirls.com. http://hotpunkgirl.com/links.html, accessed 5 June 2006.

9. Bourdieu develops the concept of habitus throughout his work, but I draw in this section specifically on some of his later essays in *Practical Reason: On the Theory of Action* (1998).

10. 'Class', in this model, is not 'class' in Marx's sense of 'a group mobilized for common purposes and especially against another class'. At the same time, Bourdieu insists that these theoretical unities are more predisposed to *become* classes in the Marxist sense than other theoretical divisions of agents. While the unity of a Bourdieuian class fraction in social space by no means engenders unity automatically, it does define 'an objective potentiality of unity … a *probable class'* (Bourdieu 1998: 11).

11. John Leland, throughout his *Hip: The History,* provocatively explores how American hipness ignites in the frisson between blackness and whiteness. As

he also suggests, queer culture – gay men in particular – have always been a driving force in hip (see Leland 2004).

12. In describing such jobs, Andrew Ross suggests that 'the no-collar mentality applies to knowledge workers whose high-tech skills or aptitude for problem-solving wins them a measure of autonomy in a data-rich workplace purged of rigid supervision and lifestyle discrimination. The intangible rewards – recognition, stimulation, responsibility – offered by their jobs are almost as important as the financial compensation' (Ross 2003: 34).

13. A close reading of Lanham's book reveals that class, while only occasionally mentioned explicitly, is central to the hipster stereotypes he exploits. He jokes about his being an anthropological work, and to some extent, it succeeds as such, with his attention to cross-class tensions among the hipster set.

14. Considering nostalgic television programming in the USA, Paul Grainge (2000: 29) comes much the same conclusion, providing a persuasive critique of theories about postmodern consciousness.

15. As Linda Hutcheon (1994: 12) argues, the ironic 'scene' depends on shared assumptions of ironists and interpreters about both their intentions.

16. Many of Vargas's Second World War pin-ups gazed out at the viewer, seeming sexually aggressive and self-aware, desiring, desirable, even dangerous. As Buszek (2006: 227) recounts, ordinary women themselves took up the pin-up style in their everyday lives, producing snapshots of each other such that 'the staging, as well as appreciation, of the pin-up seemed to be a pleasurable part of women's culture by the end of the war'. At least one Vargas print decorates the Suicide Girls headquarters in Los Angeles (2003).

17. Many pin-ups from the classic period show women framed by a keyhole shape (such as a series by Peter Driben) or otherwise watched by a peeping tom. Art Frahm's series of pin-ups about women's underwear falling down in public epitomizes the humiliated pin-up. Even Vargas's post-war pin-ups, mostly for *Playboy*, 'lost the style, aggression, and the clothes' – not to mention 'the references to women's culture and clear reverence for his subjects' – of his earlier work (Buszek, 2006: 238)

18. Hutcheon maintains that irony is thus 'transideological'.

19. I am indebted to Ken Hillis for this insight about the pleasures of cynically 'consuming one's own interpellation'.

6 Cosmo Girls Talk: Blurring Boundaries of Porn and Sex

1. Everyday uses of the Internet do not necessarily revolve around identity play. The multiple uses of the Internet involve shopping; exchange of ideas, opinions and merchandise, looking for partners and friends and in such practices faking/swapping identities is hardly useful (Lee 2005). The variety of online

forums correlates to the variety of intents among the users. Not all forums invite identity play; on others, hiding one's identity may be a necessity in order to fit in (Paasonen 2002); and yet other forums may involve sharing one's experiences and life-stories in order to support a feel of community.

2. Debates tend to focus on children being exposed to pornographic material, as well as trafficking in relation to prostitution.

7 Making Porn into Art

1. Yet, as has become quite apparent over time, what had been partially achieved in the West was a female sexual emancipation from the repression of bodily desires, expression and experience. But women's increased sexual freedom and control over their bodies, was accomplished mainly on men's terms. It did not mean the end of women's (sexual) domination by men, of unequal gender power relations (inflected by class, race, generation and ability), nor of the patriarchal foundations of society at large. It has, however, effected changes in the methods and forms of male power and control. In some respects they have become more subtle and covert.

8 How Unprofessional: The Profitable Partnership of Amateur Porn and Celebrity Culture

1. Personal communication with 'Keith,' GM Video Productions, 7 January 2005.

9 Sexed Authorship and Pornographic Address in Music Video

1. There are currently no generally recognized conventions for citing titles of music video within academic text. As such, where we refer to a song we follow standard procedures and enclose the title with speech marks. However, in instances where we make specific reference to a music video, which by default has the same name as the song it is designed to promote, we italicize the title.

2. Linda Williams argues that the 'insert of an insert' is a key device in feature length porn movies and, although the inserts are not, in this video, literally 'inserts of inserts' they function in much the same way to provide more detail of the sexual activity than can be seen in the master shot. (Williams 1989: 72).

10 Outdoor Pornification: Advertising Heterosexuality in the Streets

1. Fashion ads and spreads in international magazines even repeatedly test the border between soft- and hardcore pornography.
2. Butler's renowned theorizing gives an elaborate account of gender and sexuality as *doing,* and more precisely, as repetitious and ritualized doing, see Butler (1999: 33, 43–4, 178–9).
3. On the interconnectedness of power and knowledge, see Foucault (1990: 98–100). On visuality and its relation to production of knowledge, see Rose (2001, 7–9).
4. By sexualization I refer to practices foregrounding the culturally eroticized parts of the human body – or other objects which have gained the position of a fetish, both referring to and replacing the 'primary' sexual object. As Emily Apter so poignantly writes in her Introduction to the book *Fetishism as a Cultural Discourse*, 'a consistent displacing of reference occurs, paradoxically, as a result of so much *fixing*. Fetishism, in spite of itself, unfixes representations even as it enables them to become monolithic 'signs' of culture.' (Apter 1993: 3.) On the restriction of the erogenous body to certain parts such as penis, vagina, breasts and buttocks and thereby fragmentation of the body, see Butler (1999: 146).
5. On the ethical guidance given by these bodies, see e.g. the Finnish Council of Ethics in Advertising, http://www.kauppakamari.fi/kkk/palvelut/Mainonnan_ eettiset ohjeet/fi_FI/Mainonnan eettinen neuvosto/. Site accessed 14.12. 2006.
6. Hennes&Mauritz is represented in 24 countries. http://www.hm.com/pl/. Site accessed 14 December 2006.
7. Women may also be quite emphatically represented in these scenes as bisexual. See Jenny Kangasvuo's chapter in this book.
8. On signification of the directions of looking and the covered or downcast eyes see e.g. Linker (1983).

11 Insatiable Sluts and Almost Gay Guys: Bisexuality in Porn Magazines

1. All translations are by the author.
2. I will not contemplate the genre of 'bisexual porn' (Williams 1992: 257–62), since the genre has not much visibility in Finland. The porn magazines, however, reflect the most common and publicly visible form of porn in the country as the magazines are widely sold in grocery stores, kiosks and supermarkets. Some of the magazines, published for decades, have gained if not a respectable, at least acknowledged status.

3. This does not necessarily mean that the couples could be assumed to be heterosexual, since *Haloo!* promotes bisexual experiences at least for women.
4. I use the phrase 'different genders' instead of 'both genders' to emphasize my detachment from the dichotomized notion of genders.

12 Bend over Boyfriend: Anal Sex Instructional Videos for Women

1. Even when male partners ejaculate in the Hartley video, the camera angle shifts palpably to his straining face and then glides down his body where his female partner is lying down or kneeling, his ejaculate evidenced on her body. In one instance, while we do not see his orgasm take place visually, his face and resulting semen in the subsequent pan down Hartley's body still assure us that indeed, male orgasm has taken place.

13 Epilogue: Porn Futures

1. This emphasis was present at the 2005 *Art and Politics of Netporn* conference, organized by the institute for network cultures in Amsterdam. Similar divisions were made in the 1990s in the context of 'net.art' and 'art on the net', the former representing art practices specific to the Internet, its aesthetics, expressive and interactive possibilities and the latter referring to the recycling of artistic products created with other media (such as painting, drawing or graphics) and published online.
2. To a degree, the boundaries of individual media can bee seen as artificial to start with, considering the ways in which media historically converge, make use of same texts and aesthetics: media specificity is not necessarily a helpful starting point for analysing contemporary media culture (for general overviews, see Bolter and Grusin 1999; Jenkins 2006; Lehtonen 2001).
3. Telephone interview with Jukka Siitonen, producer of Seksi.net, the largest Finnish adult site, 1 February 2006.
4. The first hits for a Google search on 'pornography statistics' link to sites by Internet Filter Review and Family Safe Media with congruent figures (the size of the industry as being 57 billion globally; 12 billion in the USA; Internet porn 2.5 billion, etc.). These listings also include more esoteric categories such as 'sexual solicitations of youth made in chat rooms' (89 per cent) and 'Christians who said pornography is a major problem in the home' (47 per cent). The origin of these figures remains a mystery, whereas the category of pornography is broad enough to encompass sex clubs. Similar statistics are referenced by Pamela Paul (2005: 59–60). See http://www.familysafemedia.com/pornography_statistics.html; http://internet-filter-review.toptenreviews.com/internet-pornography-statistics.html.

References

Acham, Christine (2004), *Revolution Televised: Prime Time and the Struggle for Black Television*, Minneapolis: University of Minnesota Press.

Ackman, D. (2001), 'How big is porn?', *Forbes.com*, 25 May, electronic document at http://www.forbes.com/2001/05/25/0524porn.html

Ahmed, S. (2000), *Strange Encounters. Embodied Others in Post-Coloniality*, London & New York: Routledge.

Althusser, L. (1971), *Lenin and Philosophy and Other Essays*. Translated by Ben Brewster. New York & London: Monthly Review Press.

Altman, R. (1999), *Film/Genre*, London: BFI.

Apter, E. (1993), 'Introduction', in E. Apter and W. Pietz (eds), *Fetishism as Cultural Discourse*. Ithaca & London: Cornell University Press.

Arthurs, J. (2004), *Television and Sexuality: Regulation and the Politics of Taste*, Berkshire: Open University Press.

Attwood, F. (2002), 'Reading Porn: The Paradigm Shift in Pornography Research', *Sexualities* 5(1): 91–105.

—— (2004), 'Pornography and Objectification. Re-reading the picture that divided Britain', *Feminist Media Studies*, 4(1): 7–19.

—— (2005), 'Fashion and Passion: Marketing Sex to Women', *Sexualities* 8(4): 392–406.

—— (2006), 'Sexed Up: Theorizing the Sexualization of Culture', *Sexualities* 9(1): 77–94.

——, Brunt, R. and Cere, R. (eds) (forthcoming), *Mainstreaming Sex: The Sexualization of Culture*, London: I.B. Tauris.

Aucoin, D. (2006), 'The Pornification of America', *The Boston Globe,* 24 January, electronic document at http://www.boston.com/yourlife/articles/2006/01/24/the_pornification_of_america/

'AVN Adult Entertainment Expo delivered record growth 2006' (2006), *Business Wire 2006* [cited 25 January 2006]. Available from http://www.businesswire.com.

Barron, M. and Kimmel, M. (2000), 'Sexual Violence In Three Pornographic Media: Towards a Sociological Explanation', *The Journal of Sex Research* 37(2): 161–8.

Bataille, G. (1986), *Erotism: Death and Sensuality.* San Francisco: City Lights.

Bazin, A. (1971), 'Etymology Of the Pin-Up Girl', in *What Is Cinema? Vol. 2,* Berkeley: University of California Press.

BBC (2005), 'An Acceptable Career?' BBC, 1 March, electronic document at http://news.bbc.co.uk/1/hi/magazine/4305257.stm

Beaver, W. (2000), 'The Dilemma of Internet Pornography', *Business and Society Review* 105(3): 373–82.

Benhabib, S. (1998), 'Models of Public Space: Hannah Arendt, the Liberal Tradition and Jürgen Habermas', in J. Landes (ed.) *Feminism, the Public and the Private*, Oxford: Oxford University Press.

Benjamin, A. (2006), *Pornification*, New York: Falls Media.

Berlant, L. and Warner, M, (2000), 'Sex in Public', in L. Berlant (ed.), *Intimacy*, Chicago: The University of Chicago Press.

Bersani, L. (1987), 'Is the Rectum a Grave?', *October* 43(winter 1987): 197–222.

'Black Bun Busters Is First All-Black Anal Tape'. (1985), *Adult Video News Confidential,* June: 13.

Bloomberg Business News (1996), 'Red Kamels Are Back', *The New York Times,* New York, 2 February.

Bogle, D. (1992), *Toms, Coons, Mulattos, Mammies, and Bucks: An Interpretive History of Blacks in American Films*, Expanded Edition, New York: Continuum.

Bolter, J. D. and Grusin, B. (1999), *Remediation. Understanding New Media*, Cambridge MA: MIT Press.

Bordo, S. (1993), *Unbearable Weight: Feminism, Western Culture and the Body.* Berkeley: University of California Press.

Bose, B. (ed.) (2006), *Gender and Censorship*, New Delhi: Women Unlimited.

Bose, D. (2005), *Bollywood Uncensored: What You Don't See On Screen and Why*, New Delhi: Rupa & Co.

Bourdieu, P. (1998), *Practical Reason: On the Theory Of Action,* Cambridge: Polity Press.

Breeden, D. and Carroll, J. (2002), 'Punk, Pot, and Promiscuity: Nostalgia and the Re-Creation of the 1970s', *Journal of American Culture* 25(1–2): 100–4.

Bright, S. (1987), 'The Image of the Black in Adult Video', *Adult Video News,* April: 56–64.

Bright, S. (2003), *Mommy's Little Girl: On Sex, Motherhood, Porn, and Cherry Pie,* New York, Thunder's Mouth Press.

Brooks-King, S. (2007), 'Desire and the Reproduction of Race: Erotic Capital, Race, and Industry', Dissertation in progress: New School (forthcoming).

Brown, S. (1999), Retro-Marketing: Yesterday's Tomorrows, Today! *Marketing Intelligence and Planning* 17(7): 363–76.

Burger, J. R. (1995), *One-Handed Histories: The Eroto-Politics of Gay Male Video Pornography*, New York: Harrington Park Press.

Burston, P. and Richardson, C. (eds) (1995), *A Queer Romance. Lesbians, Gay Men and Popular Culture,* London & New York: Routledge.

Buscombe, E. (2004), 'Generic Overspill: *A Dirty Western*', in P. Church-Gibson (ed.), *More Dirty Looks: Gender, Pornography and Power*, London: BFI.

Buszek, M. E. (2006), *Pin-Up Grrrls: Feminism, Sexuality, Popular Culture,* Durham, NC: Duke University Press.

Butler, H. (2004), 'What Do You Call a Lesbian with Long Fingers? The Development of Lesbian and Dyke Pornography', in L. Williams (ed.), *Porn Studies,* Durham, NC: Duke University Press.

Butler, J. (1993), *Bodies that Matter. On the Discursive Limits of 'Sex'*, London & New York: Routledge.

—— (1997), *Excitable Speech, A Politics of the Performative*, London & New York: Routledge.

—— (1999), *Gender Trouble. Feminism and the Subversion of Identity*, London & New York: Routledge.

Caldwell, J. (2004), 'Convergence television: Aggregating form and repurposing content in the culture of conglomeration', in L. Spigel and J. Olsson (eds), *Television After TV: Essays on a Medium in Transition*, Durham, NC: Duke University Press.

Califia, Pat (1994), *Public Culture: The Culture of Radical Sex,* Pittsburgh: Cleis Press.

Calvert, C. (2000), *Voyeur Nation: Media, Privacy, and Peering in Modern Culture*, Boulder, CO: Westview Press.

Campbell, J. E. (2005), 'Outing PlanetOut: Surveillance, Gay Marketing and Internet Affinity Portals', *New Media and Society*, 7(5): 663–83.

Cante, R. and Restivo, A. (2004), 'The Cultural-Aesthetic Specificities of All-Male Moving-Image Pornography', in L. Williams (ed.), *Porn Studies*, Durham, NC: Duke University Press.

Castells, M. (1996), *The Network Society*, Oxford: Blackwell.

Chapkis, W. (1997), *Live Sex Acts: Women Performing Erotic Labor,* New York: Routledge.

'Charting the Adult Industry, Number of Hardcore Titles to Hit the Market'. (1991), *Adult Video News,* Dec.: 26.

Chun, W. H. K. (2006), *Control and Freedom: Power and Paranoia in the Age of Fiber Optics,* Cambridge, MA: MIT Press.

Church-Gibson, P. (2004), 'Preface: Porn Again? Or Why the Editor Might Have Misgivings', in P. Church-Gibson (ed.) *More Dirty Looks: Gender, Pornography and Power*, London: BFI, vii–xii.

—— and Gibson, R. (eds), (1993), *Dirty Looks: Women, Pornography, Power,* London: BFI.

Clark, C. (1991), 'Pornography Without Power?' in M. S. Kimmel (ed.), *Men Confront Pornography,* New York: Meridian.

Clarke, E. O. (2000), *Virtuous Vice. Homoerotics, and the Public Sphere.* Durham, NC and London: Duke University Press.

Cole, S K. (1999), 'I Am The Eye, You Are My Victim: The Pornographic Ideology of Music Video', *Enculturation* 2(2), available online at http://www.uta.

edu/huma/enculturation/2_2/Cole.html, (accessed 23 May 2006).

Collins, P. H. (2004), *Black Sexual Politics: African Americans, Gender, and the New Racism,* New York: Routledge.

Consalvo, M. and Paasonen, S. (2002), *Women and Everyday Uses of the Internet.* New York: Peter Lang.

Cooks, L., Castaneda, M. and Scharrer, E. (2002), "There's O' Place Like Home': Searching for Community on Oprah.com', in M. Consalvo and S. Paasonen (eds), *Women and Everyday Uses of the Internet.* New York: Peter Lang.

Cramer, F. (2006), 'Sodom Blogging: "Alternative Porn" and Aesthetic Sensibility', *Texte zur Kunst* 16(64): 133–136.

Culler, J. (1975), *Structuralist Poetics: Structuralism, Linguistics and the Study of Literature,* London: Routledge & Kegan Paul.

Cullity, J. and Younger, P. (2004), 'Sex Appeal and Cultural Liberty: A Feminist Inquiry into MTV India', *Frontiers – A Journal of Women's Studies* 25(2): 96–122.

Dahlquist, J. P. and Vigilant, L. G. (2004), 'Way Better Than Real: Manga Sex to Tentacle Hentai', in D. D. Waskul (ed.), *Net.seXXX: Readings of Sex, Pornography, and the Internet,* New York: Peter Lang.

Davis, A. (1971), 'Reflections on the Black Woman's Role in the Community of Slaves', *Black Scholar* 3(4).

Dery, M. (2006), 'Naked Lunch: Talking Realcore with Sergio Messina', electronic document at http://www.markdery.com/archives/blog/psychopathia_sexualis/#00006.

Dines, G. and J. M. Humez (eds) (2003), *Gender, Race, and Class in Media: A Text-Reader,* 2nd ed., Thousand Oaks, CA: Sage.

Driver, S. (2004), 'Pornographic Pedagogies? The Risk of Teaching "Dirrty" Popular Cultures', *M/C Journal* 7(4), electronic document at http://journal.media-culture.org.au/0410/03_teaching.php.

Duggan, L. and Hunter, N. D. (1995), *Sex Wars: Sexual Dissent and Political Culture,* New York: Routledge.

Duits, L. and van Zoonen, L. (2006) 'Headscarves and Porno-chic: Disciplining Girls' Bodies in the European Multicultural Society', *European Journal of Women's Studies* 13(2): 103–17.

Dworkin A. (1989/1979), *Pornography: Men Possessing Women,* New York, E.P. Dutton.

—— (2000), 'Pornography and Grief' in Cornell, D. (ed.) *Feminism and Pornography,* Oxford: Oxford University Press.

—— and Mackinnon, C. (1988), *Pornography and Civil Rights: A New Day for Women's Equality.* Organizing Against Pornography.

Dyer, R. (1985), 'Gay Male Porn: Coming to Terms', *Jump Cut: A Review of Contemporary Media,* 30 (March): 27–9.

—— (1986), *Heavenly Bodies: Film Stars and Society.* London: MacMillan.

—— (1992), 'Coming to Terms: Gay Pornography', in *Only Entertainment*, London: Routledge.

—— (2004), *Heavenly Bodies: Film Stars and Society*, 2nd edition, London: Routledge.

Ebert, R. (1997), 'Director's Talent Makes 'Boogie' Fever Infectious', electronic document   at http://rogerebert.suntimes.com/apps/pbcs.dll/article?AID=/19971019/PEOPLE /10010341.

Eco, U. (2001), 'Wie man einen Pornofilm erkennt', in U. Eco, *Sämtliche Glossen und Parodien 1963–2000*, Frankfurt/Main: Zweitausendundeins.

Edwards, A. (2002), 'The Moderator as an emerging democratic intermediary: The role of moderator in Internet discussions about public issues.' *Information Policy* 7: 3–20.

Edwards, T. (1994), *Erotics and Politics: Gay Male Sexuality, Masculinity and Feminism*, London: Routledge.

Eggins, S. and Iedema, R. (1997), 'Difference without Diversity. Semantic orientation and ideology in competing women's magazines.' In R. Wodak (ed.), *Gender And Discourse*, London: Sage.

Elliott, R. G. (1960), *The Power of Satire*, Princeton: Princeton University Press.

Fairclough, N. (1992), *Discourse and Social Change*. Cambridge: Polity Press.

Firestein, B. A. (1996), 'Introduction', in B. A. Firestein (ed.), *Bisexuality: The Psychology and Politics of an Invisible Minority*, London: Sage.

Fish, S. (1983), 'Short People Got No Reason To Live: Reading Irony', *Daedalus*, 112(1): 175–91.

Fishbein, P. (1985), 'How to Sell Adult Tapes: Marketing All-Black or Interracial Cassettes', *Adult Video News,* July: 18.

Flusser, V. (2000), *Towards a Philosophy of Photography*, London: Reaktion Books.

Ford, L. (1999), *A History of X: 100 Years of Sex in Film,* Amherst, NY: Prometheus Books.

Forman, M. (1994), '"Movin' Closer to an Independent Funk": Black Feminist Theory, Standpoint and Women in Rap', *Women's Studies*, 23(1): 35–55.

Foster, T. (2001), 'Trapped by the Body? Telepresence Technologies and Transgendered Performance in Feminist and Lesbian Rewriting of Cyberpunk Fiction', in D. Bell and B. M. Kennedy (eds), *The Cybercultures Reader*, London: Routledge.

Foucault, M. (1990), *The History of Sexuality, Introduction (Histoire de la sexualité 1. La volonte de savoir*, 1976), transl. by Robert Hurley. New York: Vintage.

Frank, T. (1997), *The Conquest Of Cool: Business Culture, Counterculture, and the Rise Of Hip Consumerism,* Chicago: University of Chicago Press.

Fung, R. (1991), 'Looking for My Penis: The Eroticized Asian in Gay Video Porn', in Bad Object-Choices (ed.), *How Do I Look? Queer Film and Video*, Seattle: Bay Press.

Gagnon, J. (1988), *Pornography in the Urban World. (La pornographie et le monde urbain*, 1984), transl. James Boake and Jeanluc Svoboda. Toronto: Art Metropole.

Gamman, L. and Marshment, M. (1989), *The Female Gaze. Women as Viewer of Popular Culture*. Seattle: The Real Comet Press.

Gamson, J. (1992), 'The assembly line of greatness: Celebrity in twentieth-century America', *Critical Studies in Mass Communication* 9(1): 1–24.

Gauntlett, D. (2004), 'Madonna's Daughters: Girl Power and the Empowered Girl-Pop Breakthrough', in S. Fouz-Hernandez and F. Jarman-Ivens, (eds), *Madonna's Drowned Worlds: New Approaches to her Cultural Transformations 1983–2003*, Aldershot: Ashgate

Geller, T. (ed.) (1990), *Bisexuality: A Reader and Sourcebook*, Novato: Times Change Press.

Ghosh, S. (2005), 'Looking in Horror and Fascination: Sex, Violence and Spectatorship in India', in G. Misra and R. Chandiramani (eds), *Sexuality, Gender and Rights: Exploring Theory and Practice in South and Southeast Asia*, New Delhi: Sage.

—— (2006), 'The Troubled Existence of Sex and Sexuality: Feminists Engage with Censorship', in B. Bose (ed.), *Gender and Censorship*, New Delhi: Women Unlimited.

Giddings, P. (1984), *When and Where I Enter: The Impact of Black Women on Race and Sex in America,* New York: William Morrow.

Glynn, K. (2000), *Tabloid Culture: Trash Taste, Popular Power, and the Transformation of American Television*, Durham, NC: Duke University Press.

Graham, H., Kaloski, A., Neilson, A. and Robertson, E. (2003), 'Preface', in H. Graham, A. Kaloski, A. Neilson and E. Robertson (eds), *The Feminist Seventies,* York: Raw Nerve Books.

Grainge, P. (2000), 'Nostalgia and Style in Retro America: Moods, Modes, and Media Recycling', *Journal of American and Comparative Cultures* 23(1): 27–34.

Gray, H. (2004), *Watching Race: Television and the Struggle for Blackness*, Minneapolis: University of Minnesota Press.

Griffin, S. (1981), *Pornography and Silence: Culture's Revenge Against Nature*. New York: Harper & Row.

Grogan, S. (1999), *Body Image. Understanding Body Dissatisfaction in Men, Women and Children*. London & New York: Routledge.

Halavais, A. (2005), 'Small Pornographies', *ACM SIGGROUP Bulletin* 25(2): 19–22.

Hall, S. (1999), The Spectacle of the 'Other', in S. Hall (ed.), *Representation. Cultural Representations and Signifying Practices*. London: Sage.

Haraway, D. (1991), *Simians, Cyborgs, and Women: The Reinvention of Nature*, London: Free Association Books.

Haslam, D. (2005), *Not Abba: The Real Story of the 1970s*, London: Fourth Estate.

Haugen, J. D. (2003), "'Unladylike Divas': Language, Gender, and Female Gangsta Rappers', *Popular Music and Society*, 26(4): 429–44.

HBO's Real Sex (2003), 'Am I Good In Bed: Real Sex 31', HBO, USA, 30 November.

Heins, M. (2001), *Not in Front of the Children: 'Indecency,' Censorship, and the Innocence of Youth*, New York: Hill and Wang.

Hellmann, H. (2002), 'Preface', in B. Riemenschneider, *1000 Pin-Up Girls*, Cologne: Taschen.

Hermes, J. (1995), *Reading Women's Magazines. An Analysis of Everyday Media Use*, Cambridge: Polity Press.

Hills, M. (2002), *Fan Cultures*, London: Routledge.

Hillyer, M. (2004), 'Sex in the suburban: Porn, home movies, and the live action performance of love in *Pam and Tommy Lee: Hardcore and Uncensored*', in L. Williams (ed.), *Porn Studies*, Durham, NC: Duke University Press.

History of Porn, Part 5. (2000), directors Fenton Bailey and Randy Barbato, videocassette, World of Wonder.

Hoffmann, F. A. (1965), 'Prolegomena to a Study of Traditional Elements in the Erotic Film', *The Journal of American Folklore* 78(308): 143–8.

Holliday, J. (1987), 'The Changing Face of Adult Video', *Adult Video News,* Mar.: 15.

hooks, b. (1992), *Yearning: race, gender, and cultural politics.* Boston: South End Press.

Horne, P. and Lewis, R. (1997) 'Visual Culture', in A. Medhurst and S. Munt (eds), *Lesbian and Gay Studies: A Critical Introduction*, London: Cassell.

Hunt, L. (ed.) (1993), *The Invention of Pornography: Obscenity and the Origins of Modernity, 1500–1800.* New York: Zone Books.

Hutcheon, L. (1994), *Irony's Edge: the Theory and Politics Of Irony,* London, Routledge.

—— (1995), *Irony's Edge: The Theory and Politics of Irony*, 2nd edition, London: Routledge.

Inness, S. A. (2003), 'Introduction. "Strange Feverish Years": The 1970s and Women's Changing Roles', in S. A. Inness (ed.), *Disco Divas, Women and Popular Culture in the 1970s*. Philadelphia: University of Pennsylvania Press.

Irving, L. (1985), 'Director's Corner: Gregory Dark', *Adult Video News,* Dec.: 53

Jacobs, K. (2004a), 'The Amateur Pornographer and the Glib Voyeur', M/C Journal 7(4), electronic document at http://www.media-culture.org.au/0410/06_amateur.php.

—— (2004b), 'The New Media Schooling of the Amateur Pornographer: Negotiating Contracts and Signing Orgasm', http://libidot.org.katrien/

tester/articles/negotiating-print.html (accessed 23 September 2006).

Jenkins, H. (2004), 'Foreword: So You Want to Teach Pornography?', in P. Church-Gibson (ed.), *More Dirty Looks: Gender, Pornography and Power*, London, BFI.

—— (2006), *Convergence Culture: Where Old and New Media Collide*, New York: NYU Press.

Johnson, E. (1999), 'The "Coloscopic" Film and the "Beaver" Film: Scientific and Pornographic Scenes of Female Sexual Responsiveness', in H. Radner and M. Luckett (eds), *Swinging Single: Representing Sexuality in the 1960s*. Minneapolis: University of Minnesota Press.

Johnson, W. (1999), *Soul by Soul: Life Inside the Antebellum Slave Market*, Cambridge, MA: Harvard University Press.

Jones, A. (2002), 'The "Eternal Return": Self-Portrait Photography as a Technology of Embodiment', *Signs: Journal of Women in Culture and Society* 27(4): 947–78.

Jones, J. (1985), *Labor of Love, Labor of Sorrow: Black Women, Work, and Family from Slavery to the Present*, New York: Basic Books.

Juffer, J. (1998), *At Home with Pornography. Women, Sexuality, and Everyday Life*. New York: New York University Press.

—— (2004), 'There's No Place Like Home: Further Developments on the Domestic Front.' In P. Church-Gibson (ed.), *More Dirty Looks: Gender, Pornography and Power*. 2nd edition. London: BFI.

Juvonen, T., Kalha, H., Sorainen, A. and Vänskä, A. (2004), 'Minä ja mun porno', *Naistutkimus – Kvinnoforskning* 2/2004: 68–73.

Kalha, H. (2005), 'Pehmeä lasku kovaan pornoon', in K. Nikunen, S. Paasonen and L. Saarenmaa (eds), *Jokapäiväinen pornomme: Media seksuaalisuus ja populaarikulttuuri*, Tampere: Vastapaino.

Kangasvuo, J. (2006), *Koettu ja kirjoitettu biseksuaalisuus. Biseksuaalisuuden määrittely lehtiteksteissä ja biseksuaalien haastatteluissa vuosituhannenvaihteen Suomessa*, Unpublished Licenciate Thesis, University of Oulu.

Kernes, M. (2004), Lecture in Film Studies 150, University of California Santa Barbara, May.

Kipnis, L. (1996), *Bound and Gagged: Pornography and the Politics Of Fantasy In America*, New York, Grove Press.

—— (1999), *Bound and Gagged: Pornography and the Politics of Fantasy in America*, 2nd edition, Durham, NC: Duke University Press

Kleinhans, C. (2004), 'Virtual Child Porn: The Law and the Semiotics of the Image', in P.Church-Gibson (ed.), *More Dirty Looks: Gender, Pornography and Power*, London: BFI.

—— (2006), 'The Change from Film to Video Pornography: Implications for Analysis', in P. Lehman (ed.), *Pornography: Film and Culture*, New Brunswick: Rutgers University Press.

Koht, P. (2005), 'Obscene But Not Heard: As the Suicide Girls Phenomenon

Peaks, A Number Of Former Models Accuse the Company Of Not Living Up to Its Feminist-Friendly Marketing', *Metro Santa Cruz,* 16 November, www.metroactive.com/papers/cruz/11.16.05/suicidegirls-0546.html.

Koivunen, A. (2003), *Performative Histories, Foundational Fictions: Gender and Sexuality in Niskavuori Films*, Helsinki: SKS.

Kontula, O. and Haavio-Mannila, E. (2001), *Seksin trendit meillä ja naapureissa.* Helsinki: WSOY.

Kooijman, J. (2005), 'Turn the Beat Around: Richard Dyer's "In Defence of Disco" Revisited', *European Journal of Cultural Studies* 8(2): 257–66.

Kulick, D. (2005), 'Four Hundred Thousand Swedish Perverts', *GLQ: A Journal of Lesbian and Gay Studies* 11(2): 205–35.

Lane, F. S. III (2001), *Obscene Profits: The Entrepreneurs of Pornography in the Cyber Age,* New York: Routledge.

Laukkanen, M. (2004), 'Kaapitetut. Seksuaalinen suuntautuminen nuorten nettikeskusteluissa', *Tiedotustutkimus,* 27(3): 49–62.

Lederer, L. (ed.) (1980), *Take Back the Night: Women on Pornography,* New York: William & Morrow.

Lee, H. (2005), 'Implosion, virtuality, and interaction in an Internet Discussion Group', *Information, Communication and Society* 8(1): 47–63.

Lehman, P. (ed.) (2006), *Pornography: Film and Culture*, New Brunswick: Rutgers University Press.

Lehtonen, M. (2001), 'On No Man's Land: Theses on Intermediality', *Nordicom Review* 22(1): 71–84.

Leland, J. (2004), *Hip: The History,* New York: Ecco.

Levy, A. (2005), *Female Chauvinist Pigs: Women and the Rise of Raunch Culture*, New York: Free Press.

Levy, A. (2006), 'Get a life, girls', *The Spectator*, 4 March: 22.

Lewis, R. and Rolley, K. (1997), '(Ad)dressing the Dyke. Lesbian Looks and Lesbians Looking', in M. Nava, A. Blake, I. MacRury and B. Richards (eds), *Buy this Book. Studies in Advertising and Consumption.* London & New York: Routledge.

Lim, M. (2006), 'Democracy, Conspiracy, Pornography: The Internet and Political Activism in Indonesia', lecture at IR 7.0: Internet Convergences Conference, Brisbane, 28 September 2006.

Linker, K. (1983), 'Representation and Sexuality', *Parachute,* no. 32.

Lloyd, R. D. (2005), *Neo-Bohemia: Art and Commerce in the Postindustrial City,* New York: Routledge.

Lockard, J. (2001), 'Britney Spears, Victorian Chastity and Brand-name Virginity', *Bad Subjects* issue 57, electronic document at http://bad.eserver.org/issues/2001/57/lockardb.html.

Lovelace, L. (1974), *Inside Linda Lovelace*, London, Heinrich Hanau Publications.

—— (1986) *Out of Bondage*, New York: Carol Publishing.

—— and McGrady, M. (2006/1980), *Ordeal*, New York: Kensington Publishing Corp.

—— and Wallin, C. (1974), *The Intimate Diary of Linda Lovelace*. New York: Pinnacle Books.

Lowenthal, D. (1986/1985), *The Past is a Foreign Country*, Cambridge: Cambridge University Press.

Lubiano, W. (1992), 'Black Ladies, Welfare Queens and State Minstrels', in T. Morrison (ed.), *Race-ing Justice, En-gendering Power: Essays on Anita Hill, Clarence Thomas and the Construction of Social Reality*, New York: Pantheon.

Machin, D. and Thornborrow, J. (2003) 'Branding and discourse: The Case of Cosmopolitan', *Discourse & Society*, 14(4): 453–71.

—— (2006), 'Lifestyle and the Depoliticisation of Agency: Sex as Power in Women's Magazines', *Social Semiotics* 16(1): 173–88.

MacKinnon, C. (2000), 'The Roar On The Other Side Of Silence', in D. Cornell (ed.), *Feminism and Pornography*, Oxford: Oxford University Press.

Marshall, M. (2005), *Suicide Girls: The First Tour*, DVD, USA, Epitaph/Ada.

Martignette, C. G. and Meisel, L. K. (1996), *The Great American Pin-Up*, Köln, New York: Taschen.

Mason-Grant, J. (2004), *Pornography Embodied: From Speech to Sexual Practice*, Lanham, MD: Rowman and Littlefield.

Mayer, V. (2005), 'Soft-core in TV time: A political economy of *Girls Gone Wild*', *Critical Studies in Media Communication* 22(4): 302–20.

—— (2006), 'Fieldnote', *Con/texts: A Journal of the American Sociological Association* 5(4): 58–9.

McGuigan, J. (1996), *Culture and the Public Sphere*. London and New York: Routledge.

McKee, A. (2006), 'The Aesthetics of Pornography: the Insights of Consumers', *Continuum: Journal of Media & Cultural Studies* 20(4): 523–39.

McLelland, M. (2006), 'The Best Website for Men Who Have Sex With Men: cruisingforsex.com', in A. McKee (ed.), *Beautiful Things in Popular Culture*, Oxford: Blackwell.

McMahon, T. (1986), 'Displaying Adult Tapes', *Adult Video News*, Nov.: 14.

McNair, B. (1996), *Mediated Sex. Pornography and the Postmodern Culture*, London and New York: Arnold.

—— (2002), *Striptease Culture: Sex, Media and the Democratization of Desire*, New York: Routledge.

McNeil, L. and Osborne, J. (2005), *The Other Hollywood: The Uncensored Oral History of the Porn Film Industry*, New York: Regan Books.

Messina, S. (2005), 'Realcore: The Digital Porno Revolution', electronic document at http://realcore.radiogladio.it/.

Mey, K. (2006), *Art and Obscenity*, London and New York: I.B. Tauris.

Mies, G. (2006), 'Evolution of the Alternative: History and Controversies of the Alt-Erotica Industry', *American Sexuality Magazine*, electronic document at http://nsrc.sfsu.edu/MagArticle.cfm?Article=631&PageID=0

Milter, K. Szoverfy and Slade, J.W. (2005), 'Global Traffic in Pornography: The Hungarian Example', in L.Z. Sigel (ed.) *International Exposure: Perspectives on Modern European Pornography 1800–2000*, New Brunswick: Rutgers University Press.

Morgan, R. (1980) 'Theory and Practice. Pornography and Rape', in L. Lederer (ed.), *Take Back the Night: Women on Pornography.* New York: Morrow.

Morrison, T. (ed.) (1992), *Race-ing Justice, En-gendering Power: Essays on Anita Hill, Clarence Thomas and the Construction of Social Reality,* New York: Pantheon.

Morrow, P. (2006), 'Telling about problems and giving advice in an Internet discussion forum: some discourse features', *Discourse Studies* 8(4): 531–48.

Mowlabocus, S. (2005) 'Being Seen to be Gay: User Profiles and the Construction of Gay Male Identity in Cyberspace' in K. Burkitt and G. Simon (eds), *Working Papers in Contemporary History and Politics*, Manchester: European Studies Research Institute.

—— (2007) 'Life Outside The Latex: HIV, Sex and the Online Barebacking Community', in K. O'Riordan and D. J. Phillips (eds), *Queer Online: Media Technology and Sexuality*, New York: Peter Lang.

Moynihan, D. P. (1965), *The Negro Family: The Case for National Action*, Washington DC: Government Printing Office.

Mulvey, L. (1989), *Visual and Other Pleasures*, Bloomington & Indianapolis: Indiana University Press.

Nead, L. (1988), *Myths of Sexuality: Representations of Women in Victorian Britain*, Oxford: Blackwell.

Negra, D. (2004), 'Quality Postfeminism? Sex and the Single Girl on HBO', *Genders Online Journal* 39(2004): http://www.genders.org/g39/g39_negra.html

Nikunen, K. (2005), 'Kovia kokenut domina ja pirteä pano-opas: Veronican ja Rakel Liekin tähtikuvat pornon arkipäiväistäjinä' in K. Nikunen, S. Paasonen and L. Saarenmaa (eds), *Jokapäiväinen pornomme: Media seksuaalisuus ja populaarikulttuuri*, Tampere: Vastapaino.

—— and Paasonen, S. (2007), 'Porn Star as Brand: Pornification and the Intermedia Career of Rakel Liekki', *The Velvet Light Trap* no. 59.

O'Toole, L. (1998), *Pornocopia: Porn, Sex, Technology and Desire*, London: Serpent's Tail.

—— (1999), *Pornocopia: Porn, Sex, Technology and Desire,* 2nd edition, London: Serpent's Tail.

Orth, M. (2004), *The Importance of Being Famous*, New York: Henry Holt.

Osgerby, B. (2001), *Playboys in Paradise: Masculinity, Youth and Leisure-style in Modern America*, Oxford: Berg.

Oullette, L. (1999), 'Inventing the Cosmo Girl: Class Identity and Girl-Style American Dreams', *Media, Culture & Society* 21: 359–83.

Paasonen, S. (2002), 'Gender, Identity and (the Limits of) Play on the internet', in M. Consalvo and S. Paasonen (eds), *Women and Everyday Uses of the Internet*. New York: Peter Lang.

—— (2005a), *Figures of Fantasy. Internet, Women, and Cyberdiscourse*. New York: Peter Lang.

—— (2005b), 'Surfing the Waves of Feminism: Cyberfeminism and its Others', *Labrys*, 7, available online at http://www.unb.br/ih/his/gefem/labrys7/cyber/susanna.htm (accessed 20 August 2006).

—— (2006), 'Email from Nancy Nutsucker: Representation and Gendered Address in Online Pornography', *European Journal of Cultural Studies* 9(4): 403–20.

—— (2007a), 'Online Pornography, Normativity and the Nordic Context', in M. Sveningsson Elm and J. Sundén (eds), *Cyberfeminism in Northern Lights: Digital Media and Gender in a Nordic Context*, Cambridge: Cambridge Scholars Publishing.

Paasonen, S. (2007b), 'Strange Bedfellows: Pornography, Affect and Feminist Reading', *Feminist Theory* 8(1): 43–57.

Paglia, C. (1993), 'Madonna 1: Animality and Artifice', in C Paglia, *Sex, Art and American Culture: Essays*, Harmondsworth: Penguin.

Patterson, Z. (2004), 'Going On-Line: Consuming Pornography in the Digital Era', in L. Williams (ed.), *Porn Studies*, Durham, NC: Duke University Press.

Patton, C. (1991), 'Safe Sex and the Pornographic Vernacular', in Bad Object Choices (ed.), *How Do I Look? Queer Film and Video*, Seattle: Bay Press.

—— (2000), 'How to Do Things With Sound', in S. Waldrep (ed.), *The Seventies. The Age of Glitter In Popular Culture*, New York: Routledge.

Paul, P. (2005), *Pornified: How Pornography is Damaging Our Lives, Our Relationships, and Our Families*, New York, Owl Books.

Perdue, L. (2002), *Erotica Biz: How Sex Shaped the Internet*, New York: Writers Club Press

Perry, I. (2003), 'Who(se) am I? The Identity and Image of Women in Hip-Hop', in G. Dines and J. M. Humez (eds), *Gender, Race and Class in the Media*, 2nd edition, London: Sage.

Phillips, D. J. (2002), 'Negotiating the Digital Closet: Online Pseudonymity and the Politics of Sexual Identity', in *Information, Communication & Society* 5 (3): 406–24.

Physicians For A Smoke-Free Canada (2006), 'Red Kamel Komes to Kanada', retrieved 20 June 2006 from http://www.smoke-free.ca/filtertips_001/red-kamel.htm.

Poster, M. (1995), *The Second Media Age*, Cambridge: Polity Press.

Poynor, R. (2006), *Designing Pornotopia: Travels in Visual Culture*, New York:

Princeton Architectural Press.

Projansky, S. (2001), *Watching Rape: Film and Television in Postfeminist Culture*. New York: New York UP.

Radner, H. (1993), 'Pretty is as Pretty Does: Free Enterprise and the Marriage plot', in A. Collins, J. Collins and H. Radner (eds), *Film Theory Goes to Movies*, London & New York: Routledge.

Railton, D. and Watson, P. (2005), 'Naughty Girls and Red Blooded Women: Representations Of Female Heterosexuality In Music Video', *Feminist Media Studies*, 5(1): 51–63.

Reading, A. (2005), 'Professing Porn or Obscene Browsing? On Proper Distance in the University Classroom', *Media, Culture & Society* 27(1): 123–30.

Reichert, T. and Lambiase, J. (eds) (2006), *Sex in Consumer Culture: The Erotic Content of Media and Marketing*, Mahwah, NJ: Lawrence Erlbaum.

Rich, F. (2001), 'Naked Capitalists', *New York Times Magazine*, 20 May, Section 6.

Rose, G. (2001), *Visual methodologies*. London, Thousand Oaks & Delhi: Sage.

Rosen, D. (2006), 'The Global Trade in Sex Toys. Made in China', *Counterpunch*, 2/3 December, electronic document available at http://www.counterpunch. org/rosen12022006.html

Ross, A. (2003), *No-Collar: The Humane Workplace and Its Hidden Costs*, New York, Basic Books.

—— (2004), 'Dot.Com Urbanism', in N. Couldry and A. McCarthy (eds), *Mediaspace: Place, Scale, and Culture In A Media Age*, New York: Routledge.

Royalle, C. (2000), 'Porn in the USA', in D. Cornell (ed.), *Feminism and Pornography*, Oxford: Oxford University Press.

Rubin, G. (1984), 'Thinking Sex: Notes for a Radical Theory of the Politics of Sexuality', in C. Vance (ed.), *Pleasure and Danger: Exploring Female Sexuality*, Boston: Routledge.

—— (1995), 'Misguided, Dangerous and Wrong: An Analysis of Anti-Pornography Politics' (1993), in G. Dines and J. M. Humez (eds), *Gender, Race and Class in Media: A Text-Reader*, London: Sage.

Ruff, T. and Houellebecq, M., *Nudes*, New York: Harry N Abrahams.

Saarikangas, K. (1996), 'Katseita, kohtaamisia, kosketuksia. Tilassa muodostuvat merkitykset', *Tiede ja edistys* 4/96, 306–18.

Schaefer, E. (2004), 'Gauging a Revolution: 16 mm Film and the Rise of the Pornographic Feature', in L. Williams (ed.), *Porn Studies*, Durham, NC: Duke University Press.

Schmidt, S. J. (2000), 'Werbekörper: Plurale Artefiktionen', in A. Krewani (ed.), *Artefakte Artefiktionen: Transformationsprozesse zeitgenössischer Literaturen, Medien, Künste, Architekturen = artefacts artefictions*, Heidelberg: Carl Winter.

Segal, L. (2004), 'Only the Literal: The Contradictions of Anti-Pornography Feminism', in Pamela Church-Gibson (ed.), *More Dirty Looks: Gender, Pornography and Power*, London: BFI.

—— and McIntosh, M. (eds), (1993), *Sex Exposed: Sexuality and the Pornography Debate,* New Brunswick: Rutgers University Press.

Seppänen, J. (2001), *Valokuvaa ei ole.* Helsinki: Musta Taide.

Shah, N. (2005), 'PlayBlog: Pornography, Performance, and Cyberspace', *Cut-Up Magazine* no. 20, electronic document at http://www.cut-up.com/news/issuedetail.php?sid=413&issue=20.

Sharpley-Whiting, T. D. (1999), *Black Venus: Sexualized Savages, Primal Fears, and Primitive Narratives in French,* Durham, NC: Duke University Press.

Shelton, E. (2002), 'A Star Is Porn: Corpulence, Comedy, and the Homosocial Cult of Adult Film Star Ron Jeremy', *Camera Obscura* 17(3): 115–46.

Shelton, M. L. (1997), 'Can't Touch This! Representations of the African American Female Body in Urban Rap Videos', *Popular Music and Society* 21(3): 107–16.

Sickels, R. C. (2002), '1970s Disco Daze: Paul Thomas Anderson's *Boogie Nights* and the Last Age of Irresponsibility', *Journal of Popular Culture* 35(4): 49–60.

Sigel, L. Z. (2000), 'Filth in the Wrong People's Hands: Postcards and the Expansion of Pornography in Britain and the Atlantic World, 1880–1914', *Journal of Social History* 33(4): 859–85.

Silverman, K. (1996), *The Threshold of the Visible World.* London & New York: Routledge.

Sinfield, A. (1998), *Gay And After*, London: Serpent's Tail.

Skeggs, B. (1993), 'Two Minute Brother: Contestation Through Gender, 'Race' and Sexuality', *Innovations*, 6 (3): 299–322.

Slade, J. (2000), 'Erotic Motion Pictures and Videotapes', *Pornography in America: A Reference Handbook,* Santa Barbara: ABC-CLIO.

Slater, D. (1991), 'Consuming Kodak', in J. Spence and P. Holland (eds), *Family Snaps: The Meanings of Domestic Photography*, London: Virago.

Sloterdijk, P. (1987), *Critique Of Cynical Reason,* Minneapolis: University of Minnesota Press.

Smith, K. (2005), 'The inescapable Paris', *Vanity Fair*, October, 280–1.

Smith, V. (2003), *Representing Blackness: Issues in Film and Video*, New Brunswick: Rutgers.

Snitow, A. (1983), 'Mass Market Romance: Pornography for Women is Different', in A. Snitow, C. Stansell and S. Thompson (eds), *Desire. The Politics of Sexuality.* London: Virago.

Sontag, S. (1964a), *Against Interpretation and Other Essays,* New York: Delta.

—— (1964b), 'Notes on "Camp"', in F. Cleto (ed.), *Camp: Queer Aesthetics and the Performing Subject: A Reader*, Ann Arbor: University of Michigan Press, 1999.

—— (1979), *On Photography*, London: Penguin Books.

Spinks, A., Partridge, H. and Jansen, B. J. (2006), 'Sexual and Pornographic Web

Searching: Trend Analysis', *First Monday* 11(9): electronic document at http://www.firstmonday.org/issues/issue11_9/spink/index.html.

Stacey, J. (1994), *Star Gazing. Hollywood Cinema and Female Spectatorship.* London & New York: Routledge.

Staiger, J. (1985), 'Standardization and differentiation: The reinforcement and dispersion of Hollywood's practices', in D. Bordwell, J. Staiger and K. Thompson (eds), *The Classical Hollywood Cinema: Film Style and the Mode of Production to 1960*, New York: Columbia University Press.

Steinem, G. (1983), *Outrageous Acts and Everyday Rebellions*. New York: New American Library.

Stoller, D. (1999), 'Feminist Fatales: BUST-ing the beauty myth', in M. Karp and D. Stoller (eds), *The* Bust *Guide to the New Girl Order,* New York: Penguin Books.

Stoltenberg, J. (1991)' 'Gays and the Propornography Movement: Having the Hots for Sex Discrimination', in M. S. Kimmel (ed.), *Men Confront Pornography.* Meridian: New York.

Stone, A. R. (2000), 'Will The Real Body Please Stand Up? Boundary Stories about Virtual Cultures' in D. Bell and B. Kennedy (eds), *The Cybercultures Reader*, London: Routledge.

Suicide Girls (2006), television broadcast, *ICONS,* USA, G4 Cable Network, 10 June.

Suicide, M. (2004), *Suicide Girls,* Los Angeles, Feral House.

Taormino, T. (1998), *The Ultimate Guide to Anal Sex for Women.* San Francisco: Cleis Press.

Thornburgh, D. and Lin, H. S. (2002), *Youth, Pornography, and the Internet.* Computer Science and Telecommunications Board, National Science Council, Washington: National Academy Press.

Tola, M. (2005), 'Re-routing the (a)sex drives of Big Dickie: Interview with Katien Jacobs', electronic document at http://www.networkcultures.org/netporn/index.php? onderdeelID=1&paginaID=13&itemID=70

Tonkiss, F. (2001), 'Analyzing Discourses', in C. Seale (ed.), *Researching Society and Culture*, London: Sage.

Turner, B. S. (1987), 'A Note on Nostalgia', *Theory, Culture & Society* 4(1): 147–56.

Turner, M. (2004), *The Pornographer's Poem*, New York: Soft Skull Press.

Van de Sompel, R. (1999), *Anne-Mie Van Kerckhoven*, Antwerp: MUHKA.

Van Scoy, K. (2000), 'Sex Sells, So Learn a Thing of Two From it', *PC Computing,* Jan.: 64.

Vance, C. S. (1992), 'More Danger, More Pleasure: A Decade after the Barnard Sexuality Conference', in C. S. Vance (ed.), *Pleasure and Danger. Exploring Female Sexuality,* revised edition, London: Pandora Press (1st edition, 1984).

Villarejo, A. (2004), 'Defycategory.com, or the Place of Categories in Intermedia', in P. Church-Gibson (ed.), *More Dirty Looks: Gender, Pornography and Power*, 2nd edition, London: BFI.

Waldrep, S. (2000), 'Introducing the Seventies', in S. Waldrep (ed.), *The Seventies. The Age of Glitter In Popular Culture*, New York: Routledge.

Warner, M. (2000), *The Trouble with Normal. Sex, Politics, and the Ethics of Queer Life*, Cambridge, MA: Harvard University Press.

Wasko, J. (1994), *Hollywood in the Information Age: Beyond the Silver Screen*, Austin: University of Texas Press.

Waters, J. and Hainley, B. (2003), *Art – A Sex Book*, London: Thames and Hudson.

Waugh, Thomas (2001), 'Homosociality in Classic American Stag Films: Off-Screen, On-Screen,' *Sexualities* 4(3): 275–91.

Weeks, J. (1990), *Coming Out: Homosexual Politics in Britain from the Nineteenth Century to the Present*, London: Quartet.

White, A. E. (2006), *Virtually Obscene: The Case for an Uncensored Internet*, Jefferson: McFarland.

White, H. (1973), *Metahistory: The Historical Imagination in Nineteenth-Century Europe*, Baltimore: John Hopkins University Press.

Whiteley, S. (1997), 'Seduced By The Sign: An Analysis Of The Textual Links Between Sound And Image In Pop Videos', in S. Whiteley, (ed.), *Sexing the Groove: Popular Music and Gender*, London: Routledge.

Williams, L. (1989), *Hard Core: Power, Pleasure, and the 'Frenzy of the Visible'*, Berkeley: University of California Press.

—— (1992), 'Pornographies on/scene of Diff'rent strokes for diff'rent folks', in L. Segal and M. McIntosh (eds), *Sex Exposed. Sexuality and the Pornography Debate*, London, Virago.

—— (1995), 'Corporealized Observers. Visual Pornographies and the "Carnal Density of Vision"', in P. Petro (ed.), *Fugitive Images: From Photography to Video*, Bloomington: University of Indiana Press.

—— (1999), *Hardcore: Power, Pleasure and the Frenzy of the Visible*, expanded edition, Berkeley: University of California Press

—— (ed.) (2004a), *Porn Studies*, Durham, NC: Duke University Press.

—— (2004b), 'Introduction', in L. Williams (ed.), *Porn Studies,* Durham and London: Duke University Press.

Winston, B. (1998), *Media Technology and Society. A history: From the Telegraph to the Internet*, London: Routledge.

Winzen, M. (2003), 'A Credible Invention of Reality', in M. Winzen (ed.) *Thomas Ruff 1979 to the Present*, Cologne: Walter König.

Wood, A. and Smith, M. (2001), *Online Communication. Linking Technology, Identity and Culture*, Mahwah: Lawrence Erlbaum.

Wyatt, J. (1999), 'Selling "Atrocious Sexual Behavior": Revisiting Sexualities in the Marketplace for Adult Film of the 1960s', in H. Radner and M. Luckett (eds), *Swinging Single: Representing Sexuality in the 1960s*, Minneapolis: Minnesota University Press.

Yee, J. (2004), 'Recycling the "Colonial Harem"? Women in Postcards from French Indochina', *French Cultural Studies* 15(1): 5–19.

Zimmermann, P. R. (1995), *Reel Families: A Social History of Amateur Film*, Bloomington: Indiana University Press.

Index